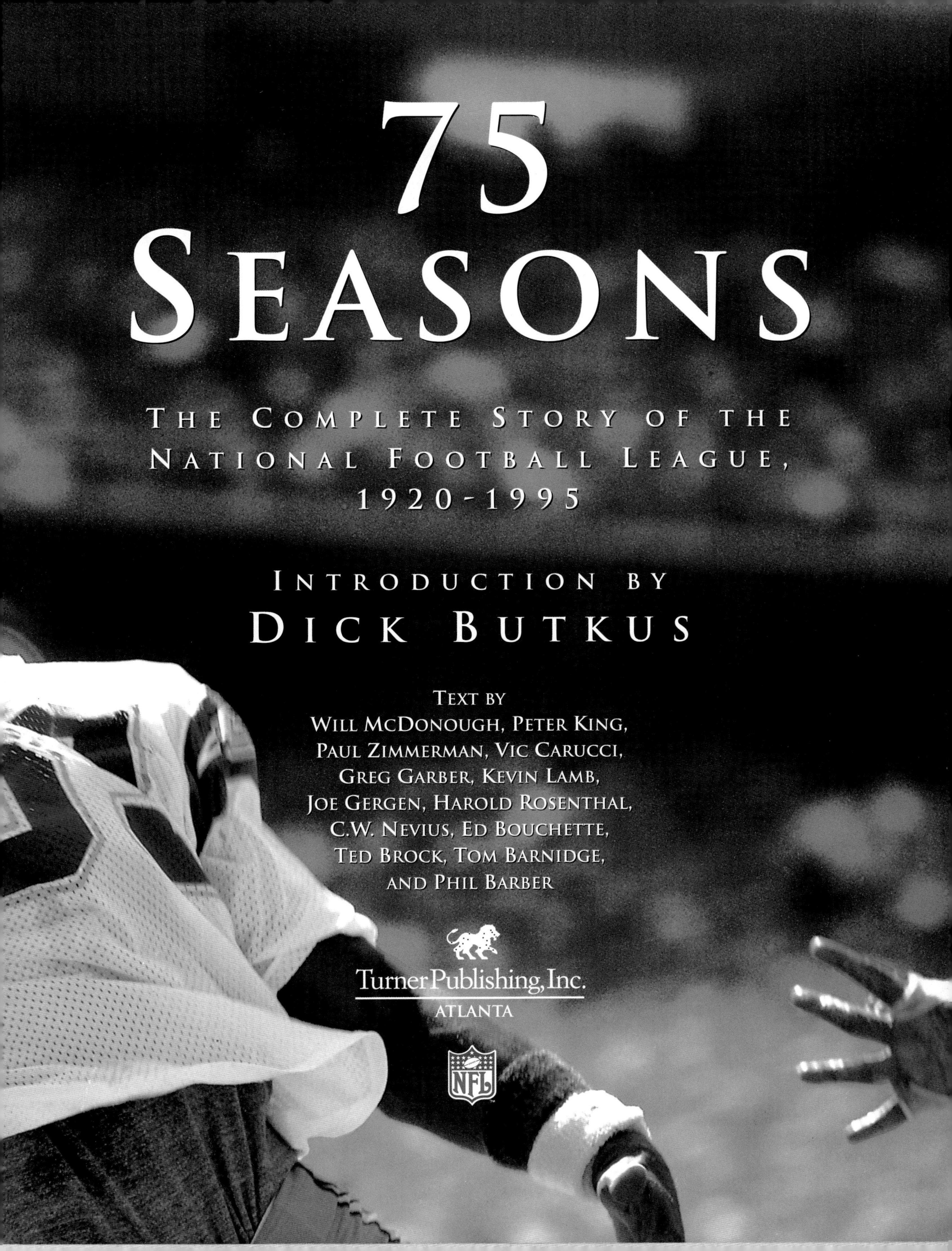

75 SEASONS

THE COMPLETE STORY OF THE NATIONAL FOOTBALL LEAGUE, 1920-1995

INTRODUCTION BY DICK BUTKUS

TEXT BY
WILL McDONOUGH, PETER KING,
PAUL ZIMMERMAN, VIC CARUCCI,
GREG GARBER, KEVIN LAMB,
JOE GERGEN, HAROLD ROSENTHAL,
C.W. NEVIUS, ED BOUCHETTE,
TED BROCK, TOM BARNIDGE,
AND PHIL BARBER

Turner Publishing, Inc.
ATLANTA

NFL

75 SEASONS
THE COMPLETE STORY OF THE
NATIONAL FOOTBALL LEAGUE,
1920-1995

Published by Turner Publishing, Inc.
A Subsidiary of Turner Broadcasting
  System, Inc.
1050 Techwood Drive, N.W.
Atlanta, Georgia 30318

Produced by National Football League
  Properties, Inc.
Creative Services Division
6701 Center Drive West, Suite 1111
Los Angeles, California 90045

ISBN 1-57036-056-1
First Edition 10 9 8 7 6 5 4 3 2 1

**Descriptions of this and preceding
pages: (1)** Paddy Driscoll; **(2-3)** 1932
NFL Championship Game at Chicago
Stadium; **(4-5)** New York Giants vs.
Brooklyn Dodgers, Polo Grounds,
1936; **(6)** Chuck Bednarik over the fall-
en Frank Gifford, 1960; **(7)** Y.A. Tittle
vs. Pittsburgh, 1964; **(8-9)** Green Bay
Packers huddle, 1965; **(10-11)** John
Jefferson, San Diego Chargers, 1980;
(12-13) Lester Hayes at the Los Angeles
Coliseum, 1983; **(14-15)** Joe Montana
leads the 49ers against the Dolphins,
Super Bowl XIX.

BY DICK BUTKUS

become so intense—it predated all of us—but we knew things definitely were different the week of the Packers game.

I suppose some of it had to do with George Halas. He was in his last stint as a head coach during my first three seasons, and he had run the team since it was founded in 1920. There was respect for Halas around the league—and a desire to beat him. You could feel the tradition the minute you stepped into the Bears' old, cramped offices at 173 West Madison. There were old pennants and trophies all over the place, but nobody had to offer you a history lesson. You could just feel it all around you. There was an aura there. If you didn't know the Bears' reputation for toughness, something was wrong.

Halas was an old-school master of motivation. I remember in my second season, he came up to me the week before we played Detroit and asked, "Did you hear what Flanagan," meaning Ed Flanagan, the Lions' center, "said about you?"

"No," I said anxiously. "What? What did he say?"

Halas just shook his head and limped away. I don't even know if Flanagan had said anything, but I was ready to murder him.

Working for Halas and seeing all those old photos of Bronko Nagurski and the other early players made me wonder what it would have been like to play in that era. I think I would have fit right in. I like the informal quality those days seemed to have. When I was growing up we didn't have Pop Warner or any organized football like that. I lived on a dead-end street, and at the end of the street was Fernwood Park. We'd play in the dirt there, then continue the game on the walk home. You know—somebody's hat would get tugged off and become a ball, and we'd be playing on people's lawns. That was my kind of competition.

Wrigley Field seemed to have an old-fashioned, informal feel to it, too, when I played there. The southeast corner of one end zone sat on top of wooden boards, which formed a ceiling over a baseball dugout. And, if you ran full speed through the north end zone, you'd hit a wall. The visiting team had to walk up a steep stairwell with a cyclone fence on either side. The good people of Chicago would toss insults—and worse—at them as our opponents made their way to the locker room.

Those Chicago fans were great. They were hard workers who appreciated an honest effort. For them, and for myself, I always aimed to play a 100-percent perfect game.

I never did put together that perfect game, but I do have some great memories stored up—like a game against the Redskins in 1971. They were coached by George Allen at the time, which made it an emotional game for me. Allen had drafted me when he was the Bears' defensive coordinator, and we had gotten to be pretty close during my rookie year when we ate lunch together every Friday.

Well, I had been kicked in the eye in this particular game, and half my face was starting to swell up like an inflated football. We scored late in the game to tie it up, and I was the left upback for the extra-point attempt. The ball was snapped and I heard the crowd roar. I looked back to see the ball sailing past Bobby Douglass, the holder, who also was our quarterback. Douglass tossed a Hail Mary pass into the end zone, and I caught it for the winning point—with one good eye.

I suppose I made some big hits along the way, too. I still remember one against Charlie Sanders, a good tight end for the Lions. One of our defensive backs intercepted a pass and Charlie sort of drifted over to help with the play. I peeled back and got him. For a moment, I almost regretted laying him out like that. Of course, I wanted to put someone on his back every time I lined up. I guess I started to get a reputation.

Having a reputation isn't always bad. Mine helped me get into the Pro Football Hall of Fame, which was the ultimate tribute. It was like insurance that I had done all right in my career. Just saying "I'm in the Hall of Fame" wouldn't mean much on its own, but when you consider the other players who have been inducted, and what they contributed to the game, it becomes a real honor.

That's similar to how I feel about being selected to the NFL All-Time Team profiled in this book. It's a great feeling even to be considered alongside some of these guys.

Take Gale Sayers, for example. We were rookies together. I might be biased because he was a teammate, but I'd have to rate Gale as the greatest halfback I ever saw. He had an amazing ability to cut on a dime and change directions. And, as an all-around offensive player—he returned punts and kickoffs, caught the ball, and even threw the halfback-option pass—there was no comparison.

Johnny Unitas was uncanny when it came to pulling a victory out of a hopeless situation. Once we had a good tip from a former Colts player about which direction Unitas was likely to throw. It worked like a charm in the first half, and I think we got a little overconfident. On one play in the second half, the tip told us he'd be throwing to the left. I called "Post," which called for a strongside rotation, but some of the guys thought I said "Pow" and put on a weakside rotation. We basically invented the double zone by accident. We were ahead of our time, but there was one problem: Johnny Unitas. He found John Mackey streaking down the middle, hit him for a touchdown, and Baltimore came back to win.

And then there was Jim Brown. I played against him only twice, in the [Chicago] College All-Star Game and the Pro Bowl. Neither game counted for much, but they were all I needed to get an idea of his incredible talent. As a College All-Star, I blitzed one play and held my arm out to push away Brown, who people said rarely blocked. Well, he pulled my arm and bent it behind me like he was going to roll me over and break it. I appreciated his effort.

There are great players today, too, guys like Joe Montana and Jerry Rice. I still announce Bears games over the radio, so I stay in touch with the league. But, hell, I'd watch anyone play if it was a good game.

I guess the NFL is in my blood by now. The sport directed my life until the day I retired. It consumed me. Whatever I've done, whatever I've been in my life, it was because of football—good, bad, or indifferent…and it mostly has been good.

Running onto that striped field and smelling the grass and hearing the pop of pads was the greatest feeling I've ever experienced. As they sang the National Anthem, my eyes would well up with emotion, and I'd be ready. I would think how lucky I was to be playing football, knowing that most of the 40,000 fans in Wrigley Field would give everything they had for the chance to trade places with me. I was blessed.

I know it sounds crazy, but my life could have ended right there on the field and I would have been happy.

The influential sportswriter Damon Runyon once said of Harold (Red) Grange: "On the field, he is the equal of three men and a horse."

In the late fall of 1925 and the early winter of 1926, Grange needed the strength and stamina of three men and a team of horses to survive what the Chicago Bears and his agent, C. C. Pyle, devised for him.

At the University of Illinois, Grange had become widely recognized as the greatest football player in history. Graced with an uncanny combination of power, speed, and agility, the redhead from Wheaton, Illinois, was held in the highest esteem in the sporting world, on a par with boxing's Jack Dempsey, baseball's Babe Ruth, and golf's Bobby Jones.

When the 1925 season began, there was much speculation about what The Galloping Ghost—the nickname coined by sportswriter Grantland Rice—was going to do with the rest of his life. One thing his college coach, Bob Zuppke, didn't want him to do was play professional football.

"Pro football was pretty questionable in those days," Grange said in the book, *What a Game They Played*, by Richard Whittingham. "Most of the college coaches and sportswriters were very down on it.... Amos Stagg had been against it since it started, too. Zup said, 'Football isn't meant to be played for money.'"

Pyle disagreed. A renowned entrepreneur who was known by the nickname "Cash and Carry," he saw Grange's football prowess as a splendid opportunity to get rich. Pyle envisioned cutting a deal with George Halas in which Grange would finish the 1925 regular season with the Bears, then join the team for a postseason exhibition tour. Pyle envisioned a bounty of gate receipts.

After Grange's final collegiate game on November 21, 1925, his life never was the same. "It was kind of a madhouse because there were all these rumors that I was going pro," Grange said. "I had to sneak out of the hotel, down the fire escape, and I got a cab to the railroad station. I went to Chicago and checked into the Belmont Hotel under an assumed name."

On November 22, the day Grange signed his pro contract, he watched from the bench as the Bears defeated Green Bay 21-0 at Cubs Park. Four days later, on Thanksgiving Day, he was in the lineup for a scoreless draw against the Cardinals.

Less than a week later, the Bears' barnstorming tour began in St. Louis. Grange thrilled the crowd by scoring 4 touchdowns in a 39-6 victory against a team hastily made up of semipros and NFL players. Only 8,000 fans turned out on a bitterly cold day in Missouri. But three days later, Chicago played Frankford before 35,000 in a Philadelphia rainstorm, edging the Yellow Jackets 14-7 as Grange scored both of the Bears' touchdowns.

The team boarded a train for New York immediately after the game, and the next day, pro football finally won over Manhattan. The New York Giants had played before mostly empty seats in 1925, their first season in the NFL, but a crowd of 73,000—the largest ever for a pro football game at that time—gathered at the Polo Grounds on December 6 to catch a glimpse of Grange. That gate saved Giants owner Tim Mara from a sea of red ink.

The tired Bears played in the same wet, muddy uniforms they had worn in Philadelphia the day before, but Grange returned an interception 35 yards for a

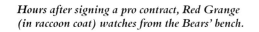

Hours after signing a pro contract, Red Grange (in raccoon coat) watches from the Bears' bench.

touchdown to help beat the Giants 19-7.

The highlight of Grange's stay in New York was meeting Babe Ruth. "I remember he said to me, 'Kid, I'll give you a little bit of advice," Grange recalled. "Don't believe anything they write about you, good or bad. And further, get the dough while the getting is good, but don't break your heart trying to get it.'"

From there, the Bears went to Washington, D.C., where Grange shook hands with Calvin Coolidge. The President said to him, "Nice to meet you, young man. I've always liked animal acts."

Chicago won that game 19-0, but Grange was held to 8 rushing yards. The Bears' trail got bumpy after that as the team lost four consecutive games—to the Providence Steam Roller at Boston, at Pittsburgh, at the Detroit Panthers, and against the Giants at Wrigley Field. Grange missed two of the contests with an injured arm.

When it was over, the eight games in 12 days had taken their physical toll on the halfback. But the $100,000 in profits that

he split with Pyle certainly helped to ease the pain. After a week of rest, Grange and the Bears hit the road again. They wound their way through the South with three games in Florida and one in New Orleans before heading to the West Coast to play in Los Angeles, San Diego, San Francisco, Portland, and Seattle. When the second tour ended in late January, Grange and Pyle split another $100,000.

In Los Angeles, a record crowd of more than 75,000 was in the Coliseum for Grange's January 16 appearance against the Los Angeles Tigers, who were led by halfback George (Wildcat) Wilson.

"That was the first time real [pro] football was ever played in the West," Grange said. "We met all kinds of people out there—the Hearst family, the Wrigleys, the Hollywood stars like Douglas Fairbanks and Harold Lloyd. And they were all football fans."

While Grange was on the West Coast, Pyle arranged for him to make a movie called *One Minute to Play*. The plot involved a halfback who is declared ineligible to play in the big game of the year, but in the last few minutes of the game, he learns he is eligible and, of course, goes out and wins it.

A SEED IN THE FERTILE FIELDS OF CHAOS

*A*mong rags-to-riches stories, the National Football League's rise from the dusty Midwestern fields of Massillon, Duluth, Canton, Racine, and Hammond certainly qualifies as one of the greatest of them all.

No fewer than 49 teams competed in the NFL at one time or another during the Roaring '20s. Toward the end of the decade, the league finally incurred a measure of stability with solid franchises in Chicago, Green Bay, and New York, and a fan base that began to realize that the pro game was every bit as good as—if not better than—the popular college game.

On November 13, 1892, William (Pudge) Heffelfinger, a former star guard at Yale, accepted $500—plus $25 for expenses—to play for the Allegheny Athletic Association in its game against the Pittsburgh Athletic Club. Heffelfinger scored the only points of the game, returning a fumble 25 yards for a touchdown as the A.A.A. scored a 4-0 victory. Thus, on that snowy day at Pittsburgh's Recreation Park, professional football was born.

For the next 28 years, this type of underhanded player deal plagued pro football. Solid leagues never took hold. Players routinely jumped from one team to another, regulations were far from uniform, schedules were haphazard, and there was no control of the competitive bidding for the top college players.

It was obvious to many coaches and players that football had a place in the American sporting scene. But somehow, organization and common sense had to be introduced.

On August 20, 1920, in Canton, Ohio, the wheels of order were set in motion by seven men representing four teams. The men held a meeting under the auspices of Canton team owner Ralph Hay. There it was decided to form a league and call it the American Professional Football Conference. The seven representatives—Hay and Jim Thorpe of the Canton Bulldogs, Frank

The backfield of the Akron Pros (opposite) helped the team to an 8-0-3 record and the championship of the American Professional Football Association in 1920.

COACH FRITZ

In early December, 1916, Frederick Douglass (Fritz) Pollard, a halfback at Brown University, became the second black player ever named to Walter Camp's All-America team. More than 50 years later, Pollard reflected, "Having been the first Negro backfield man to have been given the honor...gave me recognition wherever I went and cleared the way for me many times when otherwise I would have been very much embarrassed."

In 1920, Pollard co-coached the Akron Pros to an 8-0-3 finish and the unofficial championship of the American Professional Football Association.

Pollard had begun playing in the Pros' backfield in 1919, and he co-coached the team late that season. He was professional football's sixth black player, in a succession that began with Charles W. Follis, a halfback with the Shelby, Ohio, Athletic Club from 1902-06. More important, Pollard was the NFL's first black head coach.

He played with the Milwaukee Badgers in 1922, the Hammond Pros from 1923-25, and the Providence Steam Roller later in 1925. He rejoined Akron in 1925-26. Pollard's career after football was an odyssey through the fields of finance, journalism, and entertainment. He died in 1986, at 92.

Neid and Art Ranney of the Akron Pros, Carl Storck of the Dayton Triangles, and Jimmy O'Donnell and Stanley Cofall of the Cleveland Indians—reached agreement on several fronts.

After the meeting, the *Canton Evening Repository* reported that the reasons for forming the league were "to raise the standard of professional football in every way possible, to eliminate bidding for players between rival clubs, and to secure cooperation in the form of schedules, at least for the bigger teams."

Scenes From a Hupmobile Showroom

Nearly a month later, on September 17, a more formal meeting took place in Hay's Canton, Ohio, automobile dealership showroom. In addition to Akron, Canton, Cleveland, and Dayton, it was attended by representatives of the Decatur (Illinois) Staleys, the Hammond (Indiana) Pros, the Massillon (Ohio) Tigers, the Muncie (Indiana) Flyers, the Racine (Illinois) Cardinals, the Rochester (New York) Jeffersons, and the Rock Island (Illinois) Independents.

The owners exchanged ideas, outlined rules and regulations, elected officials, and changed the league's name to the American Professional Football Association.

Thorpe, the most famous football player of the era, was named president of the league. The group arrived at a fee of $100 for membership, but George Halas, player-coach of the Staleys, said, "I can testify that no money changed hands." Each team agreed to print stationery that proclaimed the words "Member of American Professional Football Association."

Later, the Buffalo All-Americans, Chicago Tigers, Columbus (Ohio) Panhandles, and Detroit Heralds joined the league. It was far from a perfect setup as members continued to schedule non-league games against club teams. Statistics weren't kept. Still, football had taken a logical step toward establishing its presence.

The first game featuring a team from the APFA was played on September 26, 1920, when Rock Island faced the St. Paul Ideals. The Independents rolled to a 48-0 home victory on a rainy day at Douglas Park.

The first time two teams from the APFA met head-to-head was on October 3 at Triangle Park. Dayton's Lou Partlow broke a scoreless tie in the third quarter with a rushing touchdown—considered the first official touchdown in an NFL game—as the Triangles blanked Columbus 14-0. Also that day, Rock Island whipped Muncie 45-0 in the only game the Flyers would play before disbanding. Rock Island scored 3 touchdowns on blocked punts and so thoroughly outplayed the Flyers that Halas canceled his Staleys' game against Muncie, scheduled for the following week. When that happened, the financial backers of the Muncie team pulled out and the team folded.

Leadership Makes the Difference

During the 1920 season, four teams—Canton, Akron, Decatur, and Buffalo—emerged as APFA championship contenders. Former Michigan quarterback Tommy Hughitt had formed the Buffalo team and assembled an all-star cast. During the season, though, Canton managed a victory and a tie against the All-Americans, while Akron dealt Canton two losses. In the only head-to-head meeting between Akron and Buffalo, the teams battled to a scoreless tie in Buffalo during a storm that produced rain and snow. It was after that game that the first recognized player deal in pro football history occurred. Akron sold tackle (Nasty) Bob Nash to Buffalo for $300 and five percent of that day's gate receipts.

The season came to an end on December 12 when Decatur and Akron battled to a scoreless draw, despite the Staleys' hiring Paddy Driscoll from the Cardinals to gain an advantage. Akron was the only team in the APFA that went undefeated (8-0-3) through the year.

Everyone associated with the APFA in 1920 knew that big changes were needed. And those changes started at the top. Thorpe was no more than a figurehead in his role as president. He devoted little time to league matters and lost interest in off-field developments.

Three of the guiding forces of the Chicago Bears (née the Decatur Staleys) of the 1920s, from left to right: George Halas, Paddy Driscoll, and Ed (Dutch) Sternaman. Halas owned the franchise from 1921, its first year in Chicago, until his death in 1982.

So at a meeting held in April, 1921, at the Portage Hotel in Akron, after they had presented the championship trophy to Akron, team owners got down to the business of repairing their fractured league.

The APFA braintrust decided to install Joe Carr, a sportswriter who was heavily involved in sports management, as president. In addition to serving as manager of the Columbus Panhandles, Carr had founded a semipro baseball team in Columbus at the turn of the century and later was president of the city's minor league baseball entry in the American Association. He was a top-flight administrator.

The owners then focused on which teams would be allowed in the league. Representatives from Akron, Buffalo, Canton, the Chicago Cardinals, Columbus, Dayton, Decatur, Hammond, Rochester, and Philadelphia were at the meeting. Groups in Louisville and Cincinnati sent letters requesting entrance into the APFA. The actual league map wasn't finalized then, but several rules changes were passed, the most important of which was the outlawing of players suiting up for different teams in the same week.

Carr was asked to create the league's by-laws, and he referred to Major League Baseball's constitution to gather ideas. He gave teams territorial rights to players within the league, limited player movement, developed membership criteria for franchises, established a permanent office in Columbus, and made sure standings were kept so a true champion could be crowned.

Twenty-one teams were set to play in the APFA before the 1921 season, including 11 of the original 14. But by the time the season ended, a number of teams hadn't completed full schedules, so their records were stricken from the standings.

Enter Halas

Under this system, the Chicago Staleys were awarded the 1921 championship based on their 9-1-1 record. The Buffalo All-Americans posted a 9-1-2 mark

"There wasn't one-hundred dollars in the room, but still each of us put up one-hundred dollars for the privilege of losing money."

—GEORGE HALAS,
CHICAGO BEARS OWNER, RECALLING
THE FIRST MEETING OF THE APFA

A gold-medal decathlete in the 1912 Olympics, Jim Thorpe was the most recognizable face of pro football's infancy. He played for seven APFA or NFL teams and even served as the APFA's first president in 1920.

and had an identical winning percentage of .900 (ties were ignored then). So when Carr awarded the championship to Chicago, the All-Americans protested vehemently.

On Thanksgiving Day, Buffalo had defeated the Staleys 7-6. But in the rematch in Chicago on December 4, the Staleys were victorious, 10-7, as Guy Chamberlin turned a short pass into a 70-yard touchdown and Ed (Dutch) Sternaman kicked the extra point. Chamberlin kicked the winning field goal. The All-Americans argued, first of all, that the second game was merely a postseason exhibition and shouldn't have counted in the standings. They also claimed one of Chicago's victories during the season had come against a non-APFA member (Rochester, which had failed to play the minimum six games). Carr took Buffalo's protest under advisement, but eventually ruled in favor of the Staleys, giving Halas his first pro football championship.

Halas had grown up in Chicago, then attended the University of Illinois, where he studied civil engineering and played football and baseball for the Fighting Illini. Following a World War I hitch in the Navy, Halas had played one season of pro baseball, spending the early portion of the 1919 major league season with the New York Yankees. After hitting only .091 and being slowed by a leg injury suffered while sliding into third base after hitting a triple in an exhibition game, he was sent to St. Paul of the American Association, where he finished the year.

The former college star never forgot a comment made by Illinois coach Bob Zuppke at the school's football banquet in 1917: "Why is it that just when you players are beginning to know something about football after three years, I lose you and you stop playing? Football is the only sport that ends for a man when it should be beginning."

Halas got a new beginning when he was hired to run A.E. Staley's company football team in Decatur. In trying to figure out whom the team would play, Halas wrote a letter to Ralph Hay, the manager of the Canton Bulldogs, suggesting that they form a league. This led to the formative meetings on August 20 and September 17, 1920.

The Staleys finished 10-1-2 in 1920, but despite their success, Staley decided

PRO FOOTBALL GOES TO COLLEGE

It was all in place in 1920, when professional football turned its neighborhood wars into a formal league—all the major strategy that is in place today.

The wildly innovative Amos Alonzo Stagg, operating out of the T-formation, had drawn up plays that put a halfback or a split end in motion. Bob Zuppke already had come up with the flea-flicker and the "Whoa back," a pass-lateral that goes by the name of the Hook-and-Ladder today and is considered a high form of trickery. Pop Warner's Double-Wing was the modern Shotgun, and the Run-and-Shoot is a close approximation of one of his Double-Wing variations. The Explode Package, which Joe Gibbs used so effectively against the Miami Dolphins in Super Bowl XVII? Nothing more than the old Rockne Shift.

Formations abounded. The earliest alignment, the T or "Standard Formation," was giving way to the Single- and Double-Wing, the short punt, and the Notre Dame Box. Collegiate coaching manuals of the day listed draw plays and counters, traps and screens, sucker and influence plays. Zuppke had introduced the huddle, which his colleagues scornfully called "ring around the rosie."

"The players could not always hear the signals distinctly because of the cheering multitudes, causing confusion," he explained in a 1943 letter written to Hack Applequist. It has a familiar ring.

Even the goofy stuff made some sense. A manual produced in the 1920s by the Coaches Institute in Kansas City recommended a direct snap to a deep back, through the quarterback's legs, involving the "ultimate deception. The quarterback talks to the right guard and right tackle and tells them the defensive left guard is offside. The moment the left guard is distracted the ball is snapped back to the fullback, who drives over him."

College football, stepping into its greatest era, ruled the land. The professional game followed in its wake. Pro football was a working man's game, with a sub-stratum of mill hands and factory workers—plus, of course, the occasional college star signed with much fanfare. Some NFL teams practiced only three or four nights per week.

The Bears mixed in a little T-formation—a tight variety with three backs and two tight ends—with their Single-Wing, but just about everyone else went with a direct-snap deep formation.

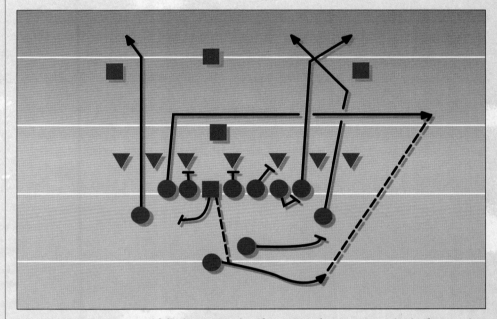

The Double-Wing was one of the direct-snap deep formations that were pervasive in the twenties.

Green Bay's Curly Lambeau was known as the league's "passing coach." He liked to gamble, which was what the passing game was in those days because the thrower received virtually no protection and the rules were prohibitive. If you threw an incomplete pass into the end zone, it was a touchback—the other team's ball!

Everyone could go downfield on pass plays; it was up to the defensive backs to sort out the eligible receivers. In his 1921 book, *The Forward Pass in Football*, Springfield College's Elmer Berry pleaded for a system in which the passer actually identified his receivers *before* he unloaded. "The usual thing is for the passer to heave the ball into the air and yell, 'Ball!'" he wrote.

Few films exist from the twenties. The Pro Football Hall of Fame has one, though, and it's as curious as a spherical football. The Providence Steam Roller versus someone or other toward the end of the decade, played at the old Cycledrome in Providence.

If a player was tackled near the sideline, that's where the next play began; the team in possession had to waste a play to get into operating territory. Stands nearly abutted the sidelines. There were no benches. Players sat alongside fans in the front row; the players were easy to spot—they were the ones without the fedoras.

It basically was a clean game—no cheap shots, no mauling, despite the accounts of grim warfare penned by the collegiate set.

The college rules book was used, including one section called "The Football Code," which recommended a standard of conduct. The highlight was a section labeled "Talking to Opponents."

"Not prohibited," it stated. "No rules can make a gentleman out of a mucker."

BRIGHT PATH'S TEAM

No NFL team ever sent a more colorful lineup onto the field than the Oorang Indians. But then, no other NFL team ever was composed exclusively of American Indians.

Ten tribes were represented on the Oorang roster. Among the players were Xavier Downwind, Baptist Thunder, Wrinkle Meat, Bear Behind, Tomahawk, Little Cyclone, Woodchuck, Long Time Sleep, Brave Man, and Bright Path.

Bright Path was Jim Thorpe, a Sac and Fox. Thorpe, the 1912 Olympic decathlon champion, generally was regarded as the "world's greatest athlete." Brave Man was halfback Joe Guyon, who eventually would join Thorpe in the Pro Football Hall of Fame. Pete Calac, an excellent fullback for seven seasons, also played for Oorang. And almost all of the Indians had attended Carlisle Institute, officially known as the United States Indian Industrial School.

In 1922, Thorpe's hunting buddy Walter Lingo, owner of the Oorang Kennels, purchased his own NFL franchise. (Oorang was a strain of Airedale terrier, developed by Lingo himself.)

Lingo hired Thorpe as his player-coach and wanted his team to play in the Kennels' hometown of LaRue (population: 750) on the site of a Wyandotte Indian village. Unfortunately, LaRue had no football field, so the Indians played their home games in Marion, 15 miles away. As it turned out, their home games totaled two. The show took to the road, where fans flocked to see Thorpe and delighted in the halftime entertainment, which featured dog shows, drums, and dancing—all of which included player participation.

Oorang finished 2-6 in 1922 and 1-10 in 1923, then disbanded.

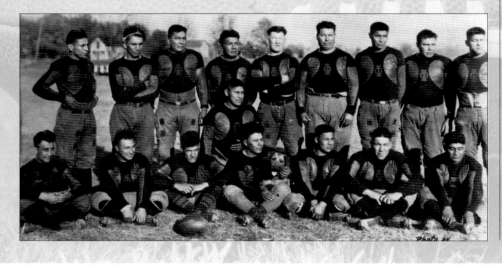

to drop the team because of a business recession. Thanks to Halas, the club did not fold. With a $5,000 check in hand from the former owner as seed money in exchange for Halas's promise to retain the name Staleys for one year, Halas took control of the club, moved it to Chicago and began building an organization that would become one of the most revered in all of sports.

"Right at the beginning I put down a set of rules for the players," Halas said. "Rules about things the pro teams never thought about in those days…curfew, meetings, practices. I asked myself, what must our players do in order to be complete football players on Sundays? One thing I insisted on was daily practice, which was something the other teams did not have."

A Name With a Ring to It

In 1922, change was the order of the day in professional football. Halas renamed his Chicago club the Bears, reasoning that he could stir up interest among local fans if the team's nickname was closer to that of Chicago's most popular major league baseball team, the Cubs.

And at a June 24 meeting in Canton, the APFA changed its name to the National Football League. It also saw its membership grow to 18. Cleveland, Cincinnati, and Detroit pulled out and were replaced by Toledo; Milwaukee; Minneapolis; Louisville; Hammond; Racine, Wisconsin; Marion, Ohio (an all-Indian team that called itself the Oorang Indians); and Evansville, Indiana. Staying in the league were the Chicago Bears and Cardinals, Canton, Buffalo,

"I had seen fat hogs go for more than they paid for me. But in those days, a fat hog was a lot more valuable than a fat tackle."

—STEVE OWEN,
AFTER THE NEW YORK GIANTS HAD BOUGHT THE TACKLE'S CONTRACT FOR $500 FROM THE KANSAS CITY COWBOYS IN 1926

Rock Island, Dayton, Green Bay, Akron, Rochester, and Columbus.

In another big development in 1922, the Packers became a publicly owned corporation.

In 1919, Earl (Curly) Lambeau and George Calhoun had met with a group of prospective players in the editorial room of the *Green Bay Press-Gazette* and had decided to organize a football team. Lambeau, who worked for the Indian Packing Company in Green Bay, talked his boss, Frank Peck, into putting up money to buy equipment and providing a field for practices. As a tradeoff, Lambeau named the team the Packers.

In 1921, the club—now backed by the Acme Packing Company, which had bought out Indian Packing—had applied for and been granted a franchise in the APFA. During that season, the Packers had compiled a 3-2-1 record but suffered financially because of poor attendance. When the Packers admitted to using players who still had college eligibility left, the franchise was forfeited.

But during the June 24, 1922, meeting in Canton, the same day Halas's Staleys became the Bears and the APFA became the NFL, Green Bay was reinstated. Lambeau put up $50 and other backers provided the rest of the $250 membership fee, with Lambeau assuming ownership of the club. To pay for the trip from Green Bay to Canton, Lambeau and a friend, Don Murphy, had to sell Murphy's car. In return, Lambeau had to keep Murphy on the team.

Lambeau struggled in 1922 as the Packers were plagued by bad weather and poor attendance in their first NFL season. After one game was rained out, the insurance company refused to reimburse the team for lost gate receipts because the official amount of rain was one one-hundredth of an inch shy of that required in the policy.

Later in the year, with Lambeau virtually broke, a group of Green Bay businessmen, led by *Press-Gazette* general manager Andrew B. Turnbull, arranged a $2,500 loan for the club. A public nonprofit organization was set up to operate the Packers. Fans were able to buy shares of the stock for $5 and get a season ticket as part of the package. By the time the 1923 season began, the Packers had $5,000 in the bank, insuring future solvency. Lambeau was relieved of his ownership responsibilities so he could concentrate solely on managing and coaching the team.

No Beating Those Bulldogs

While the Packers were struggling to stay afloat, the Canton Bulldogs emerged as the league powerhouse and finished the year 10-0-2. Guy Chamberlin was hired away from Halas's team to rebuild the Bulldogs, thus beginning a long and successful coaching career. In 12 games, Canton outscored its opponents 184-15 and posted nine shutouts with a defense that featured future Pro Football Hall of Fame tackles Roy (Link) Lyman and Wilbur (Pete) Henry. The Bulldogs caught a break by not having to play Rock Island. In an October 15 game against Evansville, the Independents scored 9 rushing touchdowns in a 60-0 rout.

Canton continued to dominate the league in 1923, stretching its two-year unbeaten streak to 24 games with an 11-0-1 finish. The key for the Bulldogs was the play of tailback Lou Smythe, who became the only player ever to lead the league in both passing touchdowns (6) and rushing touchdowns (7) in the same season. The Bulldogs outscored their opposition by an even more one-sided margin (246-19) this time, recording eight shutouts. As it turned out,

A Canton Bulldogs program from 1923, when they finished 11-0-1. The Bulldogs' only blemish of the season was a 3-3 tie with the Buffalo All-Americans.

The Bears' George Trafton, the league's first all-pro center, was known for his rough-and-tumble style of play.

WINNING WAS THE ONLY THING

The NFL (known at the time as the American Professional Football Association) produced its first unbeaten team in its first season, when the Akron Pros captured the league championship by going 8-0-3.

Since then, a half-dozen teams have gone unbeaten, though Don Shula's 1972 Miami Dolphins remain the lone squad to complete an entire year–including postseason–without a loss or a tie.

Here are the teams that have gone through the regular season without losing:

YEAR	TEAM	RECORD
1920	Akron Pros	8-0-3
1922	Canton Bulldogs	10-0-2
1923	Canton Bulldogs	11-0-1
1929	Green Bay Packers	12-0-1
1934	*Chicago Bears	13-0-0
1942	**Chicago Bears	11-0-0
1972	Miami Dolphins	14-0-0

*lost 30-13 to the New York Giants in the NFL Championship Game.
**lost 14-6 to the Washington Redskins in the NFL Championship Game.

Canton's 6-0 victory over the Bears on October 21 was the pivotal game.

Halas did create his own consolation prize, though, as he turned in the play of the season during a 33-6 victory over the Oorang Indians at muddy Cubs Park on November 12. With the Indians threatening to score, Thorpe charged into the line, only to be met head-on by tackle Hugh Blacklock. Thorpe fumbled, Halas caught the ball in mid-air and ran 98 yards for a touchdown. That play stood for 50 years as the longest fumble return in NFL history.

"I never ran faster in my life," Halas said. "I could feel Thorpe behind me all the way, and I was waiting for him to whip out his legs for one of those cross-body tackles of his."

As good as the Bulldogs were on the field, they were a disaster at the gate as tiny Lakeside Park made it impossible for owner Ralph Hay to turn a profit. Hay cut his losses and moved the team north to Cleveland, combining it with the Indians. Not all of Canton's players followed the team to Cleveland, but Chamberlin had more than enough talent left over to stretch his unbeaten streak to 30 games before the team suffered a stunning 12-7 loss to the new Frankford (Pennsylvania) Yellow Jackets.

Rock Island's championship aspirations were dealt a blow on October 26, during a 23-7 loss to the Kansas City Blues, a new franchise. The Independents' star tackle Fred (Duke) Slater was not allowed to play in Kansas City because he was black. By November 30, Cleveland had a 7-1-1 record, Chicago was 6-1-4, and Frankford was 11-2-1. In December, the Bears beat both Cleveland and Frankford, then lost to Rock Island. Whether those games counted in the standings was anyone's guess; when the season ended, there was another disputed championship.

At the league meeting in Cleveland in late January, president Carr declared that all games played after November 30 were postseason exhibitions, claiming the teams had no right to arrange league games without official permission. Thus, he awarded the title to Cleveland based on its better winning percentage on November 30.

Red Is In, Maroons Out

On November 21, 1925, Harold (Red) Grange wrapped up his brilliant collegiate career at the University of Illinois, leading the Illini to a 14-9 victory over Ohio State in front of 90,000 fans in Columbus, Ohio. The next day, Grange sat on the bench and watched his new team, the Chicago Bears, beat Green Bay 21-0 at Wrigley Field. Four days later, on Thanksgiving Day, Grange made his NFL debut in the Bears' scoreless tie against the Cardinals in front of 36,000 fans at jam-packed Cubs Park.

The Cardinals did a wonderful job of containing Grange, both from scrimmage (40 rushing yards) and on kick returns, but it didn't seem to matter. The fans were in love with the "Galloping Ghost," and the Bears became the hottest ticket in pro football. After the season, they launched an eight-game barnstorming tour with Grange as the gate attraction, and when that was over, they played a nine-game tour that lasted into late January.

Awarding the 1925 NFL title proved more difficult than tackling Grange. The key game in the championship puzzle was played on December 6 when the Pottsville (Pennsylvania) Maroons traveled to Chicago to meet the Cardinals. Pottsville won 21-7, improving its record to 10-2 while Chicago

BRING YOUR OWN UNIFORM

The National Football League was born in the Roaring Twenties and, with regard to equipment, followed one rule appropriate to the times: There were no rules.

The word "uniform" was hardly suitable to pro football in the 1920s. Teams issued jerseys and socks, and little else. Players had to provide the rest, and they usually used what they had worn in college or on the sandlots, from helmets and shoes to shoulder pads and pants.

The NFL had a rag-tag look to it. Most players wore leather "head helmets," some of which were so pliable they could be folded and shoved into back pockets. The headgear offered minimal protection. Some players wore nothing to protect their heads except long hair.

A nose-protector helmet that looked like a leather ski mask occasionally was used. Ostensibly, it was made to protect the face, but some college players donned them in order to play in the pros under aliases, thus protecting their real identities and their amateur status.

Pants were made of brown canvas, and the wool jerseys looked more like sweaters. When it rained, a football player's uniform could double its weight. Some jerseys had sticky striping on the front (soon outlawed) to help a player grip the ball.

Most of the equipment in pro football was similar to that used in the more popular college game, where most of the innovations took place. But a few NFL teams did promote one novelty that would catch on: the logo. The Chicago Cardinals used coupled Cs on their sleeves, and the Frankford Yellow Jackets had FYJ interlocked. But the most stunning example was the black-and-white igloo on the chests of the Duluth Eskimos.

The ball was much fatter than today's, though it was tapered as the decade wore on and passing became more popular. For $2, you also could purchase an individual Rawlings suitcase for your ball that was made of selected khaki with leather handles.

An important development took a foothold early in the decade when removable cleats were designed by John T. Riddell. Until then, tapered, rectangular leather cleats were nailed to the shoe, which almost always was a black hightop made of kangaroo leather.

"Riddell thought that if you had a detachable cleat, when bad weather came you could take off the short ones and put longer ones on in the mud," said George Bogar, a long-time manufacturer's representative. "They became very popular."

So popular, in fact, that they basically still are used today on grass fields.

A 1920s ensemble, including Dayton Triangles jersey, leather shoulder pads, and a hard-rubber nose guard kept in place by clamping the teeth.

Player-coach Guy Chamberlin won four NFL championships with three different teams—Canton, Cleveland, and Frankford. He was one of the pro game's first accomplished pass-catchers.

fell to 9-2-1. Realizing his team's winning percentage wasn't good enough to claim the championship, Cardinals owner Chris O'Brien scheduled two more games, one against Milwaukee on the following Thursday and another against Hammond on Saturday. Both opponents had disbanded before the season ended, but they regrouped one more time for a payday. The Cardinals blasted Milwaukee 59-0 in a farce of a game that was played with five-minute quarters, then improved to 11-2-1 by beating Hammond two days later.

Pottsville then scheduled an exhibition game against a team made up of former Notre Dame all-stars, including the famed Four Horsemen, at Shibe Park in Philadelphia. The Frankford franchise protested to the league, saying the Maroons were violating the Yellow Jackets' territorial rights. League president Joe Carr agreed and ordered the game canceled. But the Maroons, claiming the NFL office had given verbal approval, played the game, and posted a 9-7 victory.

Carr countered by suspending the Pottsville team, thus freezing the Maroons' record at 10-2. The owners were ready to award the championship to the Cardinals. But O'Brien refused to accept the title. The owners never officially awarded a title for 1925, but league records list the Cardinals as champions.

American Competition

Because of Grange's barnstorming success, Pyle told the Bears Grange would not play for Chicago in 1926 unless Halas and his partner, Sternaman gave Grange one-third of the team. They refused, so Pyle decided he and Grange should start their own NFL franchise and place it in the media center of the world, New York City, to capitalize fully on the star's popularity.

At the league's annual postseason meeting, Pyle proposed putting his team in Yankee Stadium, but Giants owner Tim Mara refused to allow it, claiming territorial infringement. When the league backed Mara, Pyle announced he was forming his own circuit—the American Football League—with a team in New York.

Joey Sternaman, quarterback of the Bears and brother of club co-owner Dutch, formed his own team in Chicago and called it the Bulls. Sternaman then obtained a lease with Comiskey Park, sending the Cardinals scurrying to smaller Normal Park. Other teams were formed in Brooklyn, Philadelphia, Newark, Boston, and Cleveland, while Rock Island jumped from the NFL to the new league. A ninth team, a traveling band without a home field but calling itself the Los Angeles Wildcats, was led by former University of Washington All-America back George Wilson.

Early in the season, the AFL looked as if it might give the NFL serious competition for the market. On October 17, the Bears hosted the Cardinals at Wrigley Field while the upstart Bulls were playing Grange's New York Yankees. Only 12,000 turned out for the Bears game, while more than 20,000 came to see the Yankees meet the Bulls at Comiskey.

"It was a big gamble and I got talked into making it," Joey Sternaman recalled of his venture into the AFL. "It seemed like a real good thing at the time. We actually had

ONE MAN'S LOSS...

Best known for his roles as head coach and owner of the Chicago Bears, legendary George Halas also was one of the finest two-way ends of his era, from 1920-29. While playing for the Bears in 1923, Halas plucked a fumble by the Oorang Indians' Jim Thorpe in mid-air at Chicago's 2-yard line and raced 98 yards to a touchdown, a record return that stood nearly half a century. The longest fumble returns in NFL history (all for touchdowns):

104	Jack Tatum, Oakland vs. Green Bay	Sept. 24, 1972
100	Chris Martin, Kansas City vs. Miami	Oct. 13, 1991
99	Don Griffin, San Francisco vs. Chicago	Dec. 23, 1991
98	George Halas, Chicago Bears vs. Oorang	Nov. 24, 1923
97	Chuck Howley, Dallas vs. Atlanta	Oct. 2, 1966

a pretty good team and we beat Red and his New York Yankees. But we didn't get the crowds and we just couldn't make it go. I came out broke…it was a bum gamble."

For the remainder of the season—with a rainy autumn not helping its cause—the AFL began to stumble. By the end of October, Newark and Cleveland had disbanded. In early November, the Brooklyn team shut down and merged with the NFL's Brooklyn Lions. Later that month, Rock Island suspended operations.

The AFL championship was decided in two games in November. First, Philadelphia beat New York 13-10 in front of 22,000 fans at Yankee Stadium on Thanksgiving Day, as Grange injured his hip. With the Galloping Ghost out of the lineup two days later in Philadelphia, the Quakers stopped the Yankees 13-6.

The Yankees then embarked on a tour of the South and West, trying to recapture the magic of the 1925 tours. They weren't nearly as successful. And while the Yankees played before mediocre crowds, the AFL folded.

Iron Men of the North

Frankford stormed to the 1926 NFL championship, posting a 14-1-1 record. Coach Guy Chamberlin persuaded two former Canton teammates, fullback Ben Jones and guard Rudy Comstock, to join the Yellow Jackets, while guard Adolph (Swede) Youngstrom jumped on board from Buffalo. Oddly enough, the title—just as it was in the AFL—was decided in Shibe Park when Frankford met the then-unbeaten Bears. Bill Senn scored for the Bears in the first half, but Chamberlin blocked the extra point. That play proved pivotal when Houston Stockton fired a touchdown pass to Henry Homan, who had beaten Paddy Driscoll on the play. Ernie Hamer made the conversion, and the Yellow Jackets held on for the 7-6 victory, giving Chamberlin his fourth championship in five years, in three different cities (Canton, Cleveland, and Frankford).

Another interesting story emerged from the 1926 season. Ernie Nevers, the

The Canton Bulldogs were the league's first powerhouse team. Canton won back-to-back titles in 1922-23, then was made inactive in 1924.

The 1924 NFL championship trophy presented to the Cleveland Bulldogs.

Johnny Blood (McNally) was a free-spirited halfback who started with the Milwaukee Badgers in 1925.

All-America fullback from Stanford, was nearly as hot a property as Grange was when his college eligibility expired in 1925. But while Grange turned to pro football immediately after Illinois's season ended, Nevers, who had one semester of classes to complete before he could obtain his degree, initially stayed in school.

However, after seeing how much money Grange pocketed on his barnstorming tours, Nevers couldn't resist the pro offers. He put his degree on hold to play in the NFL and signed for $25,000, plus 10 percent of the gate receipts, to play in two all-star games against the New York Giants in Florida. He then signed a $20,000 contract to play for the Duluth Eskimos in 1926.

The Eskimos played one home game, beating Kansas City 7-0 on September 19. The next day, they hit the road and didn't return home until February.

Duluth finished the NFL schedule with a 6-5-3 record, and Nevers set five league marks for rushing, passing, and scoring. He kicked 5 field goals against Hartford in a 15-0 victory, a mark that wasn't equaled until Bob Waterfield did it for the Los Angeles Rams in 1951. Against Milwaukee, Nevers threw a record 62-yard touchdown pass to pull out a 7-6 victory in the waning seconds. Against Pottsville, he completed 17 consecutive passes and scored 27 points. And against the Giants, he carried the ball nine straight plays on one scoring drive.

When the season ended, the Eskimos embarked on a 16-game tour, similar to those involving Grange. The exhibition tour took Nevers—who was paid $15,000 plus a percentage of the larger gates—and Duluth into most of the NFL cities, then to the West Coast.

When his 30-game season ended, Nevers had played 1,711 of 1,740 possible minutes of football. Grantland Rice dubbed the Eskimos "The Iron Men of the North."

"Ernie was probably the first of the triple-threat backs," Grange said. "He could run, kick, and pass. He was a star through and through. Guys like Nevers and [Bronko] Nagurski would have played the game for nothing."

Trimming the Fat

In 1927, the NFL examined itself, learned a lesson from the defunct AFL, and came to the conclusion that more wasn't necessarily better. Twenty-two NFL teams had competed in 1926. But the owners decided to eliminate the financially burdened franchises and concentrate on strengthening those that were playing on fairly stable ground.

Twelve clubs—the Los Angeles Buccaneers, Kansas City Cowboys, Louisville Colonels, Canton Bulldogs, Akron Pros, Hammond Pros, Columbus Tigers, Detroit Panthers, Milwaukee Badgers, Racine Tornadoes, Hartford Blues, and Brooklyn Tigers—were cast away.

That left the New York Giants, Green Bay Packers, Chicago Bears, Providence Steam Roller, Frankford Yellow Jackets, Pottsville Maroons, Chicago Cardinals, Dayton Triangles, Duluth Eskimos, and Buffalo Bisons as holdovers. Added to that group were the Cleveland Bulldogs and C.C. Pyle's New York Yankees, the only surviving team from the AFL.

For the first time, the NFL's map was spread evenly between the Midwest and the East, breaking the hold the Ohio-Illinois area once had on the league. There were six teams in each geographical area.

Still, the pro game was having a hard time catching on. Baseball remained the number-one sport in America, boxing drew huge crowds, and college football still was wildly popular. NFL games were worth about one paragraph each in the daily newspapers.

"You'd get back into the hinterlands and tell them that pro football was a good game, that the pros blocked hard and tackled hard," Grange said in *The Game That Was*, "and they'd laugh at you."

On October 16, 1927, the Yankees traveled to Chicago to take on the Bears at Wrigley Field, site of Grange's pro football baptism. Late in the game, which Chicago won 12-0, Grange suffered a season-ending knee injury when he was tackled by George Trafton.

"I had my cleat dug into the ground and it was kind of a wet day and somebody fell over my knee," Grange recalled. "It was nothing deliberate, just one of those things. I was hit from the side and, boom, out went the knee. I came back after that injury, but I could never do again what I'd been able to do before. I was just an ordinary back. The moves were gone forever."

The Giants earned the 1927 NFL championship by winning their last nine games by a cumulative score of 170-14. The Giants played Cleveland to a 0-0 tie in their second game and lost to the Bulldogs 6-0 in their fourth game. After that, New York was unbeatable.

Ride of the Steam Roller

The NFL survived the 1928 season without its two biggest stars, Grange and Nevers. Grange's bad knee kept him sidelined the whole year. Nevers spent the summer pitching in the major leagues for the St. Louis Browns, then shunned his old NFL team, Duluth, and accepted an assistant coaching position in the fall under Glenn (Pop) Warner at Stanford. Without Nevers, the Eskimos folded.

Red Grange (with ball), the "Galloping Ghost" of Illinois, bestowed instant credibility upon the professional ranks when he joined the Bears in 1925.

"Grange runs as Nurmi runs and Dempsey moves, with almost no effort, as a shadow flits and drifts and darts. There is no gathering of muscles for an extra lunge. There is only the effortless, ghostlike weave and glide upon effortless legs with a body that can detach itself from the hips with a change of pace, then come to a dead stop and pick up instant speed, so perfect in the coordination of brain and sinew."

—GRANTLAND RICE,
SPORTSWRITER

The Duluth Eskimos played a withering 29-game road schedule that took them coast to coast in 1926. Record-setting fullback Ernie Nevers is dead center.

"As a youngster I was very shy. I was scared to death of people. But football gave me an outlet for my emotions. You get the chance to go man-to-man and see if you can stand up against the best they can throw at you. On a football field I was just a different person."

—ERNIE NEVERS,
DULUTH ESKIMOS AND CHICAGO CARDINALS
RUNNING BACK

A Bears season ticket from 1926, when the team finished 12-1-3 but lost the title to the 14-1-1 Frankford Yellow Jackets.

Providence won its first and only NFL title by tying and then beating Frankford on back-to-back days in mid-November. On Saturday, November 17, at Frankford, the Yellow Jackets took a 6-0 lead on a blocked punt in the third quarter. But George (Wildcat) Wilson scored on a short run and when Olaf (Curly) Oden missed the extra point, the game ended in a 6-6 tie.

The next day in Providence, an overflow crowd of 11,000 turned out at the Cycledrome—a facility that originally was built for bicycle races—to see the Steam Roller earn a 6-0 victory. The only score came on a 46-yard touchdown pass from Wilson to Oden.

A week later, the Steam Roller beat the defending-champion Giants 16-0 to solidify its position at the top of the standings.

In 1929, Tim Mara perfectly illustrated the adage, "If you can't beat 'em, join 'em." Or even buy 'em, which was what the Giants owner did when he decided he wanted Benny Friedman, the all-everything back of the Detroit Wolverines. The Detroit ownership refused to trade Friedman to Mara, so he bought the entire team just to get his player. Mara paid Friedman $10,000 and also hired Detroit coach Roy Andrews to run the Giants.

Benefitting from the new blood, the Giants produced the best offense in the league as Friedman passed for 19 touchdowns—including 8 to Ray Flaherty—and kicked 20 extra points. New York also fielded a formidable defense, helped by tackle Bill Owen, whose older brother Steve had been with the Giants for several years.

Pride of the Dairy State

New York's path to the 1929 title was blocked by the emergence of the Green Bay Packers. Curly Lambeau signed three players—tackle Cal Hubbard, guard Mike Michalske, and halfback Johnny Blood (McNally)—all of whom would go on to Hall-of-Fame careers.

Michalske arrived from the New York Yankees, who folded after the '28 season. Hubbard came from the Giants after requesting that Mara trade him. Blood signed as a free agent when Pottsville went out of business. Blood rushed for 2 touchdowns, caught 2 touchdown passes, and threw 1, and his versatility served as a microcosm of the Packers' offense. On defense, Green Bay was even more polished, allowing only 22 points during a 12-0-1 season.

Green Bay played its first five league games at home—and the only points it allowed came on 2 safeties. The Packers then played eight consecutive games on the road and the only blemish was a scoreless tie at Frankford on November 28. That came four days after an emotional 20-6 victory over the Giants at

THE IGNORING TWENTIES

Pro football lived in the Roarin' Twenties—you just couldn't find it in the newspapers or on radio. "The press looked at the game like wrestling," said New York Giants owner Wellington Mara, whose family purchased the franchise for $500 in 1925.

"Let's just say, from the stories passed down to me, we were looked at askance in the press. Major league baseball and college football dominated. The organization that was the NCAA in those days wanted nothing to do with the pros. They were upset about Red Grange leaving college and going on the big [NFL] barnstorming tour."

Of course, it was tough to keep up with the pro football business in this era. Franchises folded almost weekly, college players worked under assumed names on weekends, and the combatants constantly were jumping from team to team.

Out of such instability came an NFL anchor: the Green Bay Packers. "The Packer corporation, which still is in existence today, was formed right in the office of the *Green Bay Press-Gazette*," recalled retired sportswriter Art Daley, who covered the Packers from the 1930s through the 1980s and still is an active member of the Pro Football Hall of Fame Selection Committee.

"The story goes that it was raining like heck one weekend and Curly Lambeau didn't know where he could come up with the thousand dollars for the visiting team. He went to the newspaper and A.B. Turnbull, the publisher, put up the money, and Turnbull was the one who then incorporated the Packers."

Daley was there before radio discovered pro football. "When the Packers went on the road, four-hundred or five-hundred fans would go to a little park in the middle of town to follow the game," he said. "Someone on the road with the team would phone back whenever there was a score and at the end of a quarter.

"They had this makeshift board with a football field on it and a guy would move a ball back and forth, then announce what was happening to the crowd, as he was told by the guy on the phone."

Those park gatherings soon became unnecessary as radio began broadcasting pro football games. Daley recalled listening to one of the first play-by-play announcers, Russ Winnie: "The sponsor was the Wadham Oil company, and they had this commercial where you could hear the hooves of the horses [pulling the oil trucks] racing down the streets."

The media certainly weren't racing to cover pro football in the twenties. But by the end of the decade the NFL was better organized, and interest was on the rise.

---

the Polo Grounds. The Packers had entered the game 9-0, the Giants 8-0-1. Blood scored a touchdown and set up another with a fumble recovery. Green Bay finished the game with only 11 healthy players. Neither team lost the rest of the season, and the Packers became champions for the first time.

The NFL owners adopted a key rules change in 1929 when they added a fourth official, the field judge. During the annual Thanksgiving Day meeting between the Bears and Cardinals, the fourth official was privileged to see Ernie Nevers score all of the Cardinals' points in a 40-6 victory. Nevers rushed for 6 touchdowns and kicked 4 conversions, showing no ill effects from sitting out the 1928 season. It is a one-game scoring record that still stands.

"The final score: Bears 6, Nevers 40!" the Bears owner recalled in his book, *Halas*. "Nevers was properly cheered by 8,000 people, including the entire Notre Dame team brought there by [Knute] Rockne for a postseason course."

A college coach learning from the pros was a rarity in 1929. That would change.

LONG PLAYING RECORDS

On Thanksgiving Day in 1929, the Chicago Cardinals' Ernie Nevers scored all of his team's points (6 rushing touchdowns and 4 extra points) in a 40-6 rout of the Chicago Bears, setting an NFL single-game mark that never has been equaled.

The league's longest-standing individual regular-season records, according to the *Official National Football League Record & Fact Book*:

RECORD	DATE
MOST POINTS, GAME	
40 Ernie Nevers, Chi. Cardinals vs. Chi. Bears	Nov. 28, 1929
HIGHEST AVERAGE GAIN RUSHING, SEASON	
8.4 Beattie Feathers, Chicago Bears	1934
HIGHEST PUNTING AVERAGE, SEASON	
51.4 Sammy Baugh, Washington	1940
MOST CONSECUTIVE SEASONS LEADING LEAGUE, PUNTING	
4 Sammy Baugh, Washington	1940-43
MOST CONSECUTIVE SEASONS LEADING LEAGUE, AVERAGE GAIN PASSING	
5 Sid Luckman, Chicago Bears	1939-1943

TEAM *of the*
TWENTIES

THE PRIZE WITNESS OF THE NFL

When Arda Bowser is speaking, you want to toss aside the TV remote, take the phone off the hook, shut off the radio, and tell the dog to throw the ball to himself for a while. Because you might never again get to listen to the only person still alive who played in the year the National Football League got its name.

Bowser was born in 1899. The American Professional Football Association was born in 1920, and it switched names—but nothing else—to the National Football League in 1922. That was the year, 1922, when the Canton Bulldogs recruited Bowser—to play fullback, linebacker, punter, and kicker—for $200 per week.

Bowser was not one of the greatest players of the '20s. When the all-time team of that decade was selected, 11 made it, men such as Cal Hubbard, Ernie Nevers, and Paddy Driscoll. But Bowser ought to have an honorary title with the group, something like Most Valuable Historian.

In 1922, Bowser, his college career over, was an assistant coach at his alma mater, Bucknell, in north-central Pennsylvania. The head coach gave him weekends off to pursue this new world of pro football. "It was a job," Bowser said. "It was a way to make money."

Then, the Frankford Yellow Jackets, a semipro team from Philadelphia, offered Bowser the same deal as Canton to play a Saturday-afternoon game. But he'd have to do it under an assumed name because he didn't want the Bulldogs to know he was double-dipping.

"I'd get on a sleeper car late Friday night in Lewisburg and get to Philadelphia around seven Saturday morning," Bowser said, in a slow and clear voice from his Winter Park, Florida, retirement home.

"I'd play the game with Frankford and catch a train Saturday night to Canton, or wherever Canton was playing that weekend. After that game, I'd have to get on a train for Harrisburg, change trains in Harrisburg, and get back to Bucknell Monday morning. We didn't have airplanes, you know.

"I remember one weekend the Canton manager, Ralph Hay, asked me to bring along a halfback," Bowser said. "So I got one, a kid from Lafayette College who I played with on Saturdays in Frankford. In those days, we got dressed in the locker room at Frankford High School, across the street from the field, and then ran through some of our plays in our stocking feet on the gym floor. We played the game, and midway through the fourth quarter we had a big lead. We asked the coach if we could go a little bit early, and he let us.

"We had a taxi waiting to take us to the Broad Street station in Philadelphia. We ran to the taxi and while we were driving to the station, we got changed in the car. When we got to the station, the Broadway Limited was just pulling out. We started yelling to the porters, 'Hold the train! Hold the train!' We ran for the train, and they held it for us. That was about five on Saturday afternoon.

"We got to Chicago the next day at noon. For some reason, the train was three hours late, and Ralph Hay, the poor guy, was nuts waiting for the train. The game, I think, was at one-thirty. He asked if we'd eaten lunch, and we said no. So before we went to the game, we ate some lunch at Harvey's Restaurant, right in the station."

This, as it happened, was a very big game. It was October 29, 1922, and the Bulldogs and Bears were fighting for first place in the new NFL. As it happened, the Bulldogs won 7-6 and went on to beat out the Bears and Chicago Cardinals to win the 1922 NFL championship with a record of 10-0-2.

We must digress for a moment. When Bowser got to Bucknell in 1919, his college coach wanted him to get more distance on kickoffs. Bowser thought he could send them deeper if the ball were raised off the ground a bit. The coach got a small steel washtub, and they started making mud on the sidelines. Whenever Bowser had a kickoff or point-after to perform, he'd race to the sidelines—he was a 60-minute, every-down player—and grab two handfuls of mud. Then he'd plop the mud on the ground, form it into a little hill, and *whammo!* Distance. In this game at Chicago, three times Bowser had to rush to the sidelines for scoops of mud, before he attempted each of three long field goals. He missed all three.

"They claim I was the first in kicking off the tee, such as it was," Bowser said.

But the game was rudimentary. "The pros made a mistake when they started," he said. "They snatched college players before their [eligibility] was over, so the colleges were against us. The press was against us. They said we didn't have the glitter of the college game, and coaches like [Amos Alonzo] Stagg were very much against us. So we had to play where we could and make our money where we could.

"On Thanksgiving weekend in 1922, I played four games in four days. On Friday, I played a game in the hard coal region, in a town called Mount Carmel, southeast of Williamsport. A buddy asked me to come and play. He said, 'Do you have your jersey fixed up? You'd better wear elbow pads and canvas gloves or you'll hurt yourself.'

"I asked him where the heck we were playing. He said, 'In a stone quarry.' And that's exactly where we played, on rocky ground."

Bowser got a job with White Motor Company, an auto and truck manufacturer, in 1923 and began playing for the Cleveland Indians of the NFL. When Jim

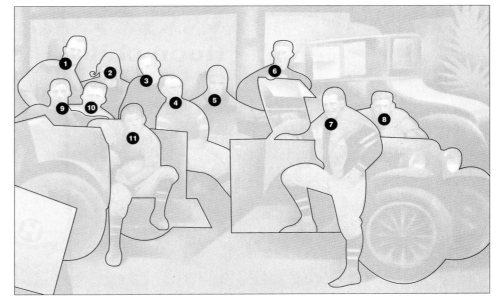

1) *Cal Hubbard, tackle; 2) Walt Kiesling, guard; 3) Lavern Dilweg, end; 4) Paddy Driscoll, back; 5) George Trafton, center; 6) Guy Chamberlin, end; 7) Harold (Red) Grange, halfback; 8) Ernie Nevers, fullback; 9) Mike Michalske, guard; 10) Wilbur (Pete) Henry, tackle; 11) Jim Thorpe, halfback.*

Thorpe's Oorang Indians came to town that fall, the Indians owner arranged a kicking exhibition featuring Thorpe and Bowser before the game. "We set up at the fifty-yard line, and he drop-kicked and I place-kicked off the mud tee," Bowser said. "He was a master of the drop-kick. We both made kicks from the fifty. The crowd seemed impressed."

Then the White Company transferred Bowser to Pittsburgh, and his new boss there wouldn't allow Bowser to commute to Cleveland to continue his career. "So I had to settle for playing barnstorming pro games some Sundays in Ohio River towns near Pittsburgh," Bowser remembered, "under an assumed name, so my boss wouldn't find out."

In 1947, Bowser thought the football life finally might have taken its toll. He went to Cuba with his wife for a fishing vacation and had a heart attack. With doctors' warnings about a short life span ringing in his ears, Bowser retired at 48, moving to a house on a central-Florida lake that fall. Forty-seven years later, his memories and

souvenirs of his days in football still intact, Bowser watches the pro game as keenly as ever.

He has been observing pro football every year since its birth, so it seemed logical to ask: Who's the best player you've ever seen?

"Easy," he said. "Jim Thorpe. Try to tackle him sometime. He'd stiff-arm you so you'd spin like a top. He was a punishing player, but a clean player, a hard player. He was fast and brainy. He had wife trouble and he drank too much, but...

"You heard the story about him and the brown jug, didn't you? Well, we'd play [Oorang], and there'd be a time out, and the waterboy would bring out a pail of water and a dipper. Then the water boy would bring out Thorpe's brown jug. We always figured he was kind of fussy; he needed his water out of a separate container. But we found out later it was firewater! He was drinking firewater right there on the field!"

Apparently, it didn't affect Thorpe's stiff arm.

If you thought indoor pro football was born in 1968 when the Houston Oilers of the American Football League permanently moved into the Astrodome, think again.

The first pro football game under a roof was played on December 18, 1932, at Chicago Stadium, where the hometown Bears beat the Portsmouth Spartans 9-0 for the NFL championship before 11,198 warm, grateful spectators.

The "field" was a layer of dirt—left over from a circus that had been staged in the arena the previous week—covering the cement floor. Not surprisingly, other substances, left behind by the circus animals, were mixed in with the dirt. The playing area was only 80 yards from goal line to goal line. It was 15 feet narrower than regulation. And the end zones were less than 10 yards deep and bordered by the hockey rink's dasher boards.

"I don't think anything could compare with the game," said Bears owner George Halas, who had seen more than his share of bizarre occurrences during the first 13 years of organized pro football. "The only thing not ridiculous about the whole mess was that we won the game."

The championship had been devised by the league office as a means of breaking a tie atop the season-ending standings. The Bears were 6-1-6, the Spartans 6-1-4, and the teams had played to a pair of ties dur-ing the regular season. The playoff was scheduled for Wrigley Field, but a paralyzing blizzard engulfed Chicago the week of the game and made it impossible to play outside.

"The snow was waist deep when we arrived," recalled Portsmouth's tailback Glenn Presnell. "There was no way we could practice."

Rather than postpone the game a week —which would have conflicted with Christmas and hurt the gate receipts— Halas arranged to have it moved indoors to the home of the National Hockey League's Chicago Black Hawks.

Because of the limited space, special rules were drawn up for the championship game. No field goals were allowed; kickoffs were initiated from the kicking team's 10-yard line; punts that bounced around in the rafters (it happened twice) were considered touchbacks; each time a team crossed midfield, it was penalized 20 yards, in effect making the field 100 yards long.

And, for the first time, inbounds lines—or hashmarks—were drawn 10 yards from each sideline. Whenever the ball was carried out of bounds, it was returned to the nearest inbounds line for the next snap, rather than being placed where it went out (right next to the hockey boards). It was a concept the NFL would adopt permanently a year later.

The Bears were heavily favored to win their second league championship, mainly because of a defense that had posted seven shutouts during the season. There was another reason for making the Spartans prohibitive underdogs: Portsmouth was without quarterback Earl (Dutch) Clark, its best player and the NFL's leading scorer. Clark had accepted an offseason basketball coaching job at his alma mater, Colorado College, and already had left to begin his duties.

Portsmouth battled gamely, though, and there was no score through three quarters. The Bears finally took control with 11 minutes to play. Dick Nesbitt

nineties

A blizzard forced the first NFL Championship Game indoors…and altered the rules forever.

intercepted a pass by Leroy (Ace) Gutowsky and returned it to the 13.

After two of his runs gave Chicago a first down at the 2-yard line, Bronko Nagurski was stopped for no gain on his next two carries, setting up a controversial play that would have huge ramifications on the game's future. Nagurski took the next snap, faked a run, then backpedaled and threw a pass into the end zone to Red Grange, who made the catch for a touchdown. George (Potsy) Clark, the Spartans' coach, argued that the play was illegal because the prevailing rules stated that forward passes had to be thrown from a point no fewer than five yards behind the line of scrimmage.

Referee Bobby Cahn, ruling that Nagurski had obeyed the five-yard rule, allowed the touchdown. Paul (Tiny) Engebretsen's conversion made it 7-0.

"I lined up as usual, four yards back," Nagurski said of the critical play. "Red went in motion and the ball came to me. I took a step or two forward as though to

begin the plunge everyone expected. The defenders converged and there was no way I could get through. I stopped, moved back a couple of steps, and Grange had gone around and was in the end zone, all by himself."

A few minutes later, an errant center snap sailed past Portsmouth punter Faye (Mule) Wilson and through the end zone for a Bears safety, wrapping up the victory.

The *Portsmouth Times*, enraged that its hometown team had lost the game on a controversial touchdown, ran a headline that read: "Sham Battle on Tom Thumb Gridiron." In the article that followed,

sportswriter Lynn A. Wittenburg called the game "a synthetic show."

But while the people of Portsmouth were upset, the NFL fathers were ecstatic over the new-found respect the league had earned during those unique 60 minutes. Being so close to the action, the fans had gained a measure of admiration for the pro players that day.

"It was the difference between sitting ringside at a heavyweight fight or in the last row of the upper deck," one sportswriter said. "All of the sounds of human beings smashing other human beings were right there and very real."

LEARNING TO WALK; LEARNING TO THROW

The 1930s finally brought a sense of organization and stability to the National Football League.

When the decade began, there was no official way to determine a champion, franchises folded and shifted cities at will, and the pro game still wasn't recognized as "real" football by college diehards.

But the NFL put itself on firm ground in the 1930s by changing rules to liberalize offense, and by creating two divisions and a season-ending championship game. When the league instituted a college draft in 1936, fans had a way of tracking where their favorite college stars would play as pros, and interest picked up.

By the end of the decade, rivalries became more pronounced as the Green Bay Packers and Chicago Bears battled annually for Western Division supremacy, while the New York Giants and Washington Redskins established themselves as Eastern Division kingpins.

And thanks to players such as Sammy Baugh, Sid Luckman, Don Hutson, and Bronko Nagurski, the league had marquee names to showcase.

Score One for the "Goons"

After the Bears' George Halas experienced the disappointment of a 4-9-2 record in 1929—his first losing season in the pros—he made two very important moves before the 1930 campaign. He removed himself as coach, hiring Ralph Jones as his replacement. Then he signed rookie fullback Bronko Nagurski from the University of Minnesota.

Jones was credited with developing the modern T-formation, and Nagurski thrived in the system, helping the Bears to a 9-4-1 finish in 1930.

"When you hit him," Nagurski's teammate, Red Grange, said of the battering-ram back, "it was like getting an electric shock. If you hit him above the ankles, you were likely to get yourself killed."

By the end of the decade, a football spiraling downfield no longer raised eyebrows. Green Bay's Cecil Isbell (opposite) launches a throw in the 1938 NFL title game.

Bronko Nagurski defined NFL football in the 1930s. The Chicago Bears fullback, a charter member of the Pro Football Hall of Fame, was a punishing runner who was even more feared as a blocker.

Sunday, OCT., 2, 1932—3 P. M.
FOOTBALL
at UNIVERSAL STADIUM
PORTSMOUTH SPARTANS
vs.
CHICAGO CARDINALS
Established Price $2.00 $1.75
Federal Tax   .25   .18
Total $2.25 $1.93
HOLD YOUR OWN TICKET

No. 3—1932
Stadium Seat
Sec.   **D**
Row   **8**
Seat   16

A 1932 ticket for the Portsmouth Spartans, who became the Detroit Lions in 1934.

When the 1930 season ended and the Packers had won their second consecutive championship, the runner-up New York Giants agreed to take part in what became the most important football game in the NFL's brief history. On December 14 at the Polo Grounds, the Giants met a team of Notre Dame all-stars. All proceeds went to the steadily dwindling New York Unemployment Fund.

With the Great Depression growing to catastrophic proportions, the Giants' participation in the exhibition was an appreciated gesture. But many of the 55,000 fans who turned out—raising more than $100,000 for the Fund—didn't give the pro team much of a chance against the polished Irish. College football still was much more popular than the pro game at the time, and the average fan likened the pros to clumsy goons.

Knute Rockne, who coached the Irish, told his team before the game: "Boys, these Giants are big, but slow. Go out there, score two or three touchdowns on passes in the first quarter, and then defend…and don't get hurt."

But Rockne's team, which included the fabled Four Horsemen and a number of more recent Notre Dame graduates, never was in the game. Benny Friedman directed the Giants to two early touchdowns, the defense permitted Notre Dame just 1 first down, and New York cruised to a 22-0 victory. That result went a long way toward legitimizing the NFL and the product it was offering.

The Packers became the first team in NFL history to win the championship three years in a row when their 12-2 record edged the 11-3 Portsmouth Spartans in 1931. Coach Curly Lambeau still had Johnny Blood (McNally), Mike Michalske, Red Dunn, Cal Hubbard, and LaVern Dilweg in his stable, and the addition of Rudy Comstock and several other newcomers gave the Packers a formidable offense and defense. Green Bay won its first nine games before losing to Ernie Nevers's Chicago Cardinals, then won three more before losing 7-6 to the Bears in the season finale.

Rules Made for Passing

The Depression took its toll on the NFL in 1932 and the league dwindled to eight teams as the Frankford Yellow Jackets, Providence Steam Roller, and Cleveland Indians, all former powers, withdrew. Before the season, George Preston Marshall, on the recommendation of Halas and NFL president Joe Carr, was allowed to form a team. Marshall, Vincent Bendix, Jay O'Brien, and M. Dorland Doyle then contributed $7,500 each to become owners of the Boston Braves. The team lost $46,000 in its first year, and Marshall was left as the sole owner when 1933 began.

The Packers' title run came to an end in '32 despite their 10-3-1 record, as the Bears beat Portsmouth in a championship playoff. The NFL kept official statistics for the first time that year and Boston's Cliff Battles won the rushing title with 576 yards, while Luke Johnsos of the Bears was the top receiver with 24 catches for 321 yards.

The 1932 NFL Championship Game, which capped the brilliant career of Bears lineman George Trafton, was played indoors at Chicago Stadium on an 80-yard field as a blizzard raged outside. That scenario proved to be a blessing for the NFL, for it stoked the creative juices of Halas, who was president of the rules committee. The small field was one reason both offenses struggled in the 9-0 game, but offensive woes had become an alarming trend

FINALLY, SOMETHING IN THE AIR

In the Depression era of the 1930s, pro football broke away from the collegiate game and began to establish its own identity. Instructional manuals now bore the names of professional coaches. League decision-makers, who had followed the NCAA Rules Committee in lockstep for 13 years, began to open up the game, and they figured the best way to do it was to make it easier to pass.

The fat ball of the twenties was slimmed down, the touchback rule for an incomplete pass in the end zone was modified, and hashmarks were introduced to ease the pressure on a team pinned on the sidelines. Later in the decade a roughing-the-passer rule was introduced and linemen were prohibited from going downfield before the pass, to give some semblance of order to the developing patterns.

Green Bay was the NFL's passingest team in 1930s. Packers head coach Curly Lambeau always favored a wide-open attack. He had talented throwers in Arnie Herber and later Cecil Isbell, and when Don Hutson arrived in 1935, he had a weapon unlike any before. Hutson was like an emissary from another planet, gifted on every pattern—the short and long post, the takeoff, the quick outs and slants. In five years he had rewritten all the career receiving records.

In 1937, Sammy Baugh, with his whip-like arm and tight spiral, arrived to put some zip into the Washington Redskins' attack. Two years later, the Bears drafted Sid Luckman and paid him $10,000 to become a pure T-formation passer.

The Single-Wing, with its unbalanced line, its two deep backs (including a run-and-throw tailback), its quarterback as blocking back and wingback set outside, was the dominant formation.

Far from being solely an instrument of power, the Single-Wing had a grace in its running concept that is not seen nowadays. Teams could attack with strength on the strong side or trap the other way, using a pulling guard and blocking back in tandem and giving the play much the same look as today's Counter-Trey. It had everything, and no team ever ran it better than the 1936 Detroit Lions, coached by George (Potsy) Clark.

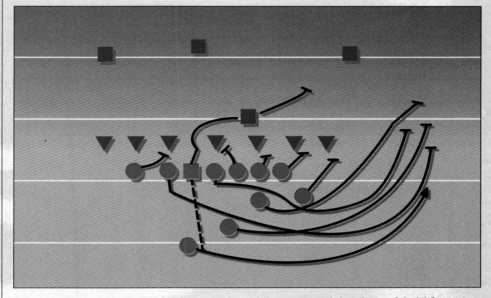

The run-oriented Single-Wing (above) dominated the NFL until the advent of the T-formation.

In 12 games, the Lions, led by nifty runners such as Dutch Clark, Ace Gutowsky, Ernie Caddel, and Glenn Presnell, gained 2,885 yards on the ground, a 242.4 per-game average that never has been matched in the NFL. The Lions finished 8-4 that year. Two losses to the passing Packers locked them out of championship competition.

The Chicago Bears employed the T-formation. In 1930, George Halas hired Ralph Jones from Lake Forest Academy to coach the team and redefine the T. Red Grange became the man-in-motion, one or both ends were flexed or split out at various times, and the result was a modern pro set. More tinkering arrived with Clark Shaughnessy, the University of Chicago coach. He added new wrinkles and codified the play-calling in the method used today.

The Bears weren't married to the T, though. It accompanied the Single-Wing, which featured 238-pound Bronko Nagurski as fullback.

For all his greatness, the Bronk never put up big numbers. He averaged 10 carries a game and had only one 100-yard performance. That was Halas's way. Share the wealth, use plenty of reserves, keep everyone fresh, and in this, he was ahead of his time.

Pass protection in the decade was primitive. "There wasn't a lot of it," Baugh said, which helps to account for the modest completion percentages. For the first six years that the league kept full statistics, no team completed 50 percent of its passes. Many of the game's leading throwers were in the 30-percent range. Coaching manuals that offered page after page of run-block analysis didn't mention pass-blocking.

The passers constantly threw on the move, with defenders in their faces, and it was only because they were tailbacks, gifted at the run, that they were saved.

"Pass-blocking wasn't organized," Luckman says. "You didn't have a guy in the press box phoning down adjustments. You were expected to dodge one or two guys rushing you."

Better days were coming.

Bill Hewitt (above) pitches on the trick play that gave Chicago the 1933 NFL title.

Art Rooney bought the Pittsburgh Pirates (later Steelers) after a big day at the track.

during the regular season. Games were slow-paced and many ended in ties—in fact, one of every five games in 1932 failed to produce a winner.

Halas thought about the rules changes, some of which were enacted for the impromptu title game, and envisioned what they might do for offensive football on a normal-sized field. He concluded that the game could be improved dramatically if the same rules were brought outside.

Marshall, who was looking to stop the financial bleeding he had experienced the previous season, felt the same way and backed Halas at every turn. At the February, 1933, league meeting, the owners approved three major rules changes. First, the goal posts were moved from the end lines to the goal lines to promote more field goals. Second, hashmarks were drawn 10 yards from each sideline, so that whenever a play ended near the sideline, the ball would be moved to the nearest hashmark for the next snap. Third, forward passes were deemed legal if they originated anywhere behind the line of scrimmage. (Previously, the passer had to be at least five yards behind the line.)

"We hoped the new rules would open up the game," Halas said. "I believe the record shows we were right."

Indeed, field-goal production increased significantly, as did the offensive output of almost every team. The number of tie games fell to five, half the total of 1932, and shutouts were reduced.

Marshall, who changed his team's nickname to Redskins before the 1933 season began, spearheaded another radical change at a July owners meeting when he proposed that the league split into two divisions, with the winners meeting in an annual season-ending championship game.

New York, the Brooklyn Dodgers, Boston, and two new teams, the Philadelphia Eagles and the Pittsburgh Pirates, composed the Eastern Division. The Bears, Cardinals, Spartans, Packers, and another new team, the Cincinnati Reds, were aligned in the Western Division.

At that same meeting, two influential owners joined the league. Art Rooney was granted a franchise for Pittsburgh, which he bought with winnings from a big day at the racetrack, and Bert Bell, with the help of Lud Wray, was awarded a franchise in Philadelphia. The key to securing both teams was the legalizing of Sunday sports in Pennsylvania. In addition, Halas became sole owner of the Bears and returned himself to the sidelines for the first time since 1929.

Tricky Title Game

At the start of the 1933 season, every NFL team knew, for the first time in league history, exactly when the championship game would be played. As it happened, the Bears (10-2-1) hosted the Giants (11-3) at Wrigley Field in the first scheduled NFL Championship Game.

The Bears fielded a strong team with tackles Roy (Link) Lyman and George Musso, guards Joe Kopcha and Jules Carlson, and center Charles (Ookie) Miller blocking for Bronko Nagurski. The Giants countered with the running of quarterback Harry Newman and halfback Ken Strong and the receiving of ends Ray Flaherty and Dale Burnett, all behind undersized but aggressive 210-pound center Mel Hein.

As a crowd of 26,000 struggled to see through misty rain and fog, Jack Manders kicked a pair of first-half field goals to give Chicago the lead. But shortly before intermission, Newman threw a touchdown pass to Morris (Red) Badgro and Strong's conversion gave New York a 7-6 advantage. Manders's third field goal again put the Bears on top, but back came the Giants behind the passing of Newman, who directed a march to the 1-yard line before Max Krause plunged in to make it 14-9.

Three minutes later, Nagurski threw a touchdown pass to Bill Karr, and Manders's extra point had the Bears back in front 16-14.

New York had another answer, however. On the first play of the fourth quarter, with the Giants at Chicago's 8, Strong swept to the right and ran into a wall of Bears. Reversing his field, he lateraled to the startled Newman. Not knowing what else to do, Newman threw the ball back to Strong, who slipped by the Bears' defense and was all alone in the end zone for an 8-yard touchdown. Strong's conversion put New York in front 21-16.

After an 8-yard punt by Strong gave the Bears possession at New York's 46 with three minutes left, Chicago used a trick play to pull out the victory. Two plays had moved the ball to the Giants' 33 when Nagurski took the snap, began to run toward the line, then stopped, jumped in the air, and threw a pass over the middle to Bill Hewitt. Hewitt went 14 yards, then lateraled to Karr, who took off down the right sideline and covered the final 19 yards for the go-ahead score. The Giants nearly pulled out the game on the final play, but a familiar face made a game-saving tackle on Badgro, allowing the Bears to survive a 23-21 thriller.

WINNING, AND LOSING, THE BIG ONE

Since the NFL's impromptu championship game in 1932 convinced league owners to adopt the idea permanently one season later, the Green Bay Packers have won more titles (8) than any other team.

Here's how each franchise has fared in NFL title games (NFL Championship Games from 1933-1965, and Super Bowls I-XXVIII):

TEAM	W	L	PCT.
Pittsburgh Steelers	4	0	1.000
San Francisco 49ers	4	0	1.000
New York Jets	1	0	1.000
Green Bay Packers	8	2	.800
Detroit Lions	4	1	.800
Los Angeles Raiders*	3	1	.750
Chicago Bears	7	4	.636
Indianapolis Colts**	3	2	.600
Philadelphia Eagles	3	2	.600
Dallas Cowboys	4	3	.571
Arizona Cardinals***	1	1	.500
Kansas City Chiefs	1	1	.500
Washington Redskins#	5	6	.455
Cleveland Browns	4	5	.444
Miami Dolphins	2	3	.400
Los Angeles Rams##	2	4	.333
New York Giants	5	11	.313
New England Patriots	0	1	.000
Cincinnati Bengals	0	2	.000
Buffalo Bills	0	4	.000
Denver Broncos	0	4	.000
Minnesota Vikings	0	4	.000

*Three games played when franchise was in Oakland (2-1).
**All games played when franchise was in Baltimore.
***Both games played when franchise was in Chicago.
#One game played when franchise was in Boston (0-1).
##One game played when franchise was in Cleveland (1-0).

Note: The Atlanta Falcons, Houston Oilers, New Orleans Saints, San Diego Chargers, Seattle Seahawks, and Tampa Bay Buccaneers have not played in an NFL title game.

"I caught a pass and the only person between me and the goal line was Red Grange," Badgro said. "I planned to lateral to a teammate who was running alongside of me—Mel Hein or Dale Burnett—but Grange grabbed me around the arms and upper body and I couldn't. Had I been able to, we would have won the championship."

Newman finished the game with 12 completions in 17 attempts for 201 yards for the Giants. Nagurski rushed for 65 yards to pace the Bears.

A Year for New Traditions

Detroit found itself back in the NFL in 1934 when G.A. Richards purchased the Portsmouth Spartans for $15,000—plus $6,500 to pay off their debts— and moved the team to Michigan, where it was renamed the Lions.

Before the regular season, *Chicago Tribune* sports editor Arch Ward organized the first Chicago College All-Star Game in the Windy City. The idea was to match the defending NFL champion against a team of just-graduated college hot shots. The game produced a lackluster 0-0 tie, but it drew 79,432 fans to Soldier Field, the beginning of an annual event that lasted until 1976 and raised more than $4 million for charity.

Another tradition began in 1934: the annual Thanksgiving Day game in Detroit. The Lions had given their new fans plenty to cheer about, racing to a 10-0 record that included seven consecutive shutouts. But a 3-0 loss to Green Bay on a 47-yard field goal by Clarke Hinkle left them a game behind the unbeaten Bears when Chicago came to town on Thanksgiving Day. The holiday showdown became the first NFL game to reach a national audience, courtesy of the NBC radio network. Graham McNamee called the play-by-play and Don Wilson (later of Jack Benny fame) added the color as 94 stations carried the action.

Earl (Dutch) Clark, who finished the season with 763 rushing yards—third to the Eagles' Tom (Swede) Hanson and the Bears' Beattie Feathers, the first player in NFL history to top 1,000 yards— was the key player for Detroit, both on offense and as a safety on defense. But with the nation listening, Clark was handled by the Bears' mighty defense.

Meanwhile, running back Leroy (Ace) Gutowsky and quarterback Glenn Presnell sparked the Lions to a 16-7 lead. Manders kicked 2 field goals in the third quarter to pull the Bears within 16-13. Then Joe Zeller intercepted a pass and ran 55 yards to the Detroit 4, setting up Nagurski's fake plunge and lob pass to Hewitt, which provided the winning points in a 19-16 decision.

Packers coach Curly Lambeau at the chalkboard with two of the keys to his vaunted passing game: end Don Hutson (left) and halfback Cecil Isbell.

SNEAKERS

On Sunday, December 9, 1934, the day of the NFL Championship Game between the New York Giants and the defending-champion Chicago Bears, the field at the Polo Grounds was a dreadful sight. Saturday night's freezing rain had left the playing surface slick with ice. The temperature at game time was 9 degrees.

New York Giants coach Steve Owen and his captain, right end Ray Flaherty, talked it over.

"Too bad we don't have sneakers instead of these things," Flaherty said, pointing to his football shoes. "I remember a game at Gonzaga [Flaherty's alma mater, in Spokane, Washington]. The ground was just like this. We switched to basketball shoes and ran away from the other team."

Owen considered it for a few moments. The Bears were undefeated. The Giants' record against Western Division teams

The Giants couldn't keep this ball in bounds, but their footwear helped tame the Bears in '34.

that season was 1-4. Why not sneakers?

One problem: Every sporting goods store in New York was closed. Trainer Gus Mauch suggested that Manhattan College might supply a set of sneakers. Mauch made a call, got permission from the college, and sent assistant equipment man Abe Cohen to pick up the shoes.

By the time Cohen returned, the Bears had staked a 10-3 halftime lead on a touchdown by Bronko Nagurski and a field goal by Jack Manders. And by the

time the Giants called time out with 10 minutes remaining in the third quarter and came to the sidelines to don their new sneakers, the Bears were ahead 13-3.

Was it the shoes? The Giants scored 4 touchdowns, including 2 runs by fullback Ken Strong, and won 30-13. Afterward, in the new champions' locker room, the exhausted Strong told reporters, "I'm no hero."

Then, pointing to Cohen, he said, "There's your hero."

The Bears went on to a perfect 13-0 record and were overwhelming favorites to win their second consecutive championship. But they lost the famous "Sneakers Game" to the Giants, 30-13 at the icy Polo Grounds.

The Beginning of the (Split) End

It took Don Hutson, a ballyhooed rookie end from Alabama, exactly one play to serve notice that pass receiving was about to become an art form in the NFL. In his inaugural start for the Packers in 1935, a home contest against the Bears, Hutson caught an 83-yard touchdown pass from Arnie Herber on his first play from scrimmage. Pass patterns never were run the same way again.

"We brought the kickoff out to the seventeen and right there we lined up for a play we had practiced all week," Hutson told Myron Cope in the book *The Game That Was.* "I lined up split to the left and Johnny Blood was way out to the right. The Bears thought we would pass to Blood, but he was a decoy. I went down and faked outside to take the halfback out, and then I cut back over the middle and got behind the safety man. Herber let the ball go and it was a forty-yard pass—but it was an eighty-three-yard gain, good for a touchdown.

"It was a simple play, but the fact that it was a long pass on the first play made it a surprise. That just wasn't done in those days. There wasn't any question anymore about my being able to play."

"Tacklers to Nagurski are like flies on the flank of a horse—a nuisance but not a serious one."

—STEVE OWEN,
NEW YORK GIANTS TACKLE, ON
CHICAGO BEARS FULLBACK BRONKO NAGURSKI

THE SKINNY BALL

The most important piece of equipment in football is...the football, of course. Once virtually the only piece of equipment, it had been so round it looked more like a basketball than what we have come to recognize in modern NFL games.

During the 1930s, the football was shaped by several rules changes. The specifications have not changed since they were updated by a 1934 rule that required the "short axis [around the middle], not less than 21¼ inches, nor more than 21½ inches." The football had become user friendlier, particularly for passers. The more tapered ball, however, sharply diminished the importance of the dropkick.

During the Great Depression, many pro teams were looking to save money anywhere they could, particularly on equipment. That may have prompted these inquiries in a letter written on March 18, 1938, by Detroit Lions player-coach Earl (Dutch) Clark to his equipment man:

"Business is very bad there in Detroit and if it doesn't pick up by fall our crowds will no doubt be smaller. For this reason I think we should keep the cost of the equipment as low as possible....Is the price quoted on the satin pants from the tool shop? If so isn't it a bit higher than last year? Isn't $8 rather high for the jersies [sic]?"

As Clark's letter attests, the fabric used in football uniforms had changed during the 1930s. Satin, Army duck, and Skookum Cloth—all synthetics—replaced canvas as the material of choice for NFL pants. Also, knits first appeared in jerseys. In 1936, the normally conservative George Halas unveiled a shocking splash of color in the uniform of his Chicago Bears, with generous amounts of striping. The new outfits lasted only one season.

The helmet of choice in the '30s fast became the hard-leather version with molded crown and reinforced fiber shell, although Rawlings was quick to point out that its Zuppke Varsity Helmet included "Soft Leather at all points of contact." Riddell developed a plastic helmet that first was used in 1939, but it did not catch on until after World War II.

Facemasks of various sorts began popping up in the thirties—and popping off helmets. They, too, would not become popular until after the war, when helmets could better support them.

"Paul Brown is often mistakenly said to be the inventor of the facemask," said Joe Horrigan, curator of the Pro Football Hall of Fame. "He patented the roll-bar facemask in the fifties, but the facemask had been around since the thirties. What wasn't available was a hard-shell helmet to attach the masks to, so they had to come up with jerry-rigged systems of attachments."

Spalding came out with what it called the Safe-T cleat in 1939, advertising "no more dangerous metal posts." Instead of the posts protruding from the bottom of the shoe, they were attached to the cleat and screwed into a hole in the shoe, much as they are today.

Shoulder pads, previously made of leather, evolved into fiber shells that offered more extensions and, for the first time, cantilevering, which held the pads high on the shoulders and gave players a more hulking appearance.

Pieces of a Bears uniform of the decade, with typical satin pants and hard-leather helmet.

Running to the Top

Bears halfback Beattie Feathers averaged 9.9 yards per carry in 1934 en route to becoming the NFL's first 1,000-yard rusher (1,004). It was 13 years before another player, the Eagles' Steve Van Buren, bettered Feathers's mark.

The evolution of the NFL's single-season rushing record:

YEAR	PLAYER	TEAM	YARDS
1932	Cliff Battles	Boston	576
1933	Jim Musick	Boston	809
1934	Beattie Feathers	Chicago Bears	1,004
1947	Steve Van Buren	Philadelphia	1,008
1949	Steve Van Buren	Philadelphia	1,146
1958	Jim Brown	Cleveland	1,527
1963	Jim Brown	Cleveland	1,863
1973	O.J. Simpson	Buffalo	2,003
1984	Eric Dickerson	L.A. Rams	2,105

Right: Chicago's Beattie Feathers, the first to reach 1,000.

Besides his blazing speed, Hutson introduced a repertoire of moves that defenders never had to deal with before. He gradually built an arsenal of new maneuvers, and defenses never caught up to him during his brilliant Hall-of-Fame career.

Incredibly, the NFL almost didn't get to enjoy Hutson's magic. "Until I started receiving letters from Curly Lambeau, I had given no thought to playing pro football," he said. "I'd never even heard of the Green Bay Packers. Down in Alabama there was nothing in the papers about pro football. They didn't even have results. It was a whole different country down there."

Lambeau got into a bidding war with John (Shipwreck) Kelly, the former Giants end and new owner of the Brooklyn franchise. Lambeau offered Hutson $175 a week and when Hutson couldn't reach Kelly to tell him of the offer, the end accepted.

When Kelly learned that Hutson had signed, he confronted the young man and suggested he sign a contract with Brooklyn for the same figure and let NFL President Joe Carr decide where Hutson would play. Hutson obliged and Carr awarded him to Green Bay because he had signed with the Packers first.

During his career, Hutson would lead the NFL in receptions eight times, and he set a league record by catching at least 1 pass in 95 consecutive games (1937-1945), a mark that stood until 1969. In 1942, Hutson became the first NFL receiver to top 1,000 yards, with 1,211.

"A Redskin game is something resembling a fast-moving revue, with cues, settings, music, pace, tableaus, and, hold your hats boys—a ballet."

—BOB CONSIDINE,
SPORTSWRITER, DESCRIBING REDSKINS OWNER
GEORGE PRESTON MARSHALL'S
FLAIR FOR DRAMATICS

THE REAL FIRST PICK

Not one Eagles fan wearing a green jersey and an adjustable cap sat in the balcony at Philadelphia's Ritz-Carlton Hotel on February 8, 1936. Not one ESPN analyst told the studio host that the New York Giants were crazy to draft three tackles or that the Brooklyn Dodgers should have traded their third and fourth choices for the Pittsburgh Pirates' second pick.

What kind of an NFL draft do you call that? You call it the first NFL draft—a friendly gathering of the nine clubs, including league pioneers George Halas of the Chicago Bears, Bert Bell of the Eagles, Curly Lambeau of the Green Bay Packers, and George Preston Marshall of the Boston Redskins. The draft was Bell's idea. In having the teams choose in inverse order of finish, the aim was to help the weak teams get stronger.

From time to time, when he wasn't hobnobbing, Marshall would croon popular songs to the piano accompaniment of Chicago Cardinals coach Jimmy Conzelman. The party was in full swing, but, as Packers president Lee Joannes later noted, "Nobody fell asleep. If you fell asleep you'd lose a couple of ball players."

That would have hurt, considering that the nine clubs chose nine players each from a list of approximately 90 players posted on the wall—a far cry from the five-figure talent pool available today at the touch of a computer key.

The first player taken in the first draft, University of Chicago halfback and first Heisman Trophy winner Jay Berwanger, never did sign with Philadelphia, which selected him initially, or the Chicago Bears, who traded for his rights. The second player chosen, Alabama quarterback Riley Smith, became the first draftee to play in the NFL. Smith went to the Boston Redskins and played three seasons.

Hutson's emergence, however, wasn't enough to derail the Lions, who went 7-3-2 to win the West. In the 1935 championship, they stopped the defending-champion Giants 26-7 on a snowy day in Detroit. The victory came two months after baseball's Detroit Tigers won their first World Series title.

First Draft

At the end of the 1934 season, Philadelphia's Bert Bell suggested that the NFL teams draft college players, with the team owning the poorest record choosing first. The proposal was accepted and put into effect in 1936, and Heisman Trophy-winning halfback Jay Berwanger of the University of Chicago became the first player ever drafted by the NFL—by Bell, whose Eagles had finished with a 2-9 record in 1935. Bell then traded Berwanger's rights to the Bears. Ironically, Berwanger elected not to play pro football.

The Bears, one of the teams Bell was trying to overtake, used the draft brilliantly, selecting West Virginia tackle Joe Stydahar and Colgate guard Dan Fortmann, both future Hall-of-Fame inductees.

Stability became reality in 1936 when, for the first time since the formation of the NFL, there were no franchise shifts. It also was the first year in which all the teams played the same number of regular-season games (12).

Boston and Green Bay won tight division races in '36. Then, in a move that would become commonplace with the birth of the Super Bowl 30 years later, the NFL Championship Game was played at a neutral site.

It was to have been played in Boston, but Redskins owner George Preston Marshall moved the game to New York's Polo Grounds. Marshall claimed the fans of Boston hadn't supported his team as it won the Eastern Division. The fans were upset that Marshall, without advance notice, had raised ticket

Green Bay's Clarke Hinkle (with ball) was a fierce competitor and valuable halfback.

prices on the day of a game earlier in the season. They protested by staying home when Pittsburgh came to Boston for a late-season game (only 5,000 showed up). In the Packers-Redskins game, Arnie Herber threw 2 touchdown passes, 1 to Hutson, and Green Bay rolled to a 21-6 victory before 29,545 mostly disinterested fans.

The NFL again had competition in the pro ranks as a second American Football League was formed in 1936 with teams in Boston, Cleveland, New York, Pittsburgh, Rochester, and Brooklyn. The Boston Shamrocks posted an 8-3 record and won the championship that first year. Three prominent former Giants—Red Badgro, Harry Newman, and Ken Strong—played in the AFL, as did future Hall-of-Fame coach Sid Gillman.

In the AFL's second season, Brooklyn and Cleveland folded and were replaced by Cincinnati and Los Angeles, the latter winning the title with an 8-0 record. The Bulldogs became the first pro football team to play home games on the West Coast, as two of their games were held at Gilmore Stadium in Hollywood. The entire league disappeared after the season.

Capital Gains

In the NFL, meanwhile, the Cleveland Rams were formed by Homer Marshman and joined the league in 1937. As expected, Marshall moved his Redskins to Washington, and once in the nation's capital, his first order of business was signing All-America tailback Sammy Baugh of Texas Christian University to an $8,000 contract.

The Redskins may have been in a new city, but they remained successful, winning their second Eastern Division title. In his first game as a pro, Baugh completed 11 of 16 passes as Washington beat the Giants 13-3 in a night game at Griffith Stadium. Marshall organized the Redskins' marching band and produced elaborate halftime shows that created a rabid support group.

Never was this more evident than in the game that decided the Eastern Division title. About 10,000 Redskins fans made the journey to New York to watch their team pummel the Giants 49-14 as huge tackle Glen (Turk) Edwards and the Redskins' offensive line controlled the game.

Baugh capped his stellar rookie season by completing 18 of 32 passes for 354 yards and 3 touchdowns to lead the Redskins over the Bears 28-21 in the 1937 NFL Championship Game at Wrigley Field. All three of the scoring passes came in the third quarter as Washington overcame a 21-14 deficit.

In 1938, Hugh (Shorty) Ray was hired as a technical advisor and supervisor of NFL officials, a position he held until 1956. Ray's primary job was to devise ways of making the sport faster and safer. He watched hundreds of games and always was making notations on what he saw. His contributions earned him a spot in the Pro Football Hall of Fame.

Neither Washington nor Chicago returned to the title game in 1938 as the Giants and Packers ascended to the tops of their respective divisions. A crowd of 48,120 came to the Polo Grounds to watch the Giants pull out a 23-17 victory for the championship. Despite playing without Hutson, who had suffered a knee injury earlier in the season, the Packers held a 378-212 advantage in total yards, but a pair of blocked punts—by Jim Lee Howell and Jim Poole—led to 9 New York points and made the difference.

At the end of the season, the first Pro Bowl was played at Wrigley Field in Los Angeles. Marshall had met during the summer with *Los Angeles Times*

WHIZZER

To those who followed his career as a United States Supreme Court Justice, it might be difficult to imagine that Byron White ever was a rookie at anything. But in 1938, as a rookie with Art Rooney's Pittsburgh Pirates, Byron (Whizzer) White, an All-America halfback and first-round draft pick from the University of Colorado, led the NFL in rushing with 567 yards.

It wasn't until late July that White reversed an early-summer decision and decided to play pro football, delaying his enrollment at Oxford University as a Rhodes Scholar until January, 1939.

The Pirates finished last in the Eastern Division with a 2-9 record in '38, but White's speed and cutting ability, as well as his composure, made an impact. He sat out the 1939 season to study at Oxford, then returned to the NFL for two seasons with the Detroit Lions.

Augie Lio, a guard with the Lions, said of White, "I was amazed that a fellow playing with you could know so much about what everyone else did or didn't do on a certain play."

Of White's demeanor off the field, Detroit coach George (Potsy) Clark said, "While the other guys were playing cards for five cents a point, White would get out his glasses, his pipe, and his law books and start studying."

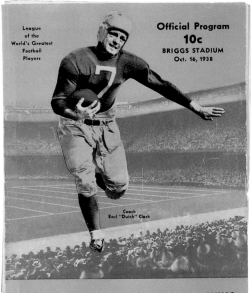

Above: A 1938 Lions-Redskins program featuring versatile back Dutch Clark. *Right*: The Giants' Kink Richards runs against Green Bay in the 1939 title game.

PASSED HISTORY

Arnie Herber's record 1,239 passing yards are dwarfed by Dan Marino's current standard of 5,084, but they made big news in 1936.

How the NFL record for passing yards in a season has grown over the years:

YEAR	PLAYER, TEAM	YARDS
1933	Harry Newman, NYG	973
1936	Arnie Herber, GB	1,239
1939	Davey O'Brien, Phil.	1,324
1940	Sammy Baugh, Wash.	1,367
1941	Cecil Isbell, GB	1,479
1942	Cecil Isbell, GB	2,021
1943	Sid Luckman, Bears	2,194
1947	Sammy Baugh, Wash.	2,938
1960	Johnny Unitas, Balt.	3,099
1961	Sonny Jurgensen, Phil.	3,723
1967	Joe Namath, NYJ	4,007
1979	Dan Fouts, SD	4,082
1980	Dan Fouts, SD	4,715
1981	Dan Fouts, SD	4,802
1984	Dan Marino, Mia.	5,084

sports editor Bill Henry and promoter Tom Gallery, pitching an idea about playing a postseason all-star game that would pit the NFL champion against a team made up of the best from the other teams. When an uncharacteristic heavy fog hung over Los Angeles, an anticipated crowd of 30,000 was reduced to about 20,000. The game went on and the Giants scored a 13-10 win, decided by Ward Cuff's 18-yard field goal with about five minutes left.

Death of a President

The NFL lost its leader before the start of the 1939 season when President Joe Carr died on May 20. Secretary-treasurer Carl Storck was named interim president until a permanent successor could be chosen.

A former sportswriter, Carr had guided the league for its first two decades, and his skills as an administrator proved invaluable during a trying era when franchises shifted and folded on a yearly basis. Storck had been Carr's right-hand man throughout his stint as president.

An NFL game was televised for the first time when the National Broad-

THE FIRST ARMCHAIR QBS

When Allen (Skip) Walz and his cohorts piled into a car and drove to Ebbets Field on October 22, 1939, they had no way of knowing what was behind the incredible door they were about to help open.

Walz would announce the first televised pro football game—to perhaps the smallest TV audience ever. The game between the Brooklyn Dodgers and Philadelphia Eagles, broadcast by RCA's experimental television station, WXBS, was beamed to the 1,000 or so TV sets then in New York.

"We had only eight people in the crew," Walz once recalled, "nine if you count the guy who drove the mobile unit. I remember getting paid twenty-five dollars to do the game. I had no spotters, no monitors, no visual aids of any sort."

What Walz described, the cameraman tried to follow. "It got sticky," Walz said, "particularly late in the game when it started to get dark."

Brooklyn outscored Philadelphia 23-14 before 13,051 fans, but the real winner was pro football, for television would take the sport in new directions.

"When my father [Art Rooney] bought the team in the 1930s," Pittsburgh Steelers owner Dan Rooney said, "it was hard to get any kind of media coverage. In fact, my father had to pay the radio station in Pittsburgh to put our games on the air."

But attention grew, thanks in part to RCA's experiment. "If that experimental broadcast showed anything," said Ed Kiely, long-time Steelers administrator, "it showed that football was the game for television. It fit the screen. It had action. It appealed to the guy who drank beer and bought cars. This is why the sponsorship was so appealing to those businesses when television boomed."

casting Company aired the Brooklyn Dodgers-Philadelphia Eagles game from Ebbets Field on October 22, 1939. The game was transmitted back to the studios in Manhattan and beamed to the few sets that were available and in use, mostly in the New York area.

During the season, future star Sid Luckman took over at quarterback for the Bears, replacing Bernie Masterson, but the Bears finished one game behind the Packers in the Western Division. In the East, the Giants rolled to a 9-1-1 record and traveled to Milwaukee to meet the Packers for the title.

The game was moved to Wisconsin State Fair Park in Milwaukee because seating was limited at City Stadium in Green Bay. A crowd of 32,279, paying an increased ticket price of $4.40, saw their Packers roll to a 27-0 victory on a windy day. Green Bay quarterback Arnie Herber suffered 3 interceptions, but he and Cecil Isbell each threw a touchdown pass. The Green Bay defense had 6 interceptions.

The NFL had overcome competition, the death of its president, and the worst of the Great Depression. It soon would learn whether it could survive war.

TEAM *of the* THIRTIES

ed an unbalanced line, with one man—an end—lined up to the left of center Mel Hein. The end took a step back, and the flanker to the far right took a step forward, to the line of scrimmage. This made Hein an eligible end. He snapped the ball to quarterback Harry Newman, who slyly handed it back to Hein. While Newman pretended to look for the ball, Hein tried to sneak away into the flat, hiding the ball. Neither time did the Giants gain significantly. But it was fun, wasn't it?

• In the fourth quarter, halfback Ken Strong took a handoff and ran left. Hemmed in, he threw a lateral pass back to Newman. Trapped himself, Newman looked, looked, looked…and then saw Strong in the far corner of the end zone. Touchdown. The Giants led 21-16.

• With a few minutes left, Nagurski threw another option pass, this time to end Bill Hewitt, who hook-and-lateraled the ball to Karr, who scored the decisive touchdown. Bears 23-21.

• On the last play of the game, the desperate Giants threw a pass to Dale Burnett near the Bears' 40-yard line, and only one man stood between Burnett and the goal line: Red Grange. "I tackled Dale high," Grange said, "so he could not lateral."

Grange, the ball, and Burnett all went down in a heap as the game ended. The Bears won.

Four of the eleven players named to the Team of the Thirties—Hewitt, Nagurski, Chicago tackle Joe Stydahar, and the Giants' Hein—played in that game. Dutch Clark and Clarke Hinkle were the gifted passers on that 1930s squad, but the best player of the decade may have been a passing target.

Curly Lambeau loved the passing game in Green Bay, and in 1935, he got a terrific target. It was Lambeau who helped create the athlete some call the best pro football player of all time. Between 1935 and 1945, end Don Hutson caught 488 passes. Over the same period, the second-best pass-catcher in the league was Jim Benton of the Cleveland Rams. He caught 190.

One day in the early thirties, Hutson left his spot on the University of Alabama baseball diamond and jogged over to the track, where the 100-yard dash was about to be run. He won the race in 9.8 seconds. Putting his baseball trousers back on, he jogged back to the baseball game and continued playing.

Hutson was a gamebreaker—his 99 touchdown receptions stood as an NFL record for 44 years—who challenged defenses. Eagles coach Earle (Greasy) Neale said Hutson was the only man he ever saw who could feint in three directions at once. Hutson helped the Packers lead the NFL in scoring each year from 1936 to 1938. He played left end and defensive back in the days of the two-way player. It's a shame most of us never have seen even a highlight of the man who once scored 29 points in a quarter.

We may not have seen Hutson, or Grange, or the indoor game, or the Packers in full regalia on the Staten Island Ferry. We can't honestly say whether the best receiver of all time was Hutson or Jerry Rice because most of us never saw a whit of Hutson. That's what history books are for.

A CHAMPION IDEA

There is little question that the NFL went from a quasi-barnstorming league to a major sports entity in the thirties, from bush league to big league. And there is no better way to illustrate that than to look at the Green Bay Packers' midseason travel schedule in 1930, and to compare it to 1939.

The Packers took a three-game, eight-day trip to the East Coast in November, 1930. After a train trip to New York City, they lost to the Giants 13-6 on a Sunday afternoon, as 37,000 fans watched the NFL's two best teams battle at the Polo Grounds.

On Thursday morning—Thanksgiving Day—Green Bay hopped a southbound train for a two-hour ride to Philadelphia. In the Philly neighborhood of Frankford, the Packers dressed in a firehouse across the street from the field, then went out and beat up on the Frankford Yellow

the 1939 NFL Championship Game, in front of 32,279 in Milwaukee.

At the dawn of the thirties, the pro game was in a precarious position. "In the early days," recalled New York Giants president Wellington Mara, a schoolboy in Manhattan during the Depression, "pro football players were looked upon with the respect of professional wrestlers."

Though the Red Grange barnstorming tour of America gave the game some pizzazz in 1925, the NFL was in trouble (as was America) as the thirties dawned. The league needed something—something big, something exciting—to give it a foothold in the entertainment market.

Every great enterprise can look back and see some fortunate turning points in its history. The NFL is no different. In 1932 and 1933, the decision to start playing championship games, the advancement of the forward pass as a weapon, and two

---

They weren't happy about it, but National Football League owners who gathered in Chicago in the summer of 1943 knew they had to do something, anything, to keep two struggling franchises from going under.

Since entering the league in 1933, the Philadelphia Eagles and Pittsburgh Steelers had only one winning season between them—Pittsburgh's 7-4 finish in 1942. With World War II depleting the rosters of all pro sports teams, the Eagles and Steelers figured to be even less competitive in '43—the Steelers had lost Bill Dudley, the NFL's top rusher in '42, and the Eagles had lost quarterback Tommy Thompson, both to military service.

So after a lot of heated discussion, the owners grudgingly agreed to merge the teams into a franchise called the Phil-Pitt Eagles-Steelers. Fans throughout Pennsylvania affectionately came to know them as the Steagles.

Much to everyone's surprise, the Steagles enjoyed some success, posting a 5-4-1 record to finish one game behind the Washington Redskins and New York Giants, who wound up tied for first in the Eastern Division at 6-3-1.

Philadelphia's Earle (Greasy) Neale and Pittsburgh's Walt Kiesling shared the head-coaching duties—Neale oversaw the offense, Kiesling the defense.

It was hardly a match made in heaven.

Bucko Kilroy, a rookie two-way lineman at the time, remembers Neale and Kiesling constantly "at each other's throats." During one practice, after Neale used an expletive to refer to a Steelers player who had blundered, an indignant Kiesling pulled all of the Steelers off the field. He brought them back to work the next day, but his relationship with Neale never improved.

On the other hand, the players got along well, as did the fans, who cheered for players from both teams during the four games at Shibe Park in Philadelphia and two at Forbes Field in Pittsburgh.

One "outsider" was quarterback Roy Zimmerman, who had been Sammy Baugh's understudy at Washington. Zimmerman completed only 43 of 124 passes for 846 yards. He threw for 9 touchdowns, compared to 17 interceptions, and made Philadelphia fans long for Thompson. The Steagles did, however, possess the best running game in the league. They ran for 1,730 yards, with Jack

Hinkle leading the way with 571 and averaging 4.9 per carry.

The highlight of the Steagles' season was when they rallied for three touchdowns in the fourth quarter to upset the powerful Giants, 26-14. Hinkle ran for a 37-yard touchdown on the first play from scrimmage.

In keeping with the patriotic times, the players, who wore the Eagles' green-and-white uniforms, were required to work at least 40 hours a week in defense plants. They trained at the University of Pennsylvania's River Field for three hours, Monday through Saturday, beginning at 6 o'clock in the evening.

"You worked all day, and you practiced all night, and by the end of the day, you were tired as hell," Hinkle remembered. "Most of us played because we loved the game."

That they were playing a game and not fighting a war created a potential image problem, considering that most of the team consisted of "4Fs"—men who had

The Steagles' backfield, including Jack Hinkle (far left) and Roy Zimmerman (far right).

some medical reason that prevented them from going to war. Hinkle's stomach ulcers resulted in his receiving an early discharge. Tackle Al Wistert was kept out of the Army by a twice-broken wrist. Guard Ed Michaels was rejected because he was deaf in one ear (he would remove his helmet in the huddle so he could hear the play, and, on the line, he would respond to movement rather than the quarterback's signals).

So the Steagles went out of their way to promote the fact the players were doing their part to help the war effort. Of course, inasmuch as the average pay was $125 per game, the defense jobs were as important to the players' wallets as they were to their image.

The merger ended on the final day of the regular season and both teams planned to play the 1944 season as separate franchises.

After the Steagles' last game, Hinkle led the NFL in rushing with 571 yards, 91 more than his closest challenger, Bill

Paschal of the Giants. But Paschal had another game left, and ran for 92 yards to win the rushing title.

Years later, someone discovered that Hinkle's 37-yard scoring run against the Giants somehow had been omitted from the game's official statistics, despite being mentioned in all newspaper accounts the next day. Hinkle had shrugged it off as "no big deal."

Flying on their own in 1944, the Eagles, with future Hall of Fame back Steve Van Buren joining Hinkle in the backfield, nearly won the East with a 7-1-2 finish, their best record ever.

Meanwhile, the Steelers still couldn't field a competitive team and they asked for, and received, permission to merge with the woeful Chicago Cardinals to form Card-Pitt. It was quite a fall from their Steagles' experience.

Card-Pitt, under co-coaches Kiesling and Phil Handler, wound up being derisively called the Carpets as the team stumbled to an 0-10 record in the Western Division. After the third loss, a 34-7 rout by the Bears, three Card-Pitt players were fined for what management termed "indifferent play." For the year, they were outscored 328-108.

EPIC BATTLES AND MINOR SKIRMISHES

The NFL had attained a level of stability in the 1930s. Gone were the days of fly-by-night franchises and championships awarded by consensus. The league was stronger than ever in 1940, but that strength soon would face obstacles that threatened to rip apart the NFL at the seams.

First would come World War II, a conflict that, for the United States alone, would mean more than 400,000 deaths and almost five years of civilian hardship. The NFL would be profoundly affected by the war.

And, relatively insignificant in the global picture but potentially disastrous for a sports league trying to pick up its pieces, the NFL would be challenged by a legitimate rival later in the decade.

It all made pro football a curious way to make a living in the 1940s. And if "strength through adversity" is an overused application, it never described a situation better.

A Scandalous Start

Detroit Lions owner George Richards was home in Los Angeles one day in 1939 when he got a phone call from an associate who was watching a college football game between Hardin-Simmons College and Loyola of Los Angeles at Gilmore Stadium in L.A. A player from Hardin-Simmons named Clyde (Bulldog) Turner was having an All-America-type day and Richards's associate, who knew that his boss had grown tired of playing the runner-up role to the Chicago Bears and Green Bay Packers in the NFL's Western Division, advised him to come to the game and see for himself.

Richards appeared for the second half and, after the game, told Turner he wanted him to play for his Lions. He envisioned the young center leading the way for Byron (Whizzer) White, the great back who would join the Lions in 1940. Richards paid Turner to tell other teams that he was not inter-

With the temperature at 6 degrees, the Cleveland Rams' sideline watched the 1945 NFL Championship Game, a contest settled by a pass that hit a goal post crossbar.

Byron (Whizzer) White (44), halfback and future U.S. Supreme Court Justice, was the NFL's leading rusher in 1940.

Early Pro Bowls featured the NFL champion vs. a team of league all-stars.

ested in pro football. On draft day, however, Lions coach Gus Henderson drafted Southern California quarterback Doyle Nave number one, thinking that Turner still would be available later. But the Bears selected Turner.

Richards was incensed. After firing Henderson, he tried to convince Turner to quit football for a year, coach a high school team in California until George Halas forgot about him, then sign with the Lions. The league got wind of the scheme and fined Richards $5,000 for tampering. Richards then sold the team to Fred Mandel. Turner went on to a Hall of Fame career. Nave never played in the NFL.

As for on-field debacles, the Washington Redskins suffered the worst defeat in NFL history when they were blown out by the Bears 73-0 in the 1940 NFL Championship Game.

To make matters worse for George Preston Marshall's Redskins, the 36,034 fans at Washington's Griffith Stadium weren't the only ones in on the action. It was the first football game ever carried on network radio. Famed sportscaster Red Barber called the play-by-play for more than 120 stations on the Mutual Broadcasting System, which paid $2,500 for the rights to air the game.

Comings and Goings

After the 1940 season, frustrated Pittsburgh Pirates owner Art Rooney, tired of losing, sold his team to Alexis Thompson for $180,000, then bought one-half interest in the Philadelphia Eagles, who were owned and coached by Bert Bell.

But Thompson, a 26-year-old steel heir whom the press frequently described as a well-heeled New York playboy, wanted to be closer to his East Coast business ties. So he agreed to a franchise switch with Rooney, who couldn't get Pittsburgh out of his blood. Thus, Rooney moved to Pittsburgh while Thompson moved to Philadelphia with the teams' players divided up in a dispersal draft.

As the story goes, the name "Steelers" was chosen through a public contest. Rooney insisted it was pure coincidence that the wife of the team's ticket manager, a close associate of Rooney's, submitted the winning entry.

Thompson hired Earle (Greasy) Neale to be his coach in 1941, and Neale's first job was to find a quarterback. Davey O'Brien, an All-America from Texas Christian University, had joined the Eagles in 1939, signing one of the most lucrative contracts in football history—$12,000 plus a percentage of gate revenues. But, after winning just 2 of 22 games in two years, O'Brien quit.

Neale acquired Tommy Thompson in the dispersal draft to run his T-formation, and within three years, the Eagles were winning more than they were losing.

Early in 1941, Elmer Layden was perfectly content at Notre Dame, where he was a living legend. Layden had made college football history in 1924 when he, Jim Crowley, Harry Stuhldreher, and Don Miller became known as the Four Horsemen playing for Knute Rockne's powerhouse Irish teams.

A decade later, Layden was coaching the Irish and serving as the school's athletic director when he got word that the National Football League was looking for someone to lead its organization the way Judge Kenesaw Mountain Landis was serving major league baseball.

Layden was beginning a new contract with the Irish, but the NFL powers-that-were convinced him to leave his alma mater and become the league's first commissioner. Carl L. Storck, one of the NFL's founding fathers, had served as treasurer and secretary of the league since 1920 and as acting president since 1939, but when his power was diverted to Layden, Storck resigned and the position of president was abolished.

There's a War On, Boys

Three scheduled NFL games were underway when the Japanese dropped the first bomb on Pearl Harbor at 12:55 P.M. Eastern time on Sunday, December 7, 1941.

Public-address announcers at New York's Polo Grounds and Chicago's Comiskey Park interrupted their accounting of the respective games to tell all servicemen present to report to their units. At Washington's Griffith Stadium, the announcer paged high-ranking government and military personnel who were in attendance, but did not mention the attack. Reporters were told to check in with their offices.

On Monday, December 8, America officially entered World War II, and the NFL had to struggle to maintain the momentum it had gained in the 1930s.

During the war, which ended August 14, 1945, more than 600 NFL players, coaches, and officials contributed in the conflict. Twenty-one of those men never came home, including 12 active players.

The Bears' Clyde (Bulldog) Turner was a seven-time all-pro at center.

THE BURNING OF WASHINGTON

George McAfee gains 7 of Chicago's monstrous total of 381 rushing yards.

A few days before the 1940 NFL Championship Game, Washington Redskins owner George Preston Marshall told *New York Daily Mirror* columnist Bob Considine, "Each of our players will get about $850 out of the game."

Considine then asked Marshall what the Chicago Bears' individual shares would be.

"Oh, the losers get about $500," Marshall said.

"The Bears," the owner told the writer, "are a team that must win by a big score. ...Don't ask me why they lose the close ones, except that they do. If I were to guess I'd probably say that there's not too much harmony on that team. Too many stars, and stars are inclined to beef at one another when the going gets tough."

On the second play from scrimmage, Bill Osmanski took a handoff from Sid Luckman, exploited a hole in the Redskins' left side, and sped outside. Near the sideline, George Wilson threw a block that leveled two Redskins, and Osmanski went 68 yards for a touchdown. The team with "too many stars" and "not too much harmony" had begun professional football's ultimate concert. The final score was 73-0, still the largest margin in the history of the game.

Ten different players scored touchdowns. Chicago defenders intercepted 8 passes, returning 3 of them for touchdowns. The Redskins, who gained only 5 yards rushing, moved inside the Bears' 20-yard line just three times.

Red Barber, who broadcast the game nationwide, recalled, "The touchdowns came so quickly there for a while, I felt like I was the cashier at a grocery store. It is a very good thing I went over the roster of the Bears. I believe I wound up having to say every player's name on the list. In fact, I believe they all scored touchdowns."

Years later, Bears owner George Halas provided the perfect counterpoint to Marshall's pregame bluster. "Everything we did, we did right," Halas said. "Everything they did was wrong....You can't blame the Redskins for what happened. They had nothing to do with the score. Or very little, anyway. It was us. The Bears played like no team before or after."

Attendance at NFL games began dropping as the war consumed America's thoughts; football suddenly didn't matter. In 1942, total paid attendance dropped to 887,920, the lowest since 1936. Roster limits were lowered from 33 to 28 and a free substitution rule was adopted. (Older players, who were forced to play while the younger men were fighting the war, had difficulty mustering the wind to play both offense and defense, although they certainly wouldn't have admitted it.) Free substitution was eliminated after the 1946 season, but was reinstalled in 1949 and has been in effect ever since.

Bears on the Rampage

It was just a week after the bombing of Pearl Harbor—one of the darkest days in American history—that the Chicago Bears and Green Bay Packers made pro football history.

Having finished the 1941 regular season tied for first in the Western Division with 10-1 records (after splitting their two games), Chicago and Green Bay met in the first divisional playoff game in league history.

The game was played in front of 43,425 shivering patrons at Chicago's Wrigley Field, where the temperature at kickoff was 16 degrees. The winner would advance to meet the New York Giants in the NFL Championship Game a week later.

The Bears, who had scored a whopping 396 points in their 11 regular-season games, were favored to defeat the Packers, and they did so with ease, 33-14. A week later, they smothered the Giants 37-9.

"Seventy-three to seven."

—SAMMY BAUGH,
WASHINGTON QUARTERBACK , WHEN ASKED BY A REPORTER WHAT THE OUTCOME OF THE 1940 NFL CHAMPIONSHIP GAME WOULD HAVE BEEN IF ONE OF HIS TEAMMATES HAD NOT DROPPED A TOUCHDOWN PASS EARLY IN THE GAME

Opposite page: **Sammy Baugh (center) missed most of the 1943 championship game after being kicked in the head.**

T TIME FOR THE NFL

In 1940 there was only one team using the T-formation: the Chicago Bears. A decade later there was only one team not using it: the Pittsburgh Steelers, who clung stubbornly to their Single-Wing. The Bears' T had been a group effort during the 1930s, with Ralph Jones and then Clark Shaughnessy fine-tuning the X's and O's, and George Halas overseeing everything. In 1940, Shaughnessy took the formation to Stanford, where he promptly gave the Indians an unbeaten season and a Rose Bowl win. The seeds already had been sewn in the NFL.

During the 1930s the collegiate ranks had sneered at the T-formation. The book *Selected Football Plays from Nine Standard Formations,* written by two Oberlin College coaches in 1934, mentioned two strengths of the T— and four weaknesses.

"Only one good cycle of plays is possible," wrote Oberlin head coach L.K. Butler, "unless the quarterback is in motion or the ball is passed through his hands on a direct snap to one of the three deep men.

"A 7-2-2 defense should kill this offense."

But he was looking at a different animal, a tight T with the ends in close and three backs set behind the quarterback. Shaughnessy's formation was more like a modern pro set, with a back going in motion out to the flank and an end split the other way. Quick traps, counters, passes to the flat, look-ins, and the occasional seam pass off a quick drop to keep the defense honest—that was the Bears' package. A relentless series of thrusts that left defenses breathless, sort of the Buffalo Bills' No-Huddle of its day.

It reached full bloom on December 8, 1940, when Chicago scored a 73-0 NFL Championship Game victory over the Washington Redskins, who actually had outscored the Bears during the regular season and had beaten them, T and all, three weeks earlier.

Halas liked to use everyone. The Giants had them dead even at 9-9 in the third quarter of the 1941 championship, but Halas had been substituting in waves, bringing in whole units at a time, and the war of attrition finally sent New York to a 37-9 defeat.

What could stop the Bears, who won three championships in a four-year period (1940-43)? Well, World War II. It scrambled things in the league. The Bears squeezed another title in postwar 1946, but the decade closed out with a

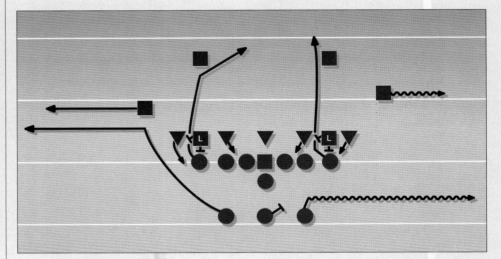

Greasy Neale's "Eagle Defense," a 5-2-4 set, was the basis of the modern 3-4 alignment.

pair of championships by the emerging team, Philadelphia.

Earle (Greasy) Neale had a solid offense, but his real genius was felt on defense. He introduced the 5-2-4 alignment (or the 5-4, depending on how the corners were playing), known evermore as the Eagle Defense. It was the basis of the modern 3-4.

Meanwhile a new league had sprung up: the All-America Football Conference, with an emphasis on offense, a flashy set of runners and throwers, and an organizational genius named Paul Brown.

Brown's innovations could fill a press guide. He started IQ testing and psychological evaluations. He first timed people in the 40-yard dash. "Write this in

your notebooks," he told his squad at its first meeting. "Youth and speed. You can't lick speed."

Otto Graham was a dazzling passer and 238-pound fullback Marion Motley was a bruising force, but the thing that made the Browns' attack go was pass protection. Form a cup, turn the opponents to the outside, let Motley hammer anybody who leaks through—it was Brown's idea, and the concept seems so simple that you wonder why no one ever had thought of it before. But no one had.

Legend has it that every time the offense broke the huddle the linemen chanted, "Nobody touches Graham."

One more Paul Brown innovation: He called all the plays, using messenger guards. It was a subject of huge controversy at the time; now it's the standard. Brown believed in total control.

Of course, Brown's emphasis on passing and speed, not to mention the Eagles' defensive creations, were directly related to the rise of the T-formation. In the end, no one could resist its temptations.

"I hated the T when we went to it in 1944," Baugh said, "but my body loved it. I probably would have lasted a year or two more as a single-wing tailback, my body was so beat up, but the T gave me nine more seasons."

Amazingly, the "Monsters of the Midway," as the fearsome Bears became known, actually seemed to improve in 1942. After finishing their schedule with an 11-0 mark, they faced a familiar foe: Washington.

The bitter sting of their 73-0 loss to the Bears in the 1940 title game was still gnawing at the Redskins when the two teams met in 1942—again at Griffith Stadium—to decide the championship. This time, the Washington defense blanked Sid Luckman (the Bears scored on a fumble return) and ended Chicago's 18-game winning streak (including two playoff victories) with a 14-6 win.

The next season, however, Luckman brought the championship back to Chicago. He led the Bears to an 8-1-1 record that included a 56-7 rout of the Giants, a game in which Luckman set an NFL record by throwing 7 touchdown passes. Chicago's 1943 roster included the legendary Bronko Nagurski, who was coaxed out of retirement to help fill a war-depleted roster. Nagurski, 34, hadn't played in five seasons.

In the title game at Wrigley Field, once more against the Redskins, Luckman passed for 286 yards and 5 touchdowns, ran for 64 yards, and even intercepted 2 passes on defense as the Bears rolled to a 41-21 victory.

Washington's Sammy Baugh missed much of the game when he was kicked in the head making a tackle in the first half. It was a huge loss for Washington. Baugh was virtually a one-man team—a terror on offense, defense, and special teams. In 1943, he pulled off an incredible feat by leading the league in passing (56 percent completion rate), interceptions made (11), and punting (45.9-yard average).

"Coaches have frequently argued about what contributed most to the great Bears clubs," Luckman said. "Method? Power? Personnel? Probably a combination of all three. But the men on the field would have laid it to experience gained in working together Sunday after Sunday with full coordination of line and backs. All over the league, they had the Bears tagged as a monopoly, and I guess they weren't far from right."

In 1944, for the first time since 1939, Chicago did not qualify for the championship as Green Bay won the West and the Giants provided the opposition. New York had beaten the Packers 24-0 during the regular season, but Ted Fritsch scored twice to lead Green Bay to a 14-7 triumph at the Polo Grounds.

Gust of Bad Luck

In a move designed to help offenses, the league voted in 1945 to move the hashmarks five yards closer to the center of the field on each side. Cleveland Rams end Jim Benton took advantage of the rule change when he caught 10 passes from quarterback Bob Waterfield for a record 303 yards during a 28-21 victory over the Lions at Briggs Stadium. That win clinched the West for the Rams, setting up an anticipated confrontation with Washington.

On August 7, 1945, a week before World War II officially ended, the Redskins had visited Cleveland's Municipal Stadium to play a preseason game against the Rams in 100-degree heat. Four months later, the Redskins returned to the shores of Lake Erie to meet the Rams in the NFL Championship Game, and it was at least 94 degrees colder. God only knows what the wind-chill factor was. That's a meteorological term that had yet to be invented.

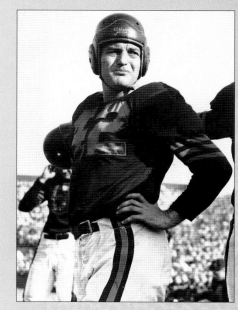

Chicago quarterback Sid Luckman

THROWIN' SEVEN

With three games left in the 1943 season, Bears quarterback Sid Luckman threw 7 touchdown passes in a 56-7 rout of the New York Giants.

That record has stood for more than half a century, though four NFL players have equaled Luckman's mark.

MOST TOUCHDOWN PASSES, GAME

7 Sid Luckman
Chicago Bears vs. N.Y. Giants,
November 14, 1943

Adrian Burk
Philadelphia vs. Washington,
October 17, 1954

George Blanda
Houston vs. N.Y. Titans,
November 19, 1961

Y.A. Tittle
N.Y. Giants vs. Washington,
October 28, 1962

Joe Kapp
Minnesota vs. Baltimore,
September 28, 1969

HEAD OF THE CLASS

Green Bay end Don Hutson elevated the pass receiving game to dizzying heights as he dominated the NFL during the 1940s.

Beginning in 1941, Hutson led the league in receiving five straight years, averaging 57 catches per year at a time when it was rare to get half that number. The apex of his career came in 1942, when he shattered NFL records with 74 receptions (runner-up Pop Ivy had 27) for 1,211 yards and 17 touchdowns.

EVOLUTION OF THE NFL SINGLE-SEASON RECEIVING RECORD		
1932	Ray Flaherty, N.Y. Giants	21
1933	John (Shipwreck) Kelly, Brooklyn	22
1935	Tod Goodwin, N.Y. Giants	26
1936	Don Hutson, Green Bay	34
1937	Don Hutson, Green Bay	41
1938	Gaynell Tinsley, Chi. Cardinals	41
1940	Don Looney, Philadelphia	58
1941	Don Hutson, Green Bay	58
1942	Don Hutson, Green Bay	74
1949	Tom Fears, Los Angeles	77
1950	Tom Fears, Los Angeles	84
1960	Lionel Taylor, Denver	92
1961	Lionel Taylor, Denver	100
1964	Charley Hennigan, Houston	101
1984	Art Monk, Washington	106
1992	Sterling Sharpe, Green Bay	108
1993	Sterling Sharpe, Green Bay	112

A blizzard had swept through Cleveland the week before, and, while the snow had stopped, the bitter cold lingered. More than 9,000 bales of straw were imported to cover the field and protect it from more snow. By game time, much of the straw wound up on the benches, where players used it to cover their legs and feet.

As cold as it was that day, the "Arctic Bowl" is remembered not for its frigidity, but for the legendary Baugh's ill-fated first-quarter pass, which resulted in a safety for the Rams. After Washington's defense had stopped a Rams drive at the 5-yard line, Slingin' Sammy led the Redskins' offense onto the field. Hoping to catch the Rams off guard, Baugh faded into his end zone to pass.

He let fly, but the ball never reached its intended destination. A gust of wind caused it to clang against the crossbar, and it fell into the end zone—an automatic safety in those days. That gave the Rams a bizarre 2-0 lead.

Those 2 points were the difference as the Rams went on to win the title 15-14. It would be their final game in Cleveland. Owner Dan Reeves moved his team to Los Angeles the next year.

All-American Revolution

If World War II staggered the NFL by diluting its product, it didn't deter certain entrepreneurs from realizing the potential of pro football.

Seeing that the American public was becoming enamored with the game, wealthy men from coast to coast tried to parlay that interest into financial gain. They lined up at Commissioner Elmer Layden's door, but one by one they were rejected.

Frustrated in their attempts to break into the NFL, a group of wartime power brokers met in a hotel room in St. Louis on June 4, 1944, and discussed the possibility of forming their own pro football league.

Arch Ward, the visionary sports editor of the *Chicago Tribune* who had organized the Chicago College All-Star Game and baseball's all-star game, chaired the meeting, which included representatives from Buffalo, Chicago, Cleveland, Los Angeles, New York, and San Francisco.

By the end of that day, the group had laid the foundation for a proposed league and chosen its name: the All-America Football Conference.

Three months later, the group was joined by former heavyweight boxing champion Gene Tunney, who represented the city of Baltimore. Each man present was granted a franchise, and Jim Crowley, another of the Four Horsemen, was elected commissioner and president of the league. Eleanor Gehrig, the widow of baseball great Lou Gehrig, was named vice president.

Eventually, an eighth franchise was awarded to William D. Cox for Brooklyn, and when the financial support for the Baltimore franchise collapsed, Miami joined the league.

In a final attempt to make the AAFC teams part of the NFL, Jack Keeshin, who owned the Chicago franchise, and Paul Brown, head coach of the Cleveland Browns, met with Commissioner Layden in April, 1945. A merger, they argued, was the only way to prevent costly bidding wars. Layden rejected their overture.

He proved no great seer of the future. In August, 1945, Layden, in response to an announcement by the AAFC, issued an infamous statement that became the AAFC's rallying cry: "[The AAFC should] first get a football, then make a schedule, and then play a game."

By the winter of 1945-46, the league had designated the fall of '46 as its inaugural season. The original teams were the Buffalo Bisons (who had made a coaching change before their first game); the Brooklyn Dodgers; the Cleveland Browns; the Los Angeles Dons; the Miami Seahawks; the New York Yankees, coached by Ray Flaherty; the Chicago Rockets; and the San Francisco 49ers, coached by Buck Shaw.

Dan Topping's Yankees played in Yankee Stadium and directly competed with the Giants for fans. Interestingly, both Big Apple teams won their respective Eastern Division titles in 1946—the Giants with a 7-3-1 record and the Yankees at 10-3-1.

Western Pioneers

Twenty-seven days after winning their first NFL championship, the Rams packed up their belongings in Cleveland and bolted for the fun and sun of Los Angeles, becoming the first major pro sports team to take up residence on the West Coast.

Since purchasing the team in 1941, owner Dan Reeves had dreamed of plugging into the lucrative Pacific market. Estimating that airplane travel finally was feasible by 1946, he shocked the hardy Cleveland patrons by going west.

It proved to be a boon to both cities. The Rams averaged nearly 40,000 fans per game in the Los Angeles Memorial Coliseum, while Cleveland went wild over its new Browns of the AAFC.

Other news at the start of the 1946 season included former Eagles coach and Steelers co-owner Bert Bell replacing Layden as commissioner, a position Bell held until he died of a heart attack while attending an Eagles game in 1959.

During 1946, the NFL also regained the majority of its star players who had been overseas fighting in World War II. One of those players was Pittsburgh's Bill Dudley, who returned in time to play the final four games in 1945. In 1946, his first full season back since leaving the Steelers after the 1942 campaign, Dudley led the NFL in rushing (604 yards), interceptions (10), and punt returns (385 yards).

Some men even returned from military service with new outlooks…or at least new tactics. An excerpt from *Halas*, the autobiography of Bears owner George Halas:

"Having been in the service thirty-nine months, I knew my veterans would be fed up with petty regulations. When the spring camp opened, I announced all rules were scrapped. Bears were men, responsible men, self-disciplined men, and would look after themselves. At a meeting, I asked, 'How do you fellas suggest we dress when traveling as a team?'

"Someone said, 'I think we should all wear shirts and jackets.'

"'Fine, gentlemen,' I said. 'We will all wear shirts and jackets. Anything else?'

"Someone said, 'A tie?'"

"'Thank you for the excellent suggestion,' I said. 'Is it agreed we all wear ties?'

"'Silence.

"'Fine,' I said. 'It is agreed we all wear shirts and ties and jackets. And I assume you gentlemen all insist that shoes be well shined.'"

Quick-kick artist Frank Sinkwich

ZERO RECALL

The NFL hasn't had a scoreless tie since Sunday, November 7, 1943.

That was the day the Soviet Red Army captured Fastov, an important railroad junction near Kiev. And in the southwest Pacific, Allied fliers pounded the major Japanese base at Rabaul, New Britain.

Compared to the Axis Powers' performance, the defensive units of the New York Giants and the Detroit Lions had a fine day: Neither the Giants nor the Lions allowed the opposition past their 15-yard lines in Briggs Stadium.

Give an assist to a cold, steady rain.

Giants halfback Bill Paschal recalled, "The players were up to their ankles in mud. I don't think there were more than a few blades of grass out there."

Despite the muck, Detroit's Frank Sinkwich, a quick-kick specialist, had punts of 54, 64, 52, 49, and 41 yards.

The Giants crossed the 50-yard line only once, in the third quarter, when future Hall of Fame center-middle linebacker Mel Hein intercepted Bill Callihan's pass at the Lions' 49 and returned it to the 34. When New York's drive stalled at the 15, Ward Cuff narrowly missed a field-goal attempt.

That was the closest anyone came to scoring.

A Quietly Shattered Barrier

In 1947, the baseball world was rocked when Branch Rickey of the Brooklyn Dodgers signed Jackie Robinson to a major-league contract, making the talented all-around athlete the first black player to compete in the modern major leagues. Robinson long since has been hailed as one of the most important athletes in American history, an acknowledgment of his courage in withstanding racial taunts and horrendous treatment in order to open the door for other black baseball players.

A year earlier, however, four black players signed with pro football teams…and none ever received the decorated distinction that was afforded Robinson, since black players had been in the NFL until the mid-30s.

The Los Angeles Rams signed two UCLA rookies, halfback Kenny Washington and end Woody Strode. At approximately the same time, the Cleveland Browns signed guard Bill Willis and fullback Marion Motley.

Washington, hobbled by bad knees, played only three seasons, and Strode, a 31-year-old rookie, performed only in 1946. But Willis and Motley enjoyed outstanding careers while playing under Paul Brown, first in the AAFC and later in the NFL.

"Jackie Robinson gets all the credit because his was a better story, but Willis and Motley were the first blacks to play [in the modern NFL]," Browns quarterback Otto Graham said. And just like Robinson, Motley and Willis put up with racial indignities.

"I remember, we went down to play Miami one time in 1946 and they [hotel personnel] told Paul that the two black guys had to stay at a different hotel," Graham recalled. "Paul said, 'Okay, let's all go.' The whole team was going to go, but then the hotel changed its mind and let us stay. That stuff went on all the time."

The Wrong Crowd

In 1946, pro football prospered as it never had before.

The end of World War II enabled hundreds of players to resume their football careers, thus bringing the quality of play in the NFL back to the standards the league had enjoyed in 1941.

The advent of the AAFC created new football jobs and brought the game to new cities. The NFL also had expanded to the West Coast. Player salaries rose due to the competition between the two leagues, and attendance soared as Americans put sports back in the mainstream of their lives.

But, during the week leading up to the 1946 NFL Championship Game between the Chicago Bears and New York, a potentially disastrous situation arose.

Although the Bears had lost to the Giants during the regular season, oddsmakers favored them by 10 to 14 points in the NFL title game, which was to be played at the Polo Grounds. This made the New York City police department suspicious, so the safe and robbery squad began a quiet investigation. The night before the game, detectives learned that a gambler had offered New York fullback Merle Hapes $2,500 to make sure the Bears would win by at least 10 points.

Hapes had told quarterback Frank Filchock of the attempted bribe. Both were taken to a police station at 2 A.M., 12 hours before kickoff. Hapes told

"For every pass I ever caught in a game, I caught a thousand in practice."

—DON HUTSON,
GREEN BAY PACKERS RECEIVER (1935-1945)

Steve Owen didn't lose Frank Filchock (left) for the 1946 title game, despite the passer's failure to report a bribe attempt.

Opposite page: **Rams halfback Kenny Washington, who, along with teammate Woody Strode, broke into the NFL in 1946.**

his side of the story, saying he had refused the offer, while admitting his failure to inform the proper authorities.

A 28-year-old salesman, Alvin Paris, who was rumored to be backed by a large out-of-state bookmaking outfit, was arrested and jailed. Filchock was freed and allowed to play in the game, but Hapes was ruled ineligible by Commissioner Bell.

Filchock threw 2 touchdowns passes, but he also threw 6 interceptions in the game, and the Bears rolled to a 24-14 victory before 58,346 fans. Filchock, like Hapes, later was suspended for not reporting the bribe. He played in the Canadian Football League in 1947.

The Browns: A League of Their Own

In the AAFC's first season, Paul Brown's Browns proved they were the class of the league, a label they never relinquished. They were the only AAFC team to show a profit in 1946, playing before a seven-game total of nearly 400,000 fans in Municipal Stadium.

The Browns posted a 12-2 record as quarterback Otto Graham, who had spent the previous two years in the Navy, dazzled the crowds by passing for 1,834 yards and 17 touchdowns. Motley and Edgar (Special Delivery) Jones combined for 1,140 rushing yards, and the Cleveland defense intercepted 41

Cleveland's offensive ringleaders—Otto Graham, Dante Lavelli, coach Paul Brown, and Mac Speedie—terrorized the AAFC.

HEADY TIMES

Enlisted men never went anywhere without them, and in this case football really was like war—the helmet became a mandatory component of the NFL uniform in 1943. After World War II, it would be transformed like no other piece of standard football equipment.

The rule actually had little effect, because practically every player in the league had worn a helmet since 1940, anyway. The last documented case of a player not using one is Chicago Bears end Dick Plasman, who played bareheaded in the 1940 NFL Championship Game. Hall of Fame end Bill Hewitt never wore a helmet, right up to his retirement in 1939. When he unretired to play with the Phil-Pitt "Steagles" in 1943, however, Hewitt had to wear one.

"He didn't like it," said Bucko Kilroy, a tackle who played next to Hewitt. "When the play was over, he'd take it off. It bothered him."

The decade that began with one player not wearing a helmet and almost everyone else sporting hard leather headgear ended with the refinement of the plastic helmet, perhaps the most revolutionary equipment change in football history. The plastic helmet was cooler, stronger, lighter, and more colorful. First developed in 1939 by Riddell, early ones tended to crack, prompting the NFL to ban them in 1948. Manufacturers perfected stronger plastic models and the ban was lifted in 1949.

The helmet was the focus of another innovation in 1948 when halfback Fred Gehrke of the Los Angeles Rams showed off the horns he had painted on his team's headgear, the NFL's first helmet logo. Other teams soon followed.

There was another breakthrough at the opposite end of the body. The Chicago Bears, under conservative coach George Halas, surprised the football world when they turned out for the 1940 title game wearing low-cut shoes, in all

Portrait of the artist as a ball carrier

likelihood the first use of the style and certainly a radical departure from the traditional black high-tops. The new shoes provided greater speed and freedom of movement, as the Bears so aptly demonstrated in their 73-0 victory over the Redskins in the championship game.

In 1941, the league spurned the Spalding football and adopted Wilson as the official ball of the NFL. The difference in balls was largely cosmetic, but the switch helped the NFL break away from the college game.

The Wilson ball was named The Duke in honor of the son of Giants owner Tim Mara—Wellington (The Duke) Mara—and it carried that name until 1970.

Other subtle changes in equipment took place. The war hastened the development of new fabrics and many of these began showing up in football uniforms. Formerly made of canvas or knit, they now sported nylon, rayon, and cotton. Chinstraps first appeared on the chin, rather than under it. And padding grew larger, offering more protection, though some players resisted the added bulk. Quarterbacks often cut down their shoulder pads, and some combatants rejected the heavy hip and kidney pads.

Rams halfback Fred Gehrke, who studied art in college, painted the first helmet logo in 1948.

Quarterback Paul Christman, fullback Pat Harder, right halfback Marshall Goldberg, and left halfback Charley Trippi collectively were known as the Dream Backfield in the Cardinals' NFL championship year of 1947. Before the regular-season started, Goldberg was replaced by Elmer Angsman, but the Dream Backfield nickname lived on.

"When you charge, you have to keep your head up. Sure you lose a lot of teeth that way, but you make a lot of tackles."

—JOE STYDAHAR,
CHICAGO BEARS TACKLE

passes and allowed only 137 points. The Browns defeated the Yankees 14-9 to win the first AAFC Championship Game.

Just as Cleveland's domination of the new circuit never changed, neither did the NFL's unwillingness to recognize the AAFC as a viable league.

"We kept reading derogatory remarks in the papers," Graham recalled. "Paul Brown, who I think was a genius, would never say a word. He'd just take those clippings and put them up on the bulletin board. They [the NFL] would say that their worst team could beat our best team. We read that kind of stuff for four years."

More than 100 NFL players were lured to AAFC teams, and many players, who eventually would attain NFL greatness, started in the new league. Six players who began their careers together with the Browns—Graham, Motley, Willis, tackle-kicker Lou Groza, center Frank Gatski, and end Dante Lavelli—later were voted into the Pro Football Hall of Fame. Brown also was inducted into the Hall.

The Original Dream Team

They didn't exactly match the popularity of the Four Horsemen of Notre Dame, but Paul Christman, Charley Trippi, Pat Harder, and Elmer Angsman gave the Chicago Cardinals one of the most potent offensive backfields in the history of the game when they teamed in 1947 to lead the Cardinals to their first NFL championship in 22 years.

Christman was the quarterback, and in 1947 he passed for 2,191 yards and 17 touchdowns. At right halfback was Angsman, who led the team with 412 rushing yards. At left halfback was the prized, well-paid rookie, Trippi, who rushed for 401 yards. Trippi had come to Chicago after signing an incredible four-year, $100,000 contract, the result of a bidding war between Cardinals owner Charles Bidwill and Dan Topping of the AAFC's New York Yanks. Harder, the fullback, amassed 371 yards. The foursome combined for 18 rushing touchdowns.

Overshadowed by the "Dream Backfield" (also called the "Million Dollar Backfield") was end Mal Kutner, who led the league with 944 receiving yards.

The Cardinals hadn't won the league title since 1925, but with their T-formation blowing holes through opposing defenses, they stormed to the Western Division crown and took on the Eagles at Comiskey Park.

And the Dream Backfield did not disappoint. Trippi broke a 44-yard touchdown run in the first quarter, then Angsman went 70 yards for a score in the second to give the Cardinals a 14-7 halftime lead.

Trippi broke five tackles on his way to a 75-yard punt return that made it 21-7 in the third, and midway through the fourth, Angsman iced the 28-21 victory with his second 70-yard touchdown run. The Cardinals rolled for 282 yards on the ground and 30,759 South Siders reveled.

In the Year of the Cardinal, the NFL added a fifth official, the back judge, and it also awarded a special bonus choice in the draft to be used by one team each year. The Bears won a lottery for the rights to the first bonus pick, and they chose halfback Bob Fenimore from Oklahoma State. Fenimore played just one season before retiring.

The Ice Man Runneth

Steve Van Buren almost didn't make it to Philadelphia's Shibe Park for the 1948 NFL Championship Game between the Eagles and Chicago Cardinals. He awoke in his suburban Philadelphia home, looked outside his window at a raging blizzard, and went back to bed, assuming the game would be postponed.

Van Buren later was awakened by a phone call from coach Greasy Neale, who wondered where Van Buren was. The soft-spoken native of New Orleans and graduate of LSU then made his familiar journey, riding the trolley to 69th Street, taking the Market Street subway to City Hall, and transferring to the Broad Street Line. He rode the subway to Lehigh Avenue, and finally trudged seven blocks through the snow to the stadium.

Van Buren and members of both teams helped pull the tarpaulin off the field, which was blanketed by snow within minutes.

"Can you imagine players from the two teams doing that today before a Super Bowl?" Van Buren later asked.

A crowd of 28,864 braved the polar elements, and they were stunned on the Eagles' first offensive play when Philadelphia quarterback Tommy Thompson threw a 65-yard touchdown pass to Jack Ferrante. However, their muffled cheers died when the play was nullified due to an offside penalty. That was the final passing threat of the day.

For more than three quarters of play, the teams took turns running into the line. The net result was no points. But late in the third quarter, Chicago quarterback Ray Mallouf and running back Angsman muffed a handoff, and Philadelphia's Frank (Bucko) Kilroy recovered at the Cardinals' 17. Four plays later, Van Buren scored on a 5-yard run and Cliff Patton kicked the conversion to give the Eagles a 7-0 lead. It may have been the most insurmountable 7-0 lead in NFL history.

Pittsburgh's (Bullet) Bill Dudley

LEADERS IN TRIPLICATE

You talk about Records That Never Will Be Broken. During the 1940s, two players accomplished a feat that is virtually impossible to duplicate in the current age of specialization: leading the league in separate offensive, defensive, and special teams categories.

In 1943, the Redskins' Sammy Baugh topped the NFL in passing (1,754 yards and 23 touchdowns), interceptions (11, which he returned for 112 yards), and punting (a 45.9-yard average on 50 punts). Three years later, (Bullet) Bill Dudley of the Steelers rushed for a league-high 604 yards, intercepted 10 passes (which he returned for 242 yards, including an 80-yard touchdown), and averaged 14.3 yards on 27 punt returns.

Baugh and Dudley both are in the Pro Football Hall of Fame.

KILROY WAS THERE

There isn't much that Bucko Kilroy has missed in the National Football League—including a paycheck.

He has been collecting them for more than 50 years, since he broke in as a player with his hometown Philadelphia Eagles in 1943. He's vice president of the New England Patriots now, but it's just the latest in a long line of pro football jobs. And at each stop—player, coach, scout, personnel director, general manager—the jovial Kilroy has enjoyed a great relationship with writers and broadcasters.

"It's amazing to me how it has all changed," Kilroy said, "When I started out, the players and sportswriters were buddies. We did everything together—drank a few beers, played cards, went to dinner. The spirit back in the forties was different…we were all in it together. Today, everyone seems to be at each other's throat.

"Back then, it was fun. The sportswriters dominated. We knew they had experimented with television, but during the war years we didn't have any. Radio was just for game days. Bryon Saam did it when I was with the Eagles and he did it alone. No color man, no analyst like they have these days."

The simplicity of it all drew a laugh from the big guy.

"I'm not positive, but I think the clubs paid for the writers' expenses in those days. We took one of the first flights ever—two DC-3s.

"It was [the NFL Championship Game of] 1949. We played the game in a driving rainstorm. We shouldn't have, but we did because it was on [network radio]. The game was a disaster. We played in the mud, and it was so bad one of the L.A. papers wrote the next day: 'What do Bert Bell and Liberty Bell have in common? They're both cracked.'"

Van Buren finished the day with 26 carries for 98 yards as the Eagles outrushed the Cardinals' Dream Backfield 225-96.

"It was sloppy, but not slippery," Van Buren said. "I could run okay, I just couldn't see. It was snowing so hard, I couldn't even see the Cardinals' safety, Marshall Goldberg."

Bits and Peace

Since joining the NFL in 1944, Ted Collins's Boston Yanks never had enjoyed a winning season. Predictably, attendance was dreadful, so in 1949 the NFL allowed Collins to move the team to New York, where the Yanks became the Bulldogs and used the Polo Grounds when the Giants were out of town. Playing in front of numerous empty seats each week, the Bulldogs finished 1-10-1. The next year they moved to Yankee Stadium, became the New York Yanks, and went 7-12.

In 1949, a rookie named George Blanda joined the Bears and was made third-string quarterback behind Luckman and Johnny Lujack. Blanda, also a kicker, made 7 of 15 field-goal attempts—a modest start to an improbable 26-year career.

While Blanda was beginning his career, Curly Lambeau was ending his illustrious term as Green Bay's coach. Lambeau stepped down after coaching the Packers since their inception 29 years earlier. The Packers had become one of the weakest teams in the league, and the governing board wanted more control of the team, which, to this point, was run almost solely by Lambeau.

With the club on the verge of bankruptcy and a sale of shares needed to restock the treasury, Lambeau decided it was best that he leave the team. He accepted the Chicago Cardinals' head coaching position a few weeks later.

The NFL Championship Game was played in Los Angeles for the first time in 1949. Pete Pihos caught a 31-yard touchdown pass and Van Buren rushed for a title-game record 196 yards to help the Eagles to their second consecutive championship, a 14-0 victory over the Rams. The game was played in a driving rainstorm, the first time the Rams had played a home game in the rain since they moved west. It was Philadelphia's second consecutive shutout victory in a championship game—a feat unmatched in NFL history.

A week earlier, Commissioner Bell had announced the historic merger agreement with the AAFC. For four years, the NFL and AAFC had waged a bitter and financially destructive war. Finally, the more powerful and established league conceded that a merger was necessary.

For its part, the AAFC was an economic shambles. One team, Cleveland, had dominated the playing field. The Browns won all four league championship games and finished their AAFC days with a regular-season record of 47-4-3. In 1948, they went unbeaten (14-0), then ended their perfect season with a 49-7 defeat of Lake Erie rival Buffalo in the championship game.

Impressive as these accomplishments were, many point to them as a pri-

mary explanation of the AAFC's eventual collapse. Fans in other cities simply tired of seeing the local boys battered by the Browns.

So, in December, 1949, the NFL set the terms and accepted into the league Cleveland, the Baltimore Colts (who had replaced Miami after 1946), and San Francisco. The players from the Buffalo, Los Angeles, Chicago, and New York franchises (Brooklyn had merged with the Yankees after 1948) were thrown into an open draft.

More than four years after peace had come to most of the world, it finally came to pro football.

Workhorse Steve Van Buren (15) sloshed his way to a record 196 rushing yards as the Eagles flattened the Rams 14-0 in the 1949 NFL Championship Game.

TEAM of the FORTIES

THE ALL-TWO-WAY TEAM

SIXTY-MINUTE MEN

*N*one of the dictionary descriptions of the adjective "two-way" focus on those unforgettable football heroes who played when "two-way" meant only one thing: playing two ways. You played on offense, gulped a breath or two and a dipper of water, and switched to defense. Then back to offense. Then to kicking off. Then to receiving.

There were fewer players in the twenties, thirties, and forties, thus a greater familiarity among the helmeted and padded. Also, the afternoons might have seemed to run a little long. Three-dozen players was the hallmark of an optimistic season. There were only four officials, compared to today's seven, and just a half-dozen crews. You remembered faces because there were no facemasks obstructing your view. Or your opponent's.

It was easier for fans to remember names and faces, too. Newspaper lineups and statistics were in their infancy; it didn't take long to determine whether your favorite player had worked the previous day. In 1943, the Detroit Lions and the New York Giants played the last scoreless game in NFL history, and the lineup in the next day's paper is offered here as evidence of things being kept simple.

New York (0)		Detroit (0)
O. Adams	LE	Fisk
Cope	LT	Ketzko
Younce	LG	R. Matheson
Hein	C	Wojciechowicz
Avedisian	RG	Lio
Blozis	RT	Kaporch
Walls	RE	J. Matheson
Shaffer	QB	Evans
Nix	LH	Sinkwich
Cuff	RH	Hackney
Kinscherf	FB	Hopp

Substitutes:

New York—Ends: Pritko, Liebel, Sulaitis. Tackles: Carroll, Roberts. Guards: Visnick, Marone. Center: Piccolo. Backs: Leemans, Brown, Paschal.

Detroit—End: Hightower. Tackle: Wickett. Guards: Rubino, Rockenbach, Stuart. Center: Conlee. Backs: Callihan, Mathews, Fenenbock, Van Tone, Colella.

That was it, a total of 44 players. The whole group was small enough to fit on one big bus, where the driver might accommodate by cashing players' paychecks (a hard-rock bit of humor that Augie Lio, the Lions' kicker—and also "RG" in the lineup—used to dispense when he was a late-stages sports columnist comparing salaries of different eras).

Another "small group" was the assistant coaches, sometimes as few as two, usually three, and four if the ownership was feeling particularly flush or the head coach had a pal who had just lost his job in Lubbock. "Coordinators" was a term unknown in football. When Weeb Ewbank worked for Paul Brown in Cleveland in the 1940s, his title was "tackles coach."

Except for championship games and one other that enjoyed a big build-up, the Chicago College All-Star Game, ticket demands were moderate. The season-ticket holder was viewed as an oddity because his friends and neighbors knew there'd be plenty of seats available at the box office the morning of the game, especially if the weather looked threatening.

Once planted in his seat, the spectator of the two-way era would consider himself blessed if any of the following players were suited up for the game:

Sammy Baugh's greatest season, 1943, takes us back a half-century, but the sheer mastery still shines across the years. He not only led the league in passing, punting, and interceptions, but he set an incredible mark of 4 interceptions in a game, a record never broken. His kicking efforts alone—he led the league in 1940 with a still-record 51.4-yard average—would keep him on a payroll today.

A considerable school supports the thinking that

Opposite: **The Chicago Bears' George (One Play) McAfee accepts a staged handoff from Sid Luckman. The lightning-fast McAfee's career punt-return average of 12.78 yards is the best in NFL history.**

Baugh brought pro football into the current age, making the transition from Single-Wing tailback to quarterback as the game moved into the T-formation era. He played 16 years and led the league in passing six times, splitting those leadership years between his old and new roles.

When Baugh appeared on the pro scene, drafted out of Texas Christian University as the Redskins were shifting from Boston to Washington, passing was almost an afterthought. Both the college and pro games recognized this by voting him among the eight greats named as charter members of their respective halls of fame.

Chuck Bednarik's career mirrored a series of adjustments. As a teenager fresh out of Bethlehem, Pennsylvania, he found himself fitting his exceptional bulk into the narrow proportions of a waist-gunner's aperture aboard a B-24 Liberator bomber in World War II. Returning, he had to adjust to a college situation in which there were seven other candidates for the center position at the University of Pennsylvania.

And with the Philadelphia Eagles, who made him a bonus pick in 1949, there was a gradual adjustment over a 14-year career: from a time when everyone

George Connor twice made all-pro on both sides of the ball.

played offense and defense to the day when he was the only one doing it, against the Green Bay Packers in the 1960 NFL Championship Game.

It was fortunate that the scant two minutes Bednarik missed in that title game didn't come at the end when the Packers, behind Bart Starr, were driving for the potential winning touchdown. Starr got off a safety-valve pass to his star runner, Jim Taylor, who shed a couple of tacklers before encountering Bednarik's bear-hug on the 9-yard line, where the game ended in a 17-13 Eagles victory.

Earl (Dutch) Clark's eyesight was such (20/100 right, 20/200 left) that it would have provided him with a safe-conduct pass out of any draft-board examination in our last three wars. There was nothing otherwise wrong with the All-America from little Colorado College at the start of the 1930s, and he wound up as an all-pro quarterback six of the first seven years he played for the Portsmouth Spartans and their successors, the Detroit Lions.

A story went around the league about Clark being blind in one eye. After the opposition had wasted all that time trying to figure out which one, they'd usually be sorry. He was one of the most feared runners of his day, and he also contributed with gifted kicking, which started with the dropped variety, then evolved to place-kicking as legislation and a burgeoning interest in passing slimmed the ball.

Clark, who often returned to his alma mater to coach basketball in the offseason, later became player-coach of the Lions and finished up with two seasons as coach of the Cleveland Rams, forerunners of today's California version. He entered the Pro Football Hall of Fame in the 1963 charter group.

From the outset, **George Connor** knew when to give a little and when to stand firm. In a Navy hitch during World War II, between stints at Holy Cross and Notre Dame, he thought he'd like a shot at service ball. So, he presented his 6 feet 2 inches and 230 pounds to the officer running the show. "Fine," was the response, "what position do you play?"

"Tackle," responded Connor.

"We've got seven tackles," was the answer.

"What don't you have?"

"Ends."

"Well, then, I'm an end."

Truth be told, Connor was a tackle, and one of the best in his or any other era in pro football. His starring role for the Chicago Bears (five times an all-pro, including offense and defense twice) traced to a firmness about not playing a home game outside his native Chicago. The Giants expended a number-one draft choice on him in 1946, and when it became obvious that New York was not his geographical dish, they traded his rights to Boston in 1948. That didn't suit him either, and Connor eventually wound up in the Windy City and Wrigley Field, just as he had envisioned as a boy.

Some of Connor's working philosophy has withstood the test of time. "If you try to follow the ball," he said, "any slick quarterback can fool you. But if you concentrate on watching a few key offensive players, they'll lead you right to the play."

George Halas never wasted anything, and in the NFL's first draft in 1936 it was down to closing time with a few names still up on the board. Chicago had one pick left. "Fortmann," said the Bears' founding father, "that sounds like a good tough name. Let's take him."

The Bears took **Danny Fortmann**, a 200-pound guard who would play eight years on the team nicknamed "Monsters of the Midway." Fortmann was a standout not for his size, but for his lack of it. A Phi Beta Kappa out of Colgate, he was one of the youngest players in the NFL at 20, and also the lightest guard. He looked more like a calisthenics coach than a savage two-way performer who called signals by day and hit the medical books at night.

Fortmann attended the University of Chicago medical school and played for the Bears in a schedule worked out by the school and the club. At the university, he was a survivor of an original horde of applicants that included another Phi Beta. The head of the medical school asked his secretary which of the applicants he should select—one was a violin player, the other a football player.

The woman was a Bears fan. She chose Fortmann. Later, his playing days done, he was a chief of orthopedics staff in Burbank, California.

Mel Hein's presence on this all-time team traces directly to a friendly postmaster in Providence, Rhode Island, sometime during the Hoover Administration. Hein's collegiate career at Washington State ended with a loss to Alabama in the 1931 Rose Bowl, and, despite his obvious talent, he had to write to three NFL teams offering his services.

The Providence Steam Roller dispatched a contract

Mel Hein became a Giant with help from a postmaster.

for $100 a game, and Hein signed it. He dropped it in the mail, then went to play for Washington State in a basketball game at Spokane. The Cougars' opponent was Gonzaga, which was coached by Ray Flaherty, a star end and assistant coach for the New York Giants. Flaherty asked if Hein had received the Giants' contract yet.

"No, I haven't," Hein said. "But if there is one on the way, it's too late. I signed one with Providence and mailed it back to them yesterday."

"Oh, no," Flaherty said. "How much are they paying you?"

Hein told him, and Flaherty told Hein that the Giants were offering $150 per game.

At Flaherty's suggestion, Hein sent a telegram to the postmaster in Providence, asking that he send the letter back. Much to Hein's surprise, the postmaster obliged. Hein tore up the Steam Roller contract, then signed the Giants' contract that had just arrived and sent it to New York.

Hein started for the Giants for 15 years. He made all-pro in eight consecutive seasons (1933-1940).

Not many early football stars left paper trails, at least ones capable of being read by the entire family gathered around the hearth. **Wilbur (Pete) Henry**, charter member of both the pro and college halls of fame, was an exception. A sizable selection of his memorabilia rests in Canton, including a diary from his college days at Washington and Jefferson. Wrote Henry: "Now that football's over I don't know what to do."

What he did was wait for other football seasons,

which brought him an All-America selection by Grantland Rice and a distinguished career in the pioneer pro game with the Canton Bulldogs, the New York Giants, and the Pottsville Maroons. And through it all he never lost his heft (250 pounds), his deceptively meaty look, or his pure joy in wrecking an entire side of the rival line.

Henry, also known as "Fats," started the latter practice at Mansfield, Ohio, as a schoolboy fullback, but he was converted to tackle in college. Rice, who saw more collegiate football players than any other observer of his era, called him the best he had seen. Henry could dominate either side of a kick. He shared the record for longest dropkick (50 yards), and he was known as one of the best kick-blockers of his day.

The helmet-less cotillion among the game's early players had excellent reasons for bareheadedness, ranging from the effect on a keen pompadour to providing a passer with a better target. The latter reason was the one offered by **Bill Hewitt**, the sturdy Michigan end who played nine seasons with the Bears and the Eagles over a span of a dozen years. His Pro Football Hall of Fame plaque pinpoints him as the first to make all-pro with two different teams.

Hewitt played with the Bears in the first scheduled NFL Championship Game in 1933, and was part of the final scoring effort that brought Chicago a come-from-behind victory over the Giants. Bronko Nagurski passed to Hewitt, who lateraled to Bill Karr, who went the distance for the title and the munificent individual payoff of $210 a man (the losers got $70 less).

Hewitt's last year with the Eagles was 1939, but he returned during the war to play on the combination Philadelphia-Pittsburgh team in 1943. Four years later he died in an auto accident at age 37.

Green Bay, one of the less-populated stops along the NFL circuit, but a surviving member of the NFL's first year of competition, takes a bit of getting used to. And vice-versa. Red Smith, the distinguished New York journalist who was a Green Bay native, used to say that as a child he rooted for 25 below because only then would school be called off.

And then there was **Clarke Hinkle**, a Hall of Fame fullback who played for the Packers in the 1930s: The town had to get used to him and the Eastern attire he brought from Bucknell, where he had achieved collegiate stardom and a contract with the Packers' boss, Earl (Curly) Lambeau, for $125 a game. This was a

considerable payday and Hinkle dressed the part. It took a while to convince his new mates that someone wearing a hat and tie could hit on a matching basis with the other stars of the day.

Well, he did. And he also kicked. And made all-pro four of his final five seasons. Hinkle was a hard-tackling linebacker and a fierce runner who retired as the NFL's career rushing leader with 3,860 yards. He helped Lambeau's Packers win two titles.

A lot of people, including songwriters who weren't born until a couple of decades later, enjoyed the frantic marionette dance that was New York in the late '20s and early '30s, but not **Cal Hubbard**, largest member of the New York Giants of that era. Hubbard was a small-town Missouri boy and his idea of a pleasant place was something like Green Bay, where you never locked your hotel room door. So when the Giants stayed over after a game to wait out a week before playing the Bears in Chicago, Hubbard asked whether they'd trade him to the Packers.

The Giants accommodated him, and Hubbard accommodated the Packers by helping them to successive NFL titles from 1929-1931, and by making all-league, all 6-5, 250 pounds of him—three times. He helped write the theoretical manual on how to play tackle in the pro game.

In another league and another sport, major league baseball, he made daily recourse to a different manual, the umpires' guide. It started as an offseason job, which practically all NFL players worked as an economic necessity. Hubbard was extra-proficient in his diamond efforts, rising from the Piedmont League to the American League, and he eventually became umpire-in-chief after a hunting accident impaired the sight of one eye. He was impressive behind the plate, the largest man in blue of his era.

Adding to his distinction of being one of eight players picked for both the college and professional Halls of Fame in charter balloting, **Don Hutson** comes through as probably the first of NFL receivers automatically assigned double-coverage. Recalled is a visit by a member of the coaching fraternity to a Chicago Cardinals training camp, where Jimmy Conzelman was preparing his troops for the opening game with Green Bay.

Privileged with a look at the game plan, the visiting coach quickly realized that someone had slipped up on pass coverage—no provision had been made for one of

GEORGE MUSSO

George Musso played against two future U.S. Presidents.

up with the one play that would swing the tide in the Bears' direction. It might be a long run, a hair-raising punt return (his 12.78-yard career average still is the NFL record), or a surprise left-handed pass. He was, at 170 pounds, one of the most dangerous two-way players in the league, despite having a three-year bite taken out of his decade by Navy service in World War II.

McAfee, a number-one draft choice out of Duke, had difficulty cracking the Chicago lineup early on, but he soared to Hall of Fame magnitude in the half-dozen seasons following his return from service. What kept him company on many a long Navy watch was the recollection of having broken a 93-yard kickoff return against the Green Bay Packers in his first pro game.

McAfee, lean and fast as lightning, was at his best running the ball, but he also intercepted 21 passes as a defensive back. He played on three of George Halas's championship teams.

There might have been a fullback or two on the level of **Marion Motley** when it came to running the ball in the late 1940s and early 1950s, but he had no equal at protecting the quarterback, as teammate and Hall of Fame quarterback Otto Graham will attest. In that role, Motley moved with the cat-like swiftness of a cornerback 50 pounds lighter.

"Motley would pick up a blitz," said Weeb Ewbank, a member of Paul Brown's Cleveland coaching staff at the time, "and when he did it was too bad for the fellow blitzing. He'd hit him so hard he'd knock him right back to the line."

Motley played strongside linebacker on defense, where his 240-pound heft was particularly useful on goal-line stands. He was a member of all four AAFC-championship Cleveland clubs, and when he came over to the NFL in 1950 he led the league in rushing.

Motley's Hall of Fame induction in 1968 was a true homecoming. He grew up in Canton, where he terrorized opponents of McKinley High.

In 1932, George Halas returned to Decatur, Illinois, where, 12 years earlier, he had directed the Staley Manufacturing Company's team, single-season precursor of the Chicago Bears. His mission was a little different this time. He came to sign a large lineman from a little college football team: **George Musso**, captain of the local Millikin eleven.

Recalled Musso, Hall of Fame member and the first NFL performer to be voted all-pro at two positions (tackle and guard), "I signed for ninety dollars a game,

the ends. He called it to the attention of Conzelman, who suggested, "He's not the one we're worried about. Not with Hutson in the game."

Hutson was with the Packers for 11 years. He made all-pro nine times, leading the league in receiving eight times. His career receptions totaled 488 for 99 touchdowns, making for an approximate payoff once in every five passes. In 1942, he caught 74 passes; league runner-up Frank (Pop) Ivy caught 27.

His nickname was "One Play," and whether you were watching from the stands or involved on the field, the idea was pretty direct: **George McAfee** could come and five dollars expenses. It worked out great: three dollars for the ride up on the Wabash and two dollars for going out on the town."

Chicago got to know Musso's name well in the 1930s, when he became an integral part of the fabled Monsters of the Midway. He was appointed captain early in his stint, and his 270 pounds, an impressive attribute at the time, demanded and got respect.

Did surviving a confrontation with Musso destine one for greater things? In 1929, he played against Ronald Reagan, a guard for Eureka College. In 1935, he went against Gerald Ford, a center from Michigan playing in the Chicago College All-Star Game.

Ernie Nevers's scoring record still held 64 years later.

While in far-off New Guinea in the early summer of 1943, Commander George S. Halas, attached to Admiral Chester Nimitz's Seventh Fleet, got a cable that had nothing to do with wresting the Pacific back from the grasp of the Japanese. This was a lot closer to the home front, where his Chicago Bears co-coaches Harley (Hunk) Anderson and Luke Johnsos were struggling with the idea of how to regain the NFL title, lost to the Redskins the previous year.

The solution was obvious: **Bronko Nagurski**, absent from pro competition since retiring in 1938. Halas had advised his fill-ins to get the Bronk, and the word from the ex-fullback's lair on the U.S.-Canadian border was that he was out of shape from pro wrestling. However, a $5,000 contract, big money in that era, just might restore the youthful bloom to his cheeks.

Halas's decision halfway around the world settled the 1943 championship immediately. "Send this," he directed the communications officer. The message read, "Give five thousand," which must also have given the Pentagon's cryptographic decoders a few interesting moments.

So Bronko Nagurski, the man who "ran his own interference" as a fullback and who terrorized the opposition as it sought to get through the Chicago line, made one final go for Papa Bear. Right down to a rout of the Redskins in the title game, where the Bronk added a career-finale touchdown.

Ernie Nevers, a blond giant from the Upper Midwest with Bunyanesque football abilities and a major-league fastball that was only occasionally successful against Babe Ruth, dominated NFL fields in the late 1920s.

His presence, with the touring Duluth Eskimos on a 29-game junket, dulled the edge of the threat presented by C.C. Pyle's rival American League, which offered Harold (Red) Grange. And when that project was turned aside, Nevers turned to other matters and set a one-game scoring record with the Chicago Cardinals: The 40 points still stand as one of the most venerable marks in the *NFL Record & Fact Book*.

Nevers, who played college ball for Pop Warner at Stanford, challenged the Notre Dame Four Horsemen in the 1925 Rose Bowl on ankles that might not have been totally recovered from previous fractures. Later, as a right-handed pitcher for the St. Louis Browns, he challenged Babe Ruth on several occasions during the 1927 season. If Ruth hadn't "won" twice, his long-held single-season homer mark would have been 58.

Warner, who had Jim Thorpe while coaching the

Carlisle Indians, rated Nevers a notch higher based on his all-around talents. Nevers ran, passed, and kicked with the best.

It almost seemed as though the Eagles were on hold as they awaited the availability of end **Pete Pihos**, drafted out of Indiana in 1945. He returned from military service and went back to Indiana to finish his education. He finally was available in 1947, and in the next three seasons Philadelphia was in three championship games, winning two.

Earle (Greasy) Neale, a Hall of Fame member, coached the Eagles in the late '40s. When he departed, Pihos played for Jim Trimble in the '50s, en route to his own Hall of Fame display. Trimble once put Pihos's ability in perspective, with heavy emphasis on his determination. "He could always go just a little further to get the ball," Trimble recalled. "And he made things happen. I eased up on his use on defense so I could have him concentrate on special teams, where he could always cause a fumble or help us get the ball back in a hurry."

Pihos was named to five consecutive Pro Bowls, catching at least 60 passes in each of his last three NFL seasons.

Pete Pihos (35) caught 185 passes in his final three seasons.

The NFL was in operation for a decade-and-a-half when the nine member clubs agreed there had to be a more equitable distribution of the available collegiate talent. A draft was instituted for the 1936 season, with the lower-finishing clubs logically drafting higher in an effort to even out the playing field.

After facing the Giants in the first two scheduled title games, the Bears had slipped in 1935 to finish in a bottom-rung tie in the Western Division. They selected a king-sized West Virginia lineman, **Joe Stydahar**, with their first pick ever, and they were back in the championship game in 1937. Stydahar, who became a primary component of the pre-World War II Monsters of the Midway, made all-league four consecutive seasons before leaving for military service. When he returned, he helped the Bears win their final title of the era in 1946. He made two stops as a coach, leading the Los Angeles Rams to the 1951 title and finishing up with a couple of seasons with the Chicago Cardinals.

Stydahar, a two-way tackle, spurned a helmet until he returned from military service after the league had mandated its use in 1943.

"The only time I ever saw someone's eyes rolling around in his head like in a Laurel and Hardy movie on the football field was when **Steve Van Buren** hit a guy who was giving us some trouble," recalled Allie Sherman, an Eagles assistant coach under Greasy Neale in the two-way days. "The linemen kept complaining and finally Steve said, 'Give me the ball, run the play at him, and get out of the way.' They did, Steve hit him, and there he was on the ground, his eyes making circles."

Van Buren ran circles around the rest of the league during an eight-year NFL tenure in which he led the league in rushing four times. He surpassed 1,000 yards twice at a time when the season consisted of 12 games, as opposed to 14 or 16. He was a ferocious runner, his mind rigidly fixed on conditioning to the point where he would do wind-sprints on the sidelines during a game, further adding to the discomfiture of the opposition. Van Buren's size (6-1, 200) made him formidable as a defensive back.

There undoubtedly have been greater games—before and since—and former Baltimore Colts defensive tackle Art Donovan, for one, will tell you that.

For instance, there was the game four weeks before the 1958 National Football League Championship Game, when the Colts rallied from a 27-7 halftime deficit to beat the San Francisco 49ers and clinch their first Western Division title.

"That was the greatest game I've ever played in," Donovan said flatly. "We were getting killed, but we came back and annihilated them to win our first division championship. That was something."

Quarterback Johnny Unitas, like Donovan a Pro Football Hall of Fame member, agreed that the 1958 title game was far from "the greatest of all time."

"I think most of the drama came from the championship setting rather than the game itself," he said. "We came down to tie it in the final seconds. Then it became the first playoff game ever to go into sudden death. You can't have much more drama than that."

If the game lacked artistic beauty, there is no question that on a gray, but unusually mild, late-December day in New York, the game of professional football ascended to a new level of public awareness. Even Donovan agrees with that.

"You can call it the most important game ever played because it may have been the best thing to ever happen to the NFL," Donovan said. "The whole country was watching it on TV. It wasn't just local. That's the game that put the league over the hump."

When end Jim Mutscheller and tackle George Preas slammed into the left side of the Giants' defensive line and created a gaping alley to the end zone for Alan (The Horse) Ameche, the first overtime game in NFL history came to a thrilling end and the Colts had their first league championship.

The stature of Baltimore's triumph grew almost instantaneously. The networks—and, more important, the advertisers—recognized that football and television went together about as well as gin and tonic.

What Donovan refuses to forget is that the game actually plodded along for nearly three quarters as the superior Colts moved to a 14-3 lead and were driving for a score that would have put away the game. On fourth-and-goal from the 1-yard line, Colts coach Weeb Ewbank chose to try for the touchdown. The gamble backfired as the Giants' Cliff Livingston fired through the line and dropped Ameche for a 4-yard loss.

"We were going in for another touchdown, and Ameche didn't hear a signal and started running and they got him," Donovan said. "We would have busted the game wide open. Then we were fighting for our lives."

Suddenly the stadium was alive, and so were the Giants. After a 1-yard touchdown dive by fullback Mel Triplett and a 15-yard scoring reception by Frank Gifford, New York led 17-14 early in the fourth quarter.

"You bet your ass we were worried," Donovan said. "We're thinking 'Here we go all over again.' A lot of us had never won four games in a season in our career, now we're almost going to win the championship, and we were blowing it. I was saying a Hail Mary."

As Donovan looked to the skies for

Baltimore fullback Alan Ameche rumbles to the winning touchdown in the 1958 title game.

divine intervention, the Colts took possession on their 14 with two minutes left. Their plan was simple: Go to Raymond Berry, their best receiver, on intermediate patterns as the Giants' secondary protected against the deep pass. Two superb plays by Berry helped the Colts reach the New York 13 with 20 seconds left.

Steve Myhra trotted onto the field and, with the nation watching, kicked a 20-yard field goal (the goal posts were on the goal line in 1958) to tie the game and force overtime.

The Giants won the coin toss and took possession first, but the Colts held on for three plays and took over at their 20.

Unitas began the historic 80-yard touchdown drive by handing off to L.G. (Long Gone) Dupre, who swept for 11 yards. On second-and-7 at the Colts' 44, Dick Modzelewski dumped Unitas for an 8-yard loss, creating a third-and-14 situation. Once again, Berry came up with a big play, catching a Unitas bullet for a first down at the New York 43.

Unitas audibled to an Ameche run and The Horse rambled to the Giants' 20. A pass to Berry gained 12, and, when a spectator raced onto the field holding up play, Unitas took advantage of the delay to consult with Ewbank. The coach wanted to run three times; if the Colts weren't in the end zone, they'd kick a field goal. But after Ameche was stopped for a 1-yard gain, Unitas called for a quick pass to Mutscheller along the right sideline. The play worked perfectly and Mutscheller was knocked out of bounds at the 1.

In the huddle, Unitas called the game-winning play: "16 Power," which had

Ameche running between the right guard and tackle. Mutscheller and Preas blocked down to the left, halfback Lenny Moore sealed off the right flank, and Ameche, two hands on the ball and head lowered, bulled into the open space. Within seconds, the field was swamped by gleeful Colts fans, who tore down the goal posts.

Donovan watches pro football today and his stomach turns when he sees players dancing after every play, no matter how inconsequential. "Boy, I remember how we celebrated," he said. "Weeb gave us a bottle of Nehi orange, and we had a ball."

BUMPING HEADS IN THE GOLDEN AGE

The 1950s were pro football's turning-point era. The NFL established itself as a big-time sports entity in the '50s, beginning with the absorption of the All-America Football Conference (the emergence of the AAFC's Cleveland Browns as a dominant NFL team proved the other league was no joke), and culminating with the NFL's emergence as a major television attraction.

Under the guidance of Commissioner Bert Bell, the NFL enjoyed unprecedented prosperity. It was a perfect fit for a country that also was in a general mood of well being. America entered the 1950s contented, at peace, and optimistic about the future. It was ready to enjoy sports again, especially a sport and a league whose product was becoming more entertaining each year.

And the biggest contribution in that area came from the 1958 NFL Championship Game between the New York Giants and Baltimore Colts, which, largely because it was decided in pro football's first overtime, helped put the sport on the map.

Give Us Your Disbanded...

It was a classic case of addition by subtraction when three All-America Football Conference teams were admitted to the National Football League in 1950. While pro football saw the disintegration of four AAFC teams—the NFL accepted only Cleveland, Baltimore, and San Francisco in the merger agreement—football fans were rewarded with a stronger, more viable organization.

The NFL always had snubbed the AAFC, but there was no doubt the junior league had a number of quality players who boosted the talent levels of the existing NFL teams.

In a few of the more notable transactions, the New York Giants were

Two staples of the NFL in the 1950s: Otto Graham and rugged play. Note the clash behind Graham (opposite), who took Cleveland to six title games in the decade.

Despite the illustration on this card, Tom Landry never played quarterback. He was a Giants defensive back from 1950-55.

awarded defensive backs Tom Landry and Harmon Rowe, and defensive tackle Arnie Weinmeister from the defunct Brooklyn-New York AAFC team (one follower called it the "greatest input of talent in the Giants' history"), and Cleveland received guard Abe Gibron, defensive tackle John Kissell, and halfback Rex Bumgardner from Buffalo in exchange for a 25 percent interest in the Browns for former Buffalo Bills owner James F. Brueil. The remaining players from the Bills, Brooklyn-New York Yankees, Chicago Hornets, and Los Angeles Dons were cast into a player pool to be dispersed to the NFL teams in a special draft in June, 1950.

But the greatest upgrade the NFL enjoyed was the inclusion of the Browns, period. Gordon Cobbledick of the *Cleveland Plain-Dealer* wrote that the Browns were "the one prize the National League wants," and whether that was true or not, one thing was perfectly clear: The Browns were as strong as any existing NFL team.

They made their NFL debut with future Hall of Fame players Otto Graham, Marion Motley, Len Ford, Bill Willis, Frank Gatski, Dante Lavelli, and Lou Groza already on the roster, and Hall of Fame coach Paul Brown putting all the pieces together. They cruised to a 10-2 mark in their first year in the league, then defeated the New York Giants in a playoff for the American Conference title. (The NFL called the Eastern Division the American Conference and the Western Division the National Conference from 1950-52, then returned to Eastern and Western Conference designations in 1953.)

San Francisco entered the NFL armed with superb running back Joe Perry and quarterback Frankie Albert, while Baltimore—although it struggled to a 1-11 finish in its final AAFC season—brought defensive tackle Art Donovan and quarterback Y.A. Tittle.

Buddy Young, who wound up playing for the New York Yankees, said the AAFC had many quality players, but its shortcomings were depth and coaching. "Some of the coaches had never been associated with pro football and didn't realize the necessity of having more than eleven or fifteen good players," Young explained. "In college you could get away with that, but in the pros, you needed depth."

Playing for the Camera

With three new clubs and scores of new players incorporated into the NFL, plus the adoption of the free substitution rule, the quality of the pro game showed dramatic improvement. And America began to take notice.

One of the keys to this rise in popularity was football's appeal on television. But while TV certainly increased the fan base, it hurt stadium attendance, especially in Los Angeles. In 1950, the Rams became the first NFL team to televise all of its home and away games. It proved to be a monumental mistake—with the games available on television, fans stayed away from the Coliseum in droves.

In 1949, the Rams—while in direct competition with the Dons of the AAFC—had drawn 205,109. In 1950, the Dons were gone and the Rams won the National Conference and eventually advanced to the NFL Championship Game, yet with many fans watching at home, attendance was cut nearly in half, to 110,162. Luckily for the Rams, they had negotiated a deal with the sponsors who advertised on the telecasts. The Rams were to receive cash from the sponsors for vacant seats when the gate fell below a

specified figure. At season's end, the team recouped $307,000 in losses.

From then on, the Rams televised only their road games. In 1951, attendance rose to 234,110. In 1953, the NFL's policy of blacking out home games was upheld by a U.S. District Court. And in 1956, Commissioner Bert Bell ruled that only road games could be televised.

Television viewers were treated to plenty of excitement, though, in 1950. There were a number of superlative statistical seasons turned in, especially in Detroit.

While the Lions failed to contend for the National Conference title, their fans were thrilled by the play of rookie halfback Doak Walker. Walker had an incredible year, scoring 5 touchdowns rushing and 6 receiving, making 38 of 41 extra points, and kicking 8 field goals for a league-leading 128 points. Meanwhile, quarterback Bobby Layne led the NFL with 2,323 passing yards, and Cloyce Box caught 50 passes for 1,009 yards.

And then there was Jim Hardy, the inconsistent quarterback of the Chicago Cardinals. In the Cardinals' opener against Philadelphia, he threw an NFL-record 8 interceptions in a 45-7 loss. The next week, during a 55-13 victory over Baltimore, he threw 5 touchdown passes to Bob Shaw.

Bell pulled off a public relations coup when he scheduled the Browns to make their NFL debut against the defending NFL-champion Eagles in the 1950 season opener. Like other former AAFC clubs, the Browns lacked the

The NFL challenged the Browns, formerly of the AAFC, by pitting them against the defending-champion Eagles in their first NFL game in 1950. Cleveland's 35-10 victory, led by fullback Marion Motley (above), served as a wake-up call for the established league.

The Los Angeles Rams' Tom Fears might have been the dominant pass-catching end of his era. Fears's 84 receptions in 1950 set a record that stood for a decade, and his 18 catches against Green Bay that season have yet to be matched.

respect of NFL loyalists. But respect was theirs after a 35-10 victory.

"When we finally played them, no team was ever as prepared emotionally for a game," Browns quarterback Otto Graham recalled. "We would have played them for a keg of beer—or in my case a chocolate milk shake.

"One of the Philadelphia papers sent a reporter to our training camp. He was there for about a month. The comments were that they were going to kill us because now we were playing with the big boys and so on. This reporter said, 'Hey, you people in Philadelphia better not get too cocky. This is a good team and they're going to give you a battle.' We played the ball game and kicked the hell out of them."

Charging Rams

For the first time in league history, special playoff games were needed to decide both conference championships in 1950.

In the American Conference, the Browns again proved they were for real as they defeated the Giants 8-3 at New York. While Cleveland's powerful offense sputtered, defensive end Len Ford and the defense corraled New York's vaunted running attack, which had averaged 195 yards per game during the regular season. Lou Groza kicked a 28-yard field goal to break a 3-3 tie with 58 seconds left in regulation, and Bill Willis capped the win when he tackled Charlie Conerly for a safety. The Browns never had lost a playoff game, having won four straight AAFC championships before joining the NFL in 1950.

In the National Conference, Tom Fears caught 7 passes from Bob Waterfield for 198 yards and 3 touchdowns to lead the Rams to a 24-14 victory over Chicago. Waterfield passed for 280 yards in the game.

The Rams had begun the year 2-2. Coach Joe Stydahar had seen enough after his club lost to Philadelphia 56-20. "Here's why you guys can't win," Stydahar raged as he pulled his front teeth bridge out of his mouth. "Look at those guys over there [the Eagles]. A half-dozen of them are wearing these things. Nobody on this team has any guts to charge in there with his head up. From now on, I want to see blood. I want to see teeth flying. If I don't we're gonna make changes around here."

The Rams edged the Lions 30-28 the next week, then beat Baltimore 70-27 and Detroit 65-24. They won seven of their final eight games and scored a league-high 466 points.

The title game between the Rams and Browns was one of the most eagerly awaited ever. For one thing, it would be the Rams' first game at Municipal Stadium since they fled Cleveland after winning the NFL championship in 1945. For another, the Browns were trying to win the league title in their first year.

Champions of All They Survey

By the time the championship game was played on Christmas Eve, Graham said, "We had proven ourselves. We were in the championship game. You had to be pretty good to get that far."

All eyes fixed upon Lou Groza's 16-yard field goal, which gave Cleveland a 30-28 victory in the 1950 NFL Championship Game.

speech to the Advertising Club, declared that if 15,000 season tickets could be sold in advance, the Texans would become the Colts. Baltimore's fans came through, and Bell talked his good friend and summer neighbor, Carroll Rosenbloom, into running the franchise.

While the Yanks-to-Colts saga was unfolding, of course, a lot of football was played. On the way to the 1951 NFL Championship Game, the Browns hosted the Bears, pinning a 42-21 defeat on George Halas's team. Halfback Dub Jones scored 6 touchdowns in the game, half his total for the season.

Elephants Crossing

The Browns and Rams assembled at the Los Angeles Coliseum for the championship game rematch. A crowd of 57,522 was on hand and millions more watched on television—this was the first NFL game to be telecast nationally, the DuMont network having paid $75,000 for the rights. The paying customers got their money's worth as the Rams came away victorious. For the first time in seven years (counting the Rams' title in 1945), a Cleveland team was not crowned king of a football world.

Joe Stydahar watched his Los Angeles Rams team dazzle the NFL with its passing game during the 1951 regular season. With Van Brocklin and Waterfield firing at will, Elroy (Crazylegs) Hirsch caught 66 passes for a league-record 1,495 yards, and he tied Don Hutson's mark with 17 touchdown receptions.

However Stydahar, realizing he had three of the best fullbacks in the league in Dick Hoerner, Deacon Dan Towler, and Paul (Tank) Younger, experimented by using all three in the same formation in a midseason game against San Francisco. The 49ers had defeated the Rams 44-17 a week earlier, but this time, employing the "Bull Elephant Backfield," Los Angeles prevailed 23-16.

In the biggest game of the year, a match with the Bears, Los Angeles fell behind 14-0 before the Bull Elephants took control. When it was over, the Rams had won 42-17, and the fullbacks had combined for 338 yards from scrimmage.

When the Browns came west for the championship game, Stydahar wanted to make sure they had to worry about Hirsch and end Tom Fears, plus the dynamic force of the Bull Elephants. "We would not be giving up speed because these three were very fast, like sprinters," Hirsch said. "We would not be de-emphasizing our passing game because these men were blessed with the hands of ends and all were established as capable receivers. And think of the strength added to the pass blocking."

For the most part, the strategy worked. Although the Rams rushed for only 81 yards on 43 attempts, they kept the ball away from the dangerous Cleveland offense. And Los Angeles's passing game was as effective as always, with Van Brocklin and Waterfield combining for 253 yards. Fears caught 4 passes worth 146 yards, including the game-winning touchdown on Waterfield's 73-yard bomb midway through the fourth quarter. The Rams won 24-17.

In 1952, the Browns reached their seventh consecutive championship game, but they were defeated for the second year in a row. Detroit, behind Bobby Layne and Doak Walker, won its first title in 17 years with a 17-7 victory at Cleveland. Walker rushed for 97 yards, including a 67-yard touch-

"As soon as it's light, I start to eat."

—ART DONOVAN,
300-POUND DEFENSIVE TACKLE
FOR THE COLTS, REFERRING TO
HIMSELF AS A LIGHT EATER

Bobby Layne: a charismatic quarterback who often led the Detroit Lions to victory, then bought the first round of drinks.

Jim Doran, subbing for the injured Leon Hart, had a big day for the Lions in the 1953 NFL Championship Game. Doran didn't seem to mind the overly enthusiastic photographers on this play.

"Football's a great life. It's much easier than working for a living. Just think— they pay you good money to eat well, stay in shape, and have fun."

—HUGH MCELHENNY,
SAN FRANCISCO 49ERS RUNNING BACK

down run in the third quarter. Layne, who had a reputation for playing just as hard off the field as he did on it, passed for 68 yards, rushed for 47, and scored the other Lions touchdown.

The Browns amassed 22 first downs to Detroit's 10 and outgained the Lions 384-258. But five drives inside the Detroit 25 were thwarted without any damage.

Ten time zones away, American troops were in the midst of the fierce Korean War. Fortunately for the NFL, this conflict would have little effect on the league's manpower or functioning, in stark contrast to World War II a decade earlier.

A Big Party

Philadelphia lost Bud Grant, its leading pass receiver in 1952 with 56 catches for 997 yards, when he defected to the Canadian Football League in 1953. But he hardly was missed as Pete Pihos stepped in and led the league in receptions (63) and receiving yards (1,049). Grant would return to the NFL 14 years later, as head coach of the Minnesota Vikings.

The Browns and Lions met again in the 1953 title game and Cleveland suffered its third consecutive championship loss as Detroit escaped with a 17-16 victory. Graham had his poorest day as a pro, completing just 2 of 15 passes for 20 yards, but thanks to 3 field goals by Lou Groza, the Browns led 16-10 with 4:10 left to play.

Starting from the Lions' 20 after the kickoff, Layne arrived in the Detroit huddle and told his teammates: "Now if you'll just block a little bit, fellas,

THE UMBRELLA OPENS

The 1950s have been called pro football's Golden Age. Per-game attendance rose every year. The formations and strategies of today became standard fare. The Los Angeles Rams put offensive numbers on the board that never have been matched, and in New York and Detroit fans cheered their defenses.

The decade opened with a flurry of strategy.

In 1949, Clark Shaughnessy had lined up the Rams in the first modern pro set —one true tight end, two wide receivers, two running backs. He was fired in 1950, but his legacy was a playbook filled with multiple wide receivers and motion, all designed to outflank the opponent and beat him with speed.

When the new coach, Joe Stydahar, checked out his material—two great quarterbacks and a busload of receivers —he knew he had to figure out a way to get everyone in on the action. The result was an explosion of offense.

In Philadelphia, the two-time defending-champion Eagles got a big surprise against Cleveland, fresh from the AAFC, on opening day. Otto Graham shredded Philadelphia's 5-4 "Eagle" defense that Saturday night with flares, sideline passes, and comeback routes to his receivers.

When the Eagles' linebackers loosened up, the Browns killed them by running 238-pound Marion Motley up the middle on draw plays. The result was a 35-10 thrashing. The most interested observer in the stands may have been Giants coach Steve Owen, who had to stop the Browns two weeks later.

"Steve Owen's defensive brilliance has never really been recognized," said Frank (Bucko) Kilroy, an Eagles guard and tackle in the fifties and one of the NFL's first player personnel directors. "The year before, when we were having trouble getting ready for the College All-Stars and Bud Wilkinson's spread-T option offense, our coach, Greasy Neale,

asked Steve for advice. He drew up a five-two with the ends dropping back, and it became the modern three-four.

"We beat the All-Stars 38-0, and the next day Wilkinson and his coaches were over at our place with their notebooks, and they took the defense back to Oklahoma with them. It became the famous five-two 'Okie,' which Chuck Fairbanks, another Oklahoma coach, introduced to the NFL as the three-four."

Owen's defense for the Browns was a 6-1-4, with the ends "flexing," or dropping back as linebackers. The result was a 6-0 Giants victory that marked October 1, 1950, as the official birthdate of the 4-3 "Umbrella" defense. It was the first time a Paul Brown-coached team had been shut out, and when the teams met again three weeks later, Owen greeted him

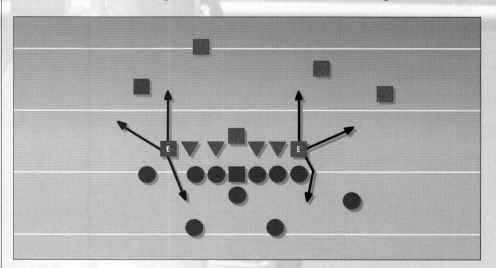

Steve Owen's "Umbrella" defense: The ends sometimes rushed, sometimes dropped into coverage.

with a 5-1-5 "Nickel." The Giants won 17-13, handing the champion Browns their only defeats of the season.

The Rams obliterated single-season records for scoring, passing, and total offense in 1950 and 1951. It took Dan Marino and Air Coryell in the 1980s to get them off the books, although some of the Rams' per-game marks still stand. The offense, which sometimes featured as many as five receivers in a pattern, was personnel-driven. The talent simply dic-

tated it, and in Bob Waterfield and Norm Van Brocklin, Los Angeles had a pair of quarterbacks who played together in two Pro Bowls and once finished 1-2 in the NFL in passing.

When age eventually caught up with the Rams, the new kids on the block were the Lions, who built their successive titles (1952-53) on defense. It was a basic 5-2-4, keyed by exceptional middle guard Les Bingaman, whose weight climbed from 250 to 350 during his seven-year career, and a four-man secondary that was honored with a nickname—"Chris's Crew," after safety Jack Christiansen.

The 4-3 became the standard NFL defense when Sam Huff arrived as the Giants' middle linebacker. The Giants had been tinkering with a 6-1 and a 5-2, and other teams had gone with a five-man front, dropping their middle man to create a four-man look. But by the end of the decade, when the Baltimore Colts' era peaked, everyone was in a 4-3.

Coach Weeb Ewbank's great gift to the NFL was his skillful handling of quarterbacks, particularly John Unitas, whom he'd rescued from the Pittsburgh sandlots. Ewbank spent endless hours on the mechanics of the position, especially the set-up. He wanted a pure pocket passer, and Unitas was the greatest of the era.

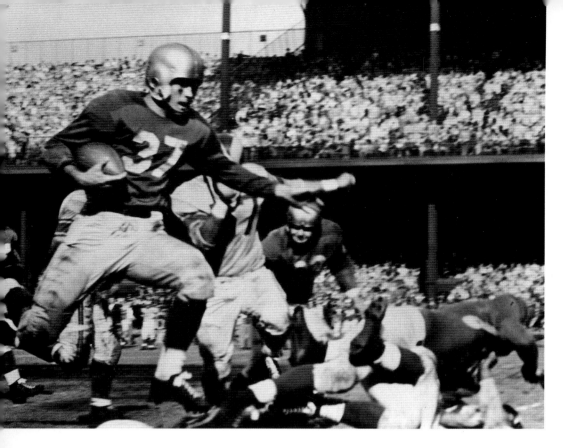

Detroit's Doak Walker was a versatile halfback who ran, caught, and kicked with authority. Excluding the 1952 season, he never finished lower than third in the NFL in scoring.

Jim Lee Howell (rear center) was the Giants' head coach from 1954-1960. His assistants included Tom Landry (rear left) and Vince Lombardi (front left).

ol' Bobby'll pass you right to the championship."

And he did. Layne completed a 17-yard pass to Jim Doran on first down, and after 2 incompletions, hit Doran for another 18-yard gain. A 9-yard pass to Cloyce Box and a foiled rushing attempt created third-and-1 at the Browns' 36. Layne sneaked through the middle for the first down, then called time out to confer with head coach Buddy Parker.

The coaching staff, recognizing that Len Ford was rushing hard from the end and paying little attention to the flat, thought a screen pass might work. Layne was set to call the play, but he changed his mind in the huddle because he knew Doran could get open deep.

Sure enough, Doran, who was in the game because of an injury to starter Leon Hart, got behind Cleveland's Warren Lahr and hauled in the winning 33-yard touchdown pass with 2:08 remaining.

Walker's conversion provided the margin of victory, giving the Lions their second consecutive NFL championship.

"Doak Walker used to say that Bobby Layne never lost a game, it was just that sometimes time ran out on him," Donovan said in his book, *Fatso*. "Bobby [finished] out his career in Pittsburgh, and I remember playing the Steelers once in an exhibition game in the Orange Bowl in Miami. Layne was dropping back to pass when three of us fell on him, really crushed him before he could get the ball off. I looked at him and said, 'You all right, Bob?'

"And he just looked up, smiled, and said, 'Yeah, Fatso, I'm all right. But don't do it again because I'm going to meet you afterward. I'm having a big party and you're all invited.'"

Layne's devil-may-care attitude was the perfect antidote for a society that suddenly had become more than a little paranoid. Senator Joseph McCarthy's televised hearings painted an America that had Communists lurking in every other doorway. But who could worry about Reds when Layne was leading his Lions downfield with good-natured confidence?

The Right Assistants

While Detroit and Cleveland continued their relentless marches through the Western and Eastern Conferences for the third year in a row, there were some exciting developments elsewhere in 1954.

San Francisco's Joe Perry became the first back in NFL history to post back-to-back 1,000-yard rushing seasons. Philadelphia quarterback Adrian Burk led the league with 23 touchdown passes, including an NFL-record-tying 7 in a 49-21 romp over Washington on October 17. And in Baltimore, the Colts introduced former Paul Brown assistant Weeb Ewbank as their new head coach. Ewbank promised he would have the Colts playing at a championship level within five years, but in that first season, Baltimore stumbled to 3-9.

The New York Giants also made some significant changes in their coaching staff in 1954. Jim Lee Howell, who had played end for the Giants from 1937 to 1948 (with a layoff for a period during the war), was promoted to head coach. He named Vince Lombardi, who had been coaching at Army, as his offensive coordinator, and Tom Landry as his defensive coordinator.

Landry had joined the Giants as a defensive back in 1950 and, although his playing career wasn't spectacular, it was consistent, a trait he later would use as a coach. The year before Howell and his staff took over, the Giants had posted a 3-9 record and were outscored 277-179, which included an embarrassing 62-14 loss to Cleveland. In 1954 they improved to 7-5 and outscored their opponents 293-184.

Fullback Fred (Curly) Morrison had 1 of Cleveland's 8 touchdowns in the muddy 1954 title game, a 56-10 rout of Detroit.

SAVING TEETH

Maybe it was the advent of TV, but football players in the 1950s finally found a way to keep their pretty faces unmarked—relatively, anyway.

A facemask that wouldn't break or shatter and provided reasonable protection for a player's nose and teeth was developed during the decade and quickly adopted by most players.

Facemasks of many sorts had appeared in the early days of pro football, mostly crude contraptions of dubious value. In the early 1950s, a wide, clear lucite model was popular until it began shattering. Finally, the tubular bar was invented in 1955 and popularized by Cleveland Browns quarterback Otto Graham. It wasn't long before the single bar doubled, tripled, and blossomed into the full-fledged "bird cage" worn by modern players.

Dentists across the country were forever grateful. You now could tell the difference between hockey players and football players. The latter still had most of their teeth, thanks to the facemask.

The facemask changed the game. Fortified with the knowledge that his nose would stay in place, a defender could rely on his helmet while making a tackle. And that helmet was almost always plastic as the old leather variety faded into the history books.

Paul Brown, one of the most innovative coaches in NFL history, showed that a player's head wasn't the only thing you could put inside a football helmet. In 1956, Brown hired an inventor to rig up a radio receiver in the helmet of George Ratterman, his Cleveland quarterback, during preseason games in Akron, Ohio, and Chicago, and in the Browns' home opener versus the New York Giants. Brown would talk to Ratterman and call plays from the sidelines rather then the usual method of sending in a messenger.

San Francisco halfback Joe Perry took face protection to a new level in the fifties.

But the experiment ran into problems in Chicago.

"We would be in the huddle," recalled Mike McCormack, a Cleveland tackle before he launched a long career as an NFL coach and general manager, "and Ratterman would get this crazy look on his face. He finally said, 'Hell, I'm getting cab calls from Michigan Avenue to State Avenue.'"

Commissioner Bert Bell soon banned the Dick Tracy-like device, and radio helmets wouldn't pop up in the NFL again for 30 years.

Other ideas that came along in the 1950s did last. Players welcomed the lighter synthetic jerseys made of material such as rayon-durene and nylon-durene. The NFL adopted a rule in 1952 for wearing numbers on those jerseys. It required centers to wear numbers in the 50s, guards in the 60s, and so on. Exceptions were made for well-known players.

Baltimore Colts running back Lenny Moore became the first player to popularize "spatting," wrapping his black shoes completely in white tape. They called him "Spats." Meanwhile, white footballs with black stripes, often used for night games, were banned in favor of brown footballs with white stripes around the ends for night use.

The estimated cost of outfitting a pro football player in full uniform in 1953 was $200. An NFL football was $14.

George Ratterman's 1956 helmet, including the radio receiver that was banned by the NFL.

Landry, a player-coach who intercepted 8 passes in 1954, fine-tuned the Giants' 4-3 defense. Lombardi, meanwhile, introduced the power sweep, and backs Eddie Price and Frank Gifford—running behind star tackle Roosevelt Brown—combined for more than 900 rushing yards. Because Howell had been able to talk Charlie Conerly out of retirement, Lombardi had a veteran signal-caller throwing to Kyle Rote and Bob Schnelker, who combined for 59 catches, 1,101 yards, and 10 touchdowns.

One of Lombardi's greatest tools was the use of game film to study opponents' tendencies. "The guy's got sixteen-millimeter eyeballs," Gifford observed at the time, noting that Lombardi could quickly determine who had blown an assignment and who had executed properly on every play. Howell and his staff later would add players such as defensive end Andy Robustelli, linebacker Sam Huff, fullbacks Alex Webster and Mel Triplett, and defensive tackle Roosevelt (Rosey) Grier, and the Giants would go on to win conference titles in 1956, 1958, and 1959.

Detroit was unable to pull off the hat trick against the Browns in the 1954 NFL Championship Game. Cleveland ended its streak of three title-game losses—including the last two to the Lions—with a remarkable 56-10 rout. Otto Graham had indicated that he would retire after the game, and he played as if it were his last, passing for 163 yards and 3 touchdowns and running for 3 more scores. The Browns converted 6 Detroit turnovers into touchdowns. Incredibly, the Lions held a 331-303 advantage in total yards.

A Very Short Retirement

After four preseason games in 1955, Paul Brown talked Graham out of quitting. Graham proved he still had another great season in him: He made the all-NFL team for the sixth consecutive year and directed the Browns to yet another league title.

The '55 Rams were guided by Sid Gillman, one of the foremost offensive thinkers in football history. Gillman utilized a diverse attack with Norm Van Brocklin throwing to Tom Fears and Crazylegs Hirsch, and with Ron Waller and Tank Younger powering a strong running game.

But Gillman's wizardry didn't work against Cleveland in the NFL Championship Game. The Browns intercepted 7 passes against Los Angeles, including 6 thrown by Van Brocklin, and Don Paul returned 1 of the interceptions 65 yards for a touchdown. When it was over, the 85,693 fans at the L.A. Coliseum had witnessed a 38-14 Cleveland triumph.

Graham passed for 209 yards and 2 touchdowns and scored twice on runs. After the game he retired again. This time he was true to his word. Graham ended his pro career having played in 10 championship games in 10 seasons.

Pittsburgh, which hadn't produced a winning season since 1949, made a regrettable decision before the 1955 campaign. Coach Walt Kiesling, looking for a quarterback to back up starter Jim Finks, brought in Johnny Unitas, Ted Marchibroda, and Vic Eaton. Kiesling kept Marchibroda and Eaton…and cut Unitas. The Steelers surpassed 20 points only three times in 12 games and finished 4-8.

Unitas played semipro ball in 1955, but Weeb Ewbank gave him a tryout in 1956 when Colts quarterback George Shaw suffered a knee injury. Unitas completed 55.6 percent of his passes to set an NFL rookie record, and the Colts fought their way toward respectability at 5-7. Along the way, they

LABOR PAINS

The idea of a players' union was germinating all around the league in the mid-fifties, which helps to explain why there are as many accounts of the origins of the National Football League Players Association as there were NFL cities at the time.

Dante Lavelli, a Hall of Fame end for the Browns, claimed the concept was born in Cleveland. Lavelli said he volunteered the basement of his home for Wednesday-night meetings with two teammates, Abe Gibron and George Ratterman, plus Creighton Miller, an attorney who had been the Browns' general manager and later general counsel.

"After we had won the NFL championship in 1955, I thought about retiring," Lavelli recalled. "The reason I went back to play was that I wanted to keep [the players' union idea] going."

The basic bargaining points discussed by the four men included:

• a minimum salary of $5,000 per year;

• consistent per diem pay for players;

• a rule requiring clubs to pay for playing equipment;

• a clause in the standard player contract that would provide for continued payment of salary to an injured player.

It wasn't a perk-filled package by today's standards, but it was a start.

November of 1956 was the NFLPA's birth month. By that time, a majority of NFL players had signed petitions authorizing Miller and the NFLPA to represent them. After a players' meeting at the Waldorf-Astoria Hotel in Manhattan, they issued a statement:

"The players obviously want a continuous improvement in their economic condition with some control over their own destiny. The football man, when dissatisfied, thinks not of a revolt, but of recognition. It is hoped that the modern club executive faced with player grievances will think not of the divine right of management, but of making feasible adjustments."

added halfback Lenny Moore to complement workhorse fullback Alan Ameche. It was clear the Colts would soon become a formidable team.

The Giants moved out of the Polo Grounds and into Yankee Stadium in 1956—the same year the NFL outlawed grabbing an opponent's facemask—and the fabled ball yard in the Bronx rocked all year.

Mickey Mantle won the triple crown for the baseball Yankees, who went on to beat the Brooklyn Dodgers in the World Series. The Giants followed that by winning their first Eastern Conference title since 1946, preventing the Browns from winning a division crown for the first time in their history, a string of 10 years. The Browns fell to 5-7 as quarterbacks Tom O'Connell, George Ratterman, and Babe Parilli failed to fill the cleats left vacant by Graham.

Slip-Sliding Away

The Giants were led by Frank Gifford, who rushed for 819 yards and caught 51 passes for 603 yards, all team highs. On the day of the 1956 NFL Championship Game between the Giants and Bears, the turf at Yankee Stadium was frozen solid, so the Giants wore sneakers instead of cleats.

While the Bears wore sneakers, too, for most of the game, they could not hang onto the ball, and New York used those turnovers to deal Chicago one of its worst defeats ever, 47-7. Alex Webster rushed for 2 scores, Gifford caught a 14-yard touchdown pass from Charlie Conerly, and the Bears gained only 67 yards on the ground.

The Giants' defensive performance was stunning considering the firepower that Chicago possessed on offense. The Bears had scored 363 points and gained 4,537 yards during the season, both league highs. Quarterback Ed Brown was an efficient passer; wide receiver Harlon Hill, who caught 47 passes for 1,128 yards and 11 touchdowns, was a gamebreaker; and fullback Rick Casares led the NFL with 1,126 rushing yards and 14 touchdowns, 12 on the ground.

But the Giants' defensive game plan—drawn up by Tom Landry and spearheaded by Emlen Tunnell, Sam Huff, Andy Robustelli, and Rosey Grier—thoroughly frustrated the physical Bears. Things got so bad for Chicago that it switched from its T-formation to a Double-Wing. But on this day, the Giants had answers for that, too.

"The 'Monsters of the Midway,' as the Bears were nicknamed, were supposed to be the roughest team in football," Gifford wrote in his book, *The Whole Ten Yards*. "As we quickly discovered, however, they had no idea what we were up to. Our offense and defense just kept outsmarting them, doing things they had never seen before and that are done all the time today.

"The Bears were playing Bears football, which meant they were trying to mug us. But thanks to Vince Lombardi and Tom Landry, pro football had moved up to another plateau—and that game confirmed it."

The Walls Had Ears

The 1957 season got off to a bizarre start when Detroit coach Buddy Parker abruptly quit two days before the first preseason game. He announced his resignation at a Lions' booster club banquet. Parker, who posted a 50-24-2 record and won two NFL championships in six seasons, was fed up with the Lions' ownership circus (12 owners split into two factions). Despite quitting

Opposite: Cleveland's Jim Brown had a swift impact on the NFL as a 1957 rookie. His 942 rushing yards that year gave him the first of eight league rushing titles.

The 49ers' Y.A. Tittle was one of the most productive quarterbacks of his generation. He recorded four 2,000-yard passing seasons during the 1950s.

in August, Parker was not unemployed for long, taking over as coach of the Steelers before the season.

"I don't want to get involved in another losing season [he had only one in Detroit, 1955], so I'm leaving Detroit." Parker said. "In fact, I'm leaving tonight."

While Parker was ending his relationship with the Lions, Pete Rozelle advanced his with the Los Angeles Rams when he was named general manager.

And the Browns began their retooling effort—by drafting fullback Jim Brown out of Syracuse. Brown rushed for a league-high 932 yards and was named rookie of the year as he led Cleveland into the NFL Championship Game after a one-year hiatus. Oddly enough, the Browns met the Lions, the same team Parker had given up on.

Assistant coach George Wilson had been promoted to replace Parker. Utilizing Layne and Tobin Rote at quarterback, plus the superb secondary play of safety Jack Christiansen (10 interceptions), Wilson coaxed Detroit to an 8-4 record and a tie with San Francisco for first place in the Western Division.

Forty-Niners co-owner Tony Morabito collapsed and died of a heart attack during San Francisco's come-from-behind 21-17 victory over the Bears at Kezar Stadium on October 27. It was a tragedy for the club, which somehow kept its bearings in an 8-4 season and earned a playoff spot opposite the Lions for the Western Conference title.

San Francisco dominated Detroit for the first 30 minutes, taking a 24-7 halftime lead. At halftime, the visiting Lions could hear the 49ers whooping it up through the thin walls of Kezar's locker rooms. San Francisco quarterback Y.A. Tittle already had thrown 3 touchdown passes, and the talented Detroit defense—which had allowed just 26 points over the final three regular-season games—seemed helpless in trying to stop Tittle, halfbacks Hugh McElhenny and R.C. Owens, and end Billy Wilson. And the 49ers' defense—led by imposing tackle Leo Nomellini—had frustrated Rote and the Lions' offense.

"Listen to those s.o.bs, listen to them," bellowed Detroit linebacker Joe Schmidt.

The Lions listened...and got angry. "Naturally, if I was ahead of a team 24-7, I think we'd be celebrating, too," Christiansen said. "We found out later from some of the players that they were very confident that they were going to be opening the champagne, and that their wives had already spent the championship money for fur coats and houses and cars and so on."

If the Lions were motivated, they certainly didn't show it on the first play of the second half when McElhenny broke a 71-yard run before being forced out of bounds at Detroit's 7. But on the next three plays, Detroit's humbled defense rose up and forced the 49ers to settle for a 10-yard field goal by Gordy Soltau, which increased the margin to 27-7. "I really believe that if I would have gone in to score on that [71-yard] run, that would have been the end of the game," McElhenny said. "I don't think they would have been able to catch up with us."

Instead, the goal-line stand seemed to revitalize the Lions. They scored 21 points—2 touchdown runs by Tom (The Bomb) Tracy, including a 58-yard scamper, and a third by Gene Gedman—within a span of 4:29 in the late third and early fourth quarters. They continued to thwart the 49ers' offense, intercepting Tittle 3 times in the final period. Schmidt returned an interception to the San Francisco 2, setting up Jim Martin's field goal that produced

Quarterback Tobin Rote led Detroit's amazing comeback in a 1957 playoff game.

Trailing San Francisco 24-7 at halftime of their NFL Western Conference Playoff Game in 1957, the Detroit Lions heard 49ers players celebrating through Kezar Stadium's thin locker-room walls. The Lions fell further behind (27-7) in the third quarter but roared back to win 31-27. For 35 years it stood as the greatest comeback in NFL playoff history. The biggest single-game turnarounds ever:

POSTSEASON

Buffalo trailed Houston 35-3...
        won 41-38 in overtime (1/3/93)
Detroit trailed San Francisco 27-7...
        won 31-27 (12/22/57)
Dallas trailed San Francisco 21-3...
        won 30-28 (12/23/72)
Miami trailed Cleveland 21-3...
        won 24-21 (1/4/86)

REGULAR SEASON

San Francisco trailed New Orleans 35-7
        ...won 38-35 in overtime (12/7/80)
St. Louis trailed Tampa Bay 28-3...
        won 31-28 (11/8/87)

Teams have rallied from 24-point deficits in regular-season games 11 times.

the final score of 31-27. It stands as one of the greatest comeback victories in playoff history.

Many people thought that the Lions might have spent all of their emotion in the frenzied second half, but that couldn't have been further from the truth. A week later, Rote passed for 280 yards and 4 touchdowns and ran for another score as the Lions routed the Browns 59-14 at Briggs Stadium to win the NFL championship.

Detroit motored to a 31-7 halftime lead and, unlike the 49ers, never let up, tacking on 4 more touchdowns in the second half. The Lions forced 6 turnovers and held Jim Brown to 69 rushing yards.

A Time to Mourn

After a two-year hiatus, George Halas returned to the sidelines to coach the Chicago Bears in 1958, claiming, "There's some new stuff I have in mind that I would like to try."

He forced John (Paddy) Driscoll, who had struggled to a 5-7 record in his second year as coach in 1957, to return to the front office, and Halas guided

The Lions beat the Browns 59-14 for the 1957 title largely on the strength of 5 interceptions, including this one by Terry Barr.

116

49ERS' LEAP YEAR

If necessity is the mother of invention, the San Francisco 49ers must be among her favorite children. The 49ers gave us the NFL's two most inventive meetings of hand and ball: The Alley-Oop and The Catch.

Alley-Oop was the name of a high-arcing pass from quarterback Y.A. Tittle to R.C. Owens, a 6-foot 3-inch rookie from the College of Idaho. The 49ers had lost their 1957 regular-season opener to the Chicago Cardinals and were practicing for their game with the Los Angeles Rams in week two.

Owens recalled: "Our offense would emulate the Rams' offense against our defense. Tittle just started launching these rainbows. I was coming up with [leaping catches] with two or three guys on me. I didn't want to look bad. Pretty soon, when I came back to the huddle, Tittle said, 'If we are completing this, why not put it in for Sunday?'

"Red Hickey, our offensive coach, and Frankie Albert, our head coach, said, 'Okay, but what do we call it?'"

They called it Alley-Oop for the comic strip character who swung from the treetops. Today, you can call it the play that gave birth to Dallas's Hail Mary, Atlanta's Big Ben, and every other lob-pass-with-tip-drill that came later.

The next Sunday, the 49ers trailed 20-16 with 3:15 remaining and the ball at the Los Angeles 11. Tittle came into the huddle on second down and said, "We'll go for the Alley-Oop." Owens stepped over the goal line, outjumped Jesse Castete, and caught Tittle's looping pass. Final score: San Francisco 23, Los Angeles 20.

After victories over the Bears, Green Bay, and the Bears again, the 49ers faced Detroit at Kezar Stadium. Trailing 31-28 with 19 seconds remaining, Tittle called for the Alley-Oop. Owens went up between two of the NFL's best defenders, Jack Christiansen and Jim David, came down with a 41-yard touchdown catch, and gave the 49ers a 35-31 victory.

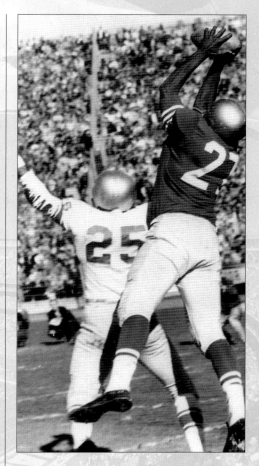

Former basketball player R.C. Owens was virtually unstoppable on the "Alley-Oop."

the Bears to an 8-4 record. That wasn't good enough to win the West, however, as Baltimore, with a pair of victories over Chicago, finished first at 9-3.

While the Colts won the West outright, the Giants needed to beat Cleveland in a playoff game to advance to the NFL Championship Game. New York's smothering defense held Jim Brown to 8 rushing yards in a 10-0 victory. Brown had set a league record by gaining 1,527 yards during the regular season, but the Giants successfully focused all their efforts on stopping him.

The 1958 Championship Game, a dramatic 23-17 victory by Baltimore, often is credited with putting the NFL on the map. Most of New York, however, was in the dark during the Giants' loss. Besides the local television blackout, the Big Apple was in the midst of a newspaper strike.

The 1959 season got off to a sad start when New York Giants founder and owner Tim Mara, 71, died after a long illness on February 17. His sons, Jack and Wellington Mara, took over operation of the club. There was another loss on October 11 when 64-year-old NFL Commissioner Bert Bell died of a heart attack. Appropriately, Bell was at Philadelphia's Franklin Field watching a game between the Eagles and the Steelers, the two teams with which he had had the most involvement.

Bell had established the Eagles in 1933 and served as their owner and general manager until 1940. He also was the head coach for five years. In 1941, Bell had joined forces with Art Rooney in operating the Steelers. He even

"I never will forget a game in 1952 in Cleveland when I had my first chance to tackle Marion Motley. He looked like a big tank rolling down on me. But you got to take him on. I hit him with my head in his knees, and he came down. I saw a few stars, but I felt good because I tackled Marion Motley."

—DICK (NIGHT TRAIN) LANE,
LOS ANGELES RAMS DEFENSIVE BACK

TINT OF BROWN

He was just 27, not far removed from calling high school and college games in places like Quincy, Massachusetts, and Rutland, Vermont. And as Ken Coleman watched Paul Brown, The Legend himself, he wondered what he was doing there, surrounded by members of the Cleveland Browns.

"Brown told the team, 'This is Ken Coleman, our new play-by-play man,'" Coleman said.

"At this point, Len Ford, who was sitting beside me, and is one of the great defensive ends in the history of the game, looks down at me and says, 'Oh, that's what you do. I thought you might be a cornerback.'"

Coleman as an NFL cornerback is not as unbelievable as a writer or broadcaster today being introduced to a group of NFL players as a member of their "team."

Coleman later became a pioneer in football broadcasting. He saw Paul Brown up close ("He would tell his players to always cooperate with the media, but, at the same time, never do anything in the press that would be detrimental to Browns football.") and he worked around some awkward arrangements. "Like split broadcasts," he said. "If we were playing the Cardinals, I would do one half and Jack Drees, the voice of the Cardinals, would do the other."

Coleman was in on some firsts, such as the first former player to broadcast a game. Coleman thinks former Cleveland Browns quarterback Otto Graham, "who worked with me in 1956, the year after he retired," holds that distinction.

It was in the fifties that TV and the NFL discovered their match made in heaven. "I still think the biggest game we ever had in the league was the Colts' win over the Giants [in the 1958 NFL Cham-pionship Game]," said former NFL Commissioner Pete Rozelle, who served first as the Rams' public relations director and later as general manager. "I think that was the first game that got television coverage across America. It reached fans who had never seen pro football before."

Tex Schramm, who went on to fame as Dallas's general manager, preceded Rozelle as PR director in Los Angeles. "We did things in those days that would never be done now," he said. "Papers didn't staff our training camps. I wrote stories for the papers and sent them via Western Union. The papers would put some other writer's by-line on the story.

"In the offseason, I got in my car, drove to four or five papers, and wrote stories. They would give me a desk, I'd give them a story. Not only that, but I wrote the headline and helped ship the copy to the composing room."

"The Packers were the most soft-bitten team in the league; they overwhelmed one, underwhelmed ten, and whelmed one."

—Legendary sportswriter Red Smith on the 1958 Green Bay Packers— one season before Vince Lombardi became the team's head coach

coached two games before Buff Donelli was brought in. As commissioner, Bell had guided the league through its most prosperous period.

Before the 1959 season began, Rams general manager Pete Rozelle orchestrated one of the most bizarre trades in sports history, dealing eight players and a draft choice to the Chicago Cardinals in exchange for halfback Ollie Matson. In six seasons with the Cardinals, Matson had scored 46 touchdowns. In 1958 he had gained 1,467 all-purpose yards. But even with Matson and split end Del Shofner (47 catches for 936 yards and 7 touchdowns), the Rams fell to the basement in the West, finishing with a 2-10 record that included a season-ending eight-game losing streak.

In Complete Command

In Green Bay, the Packers executed the move that turned around their franchise. It had been 12 years since the Packers enjoyed a winning season and 15 years since they won a championship. Curly Lambeau had coached the team from its inception in 1919 until 1949 and had posted an NFL record of 212-106-21, with six league titles. But after Lambeau was forced to resign following the 1949 season, the Packers spiraled into despair. From 1950-58, the team went 32-74-2.

Tired of their losing image, the Packers' executive committee hired Vince Lombardi from the New York Giants to lead the team back from the black hole.

Lombardi had made a name for himself playing college football. A guard, he was one of Fordham's famous "Seven Blocks of Granite." His coaching stops had included St. Cecilia's High School in Englewood, New Jersey, where his teams once won 36 straight games; Fordham, where he coached the freshmen, then joined the varsity as an assistant; Army, under head coach Earl (Red) Blaik; and New York, where he taught the power sweep as offensive coordinator with the Giants.

Lombardi let it be known that he was the boss shortly after he signed a five-year contract with the Packers. At the first team meeting, he said: "Let's get one thing straight—I'm in complete command here. Gentlemen, I've never been associated with a losing team. I do not intend to start now."

Sure enough, the Packers (who were 1-10-1 in 1958) posted a 7-5 record in 1959. The next time Green Bay endured a losing season would be 1968, the first year of the post-Lombardi era. During his historic nine-year term, the Packers went 98-30-4. They won five NFL championships, including the first two Super Bowls.

Lombardi's first team featured Bart Starr at quarterback, Paul Hornung at halfback, Jim Taylor at fullback, flanker Boyd Dowler, and split end Max McGee, and an offensive line that included Forrest Gregg, Jim Ringo, Fred (Fuzzy) Thurston, and Jerry Kramer. The group jelled by the end of the season and the Packers won their final four games, outscoring their opponents 119-51.

Hornung had struggled during his first two years in the league, but when

FRANK GIFFORD
HALFBACK   NEW YORK GIANTS

Giants halfback Frank Gifford was one of the most glamorous football stars of the 1950s. He made all-pro four times in the decade.

In the eight seasons vociferous George Halas coached the Chicago Bears in the 1950s, they posted a winning record six times.

Lombardi installed him at left halfback, the former Notre Dame Heisman Trophy winner's true talents became clear. Hornung, a college quarterback, led the league in scoring with 7 touchdowns, 31 extra points, and 7 field goals for 94 points.

Johnny U

The NFL had the pro football market all to itself throughout the 1950s. But with many league owners reluctant to expand, it was only a matter of time before entrepreneurial outsiders tried to tap into this emerging, booming industry.

Early in 1959, Lamar Hunt of Dallas, the millionaire son of oilman H.L. Hunt, spoke to George Halas, chairman of the expansion committee, and commissioner Bert Bell about the possibility of putting a new franchise in Dallas. Halas and Bell concurred that the league wasn't ready to expand. So Hunt, who also had failed in attempts to purchase the Chicago Cardinals, decided to start his own league.

On August 14, he gathered in Chicago to meet with K. S. (Bud) Adams (Houston), Max Winter and William Boyer (Minneapolis), Bob Howsam (Denver), Barron Hilton (Los Angeles), and Harry Wismer (New York). Eight days later, during a second meeting, they agreed to form the American Football League. Buffalo and Boston were added a few months later, and when Minneapolis dropped out to join the NFL, Oakland came aboard. Later in the fall, Joe Foss, the former governor of South Dakota, was named AFL Commissioner.

The 1959 season concluded with a rematch of the '58 NFL Championship Game as the Colts again met the Giants, this time in front of 57,545 rabid Baltimore fans at Memorial Stadium. The game couldn't match the excitement of the previous year as the Colts rolled to a 31-16 victory.

Johnny Unitas hit Lenny Moore with a 60-yard touchdown pass in the first quarter, but the Colts' offense stalled and didn't score again until the fourth quarter. Meanwhile, Pat Summerall kicked 3 field goals, giving the Giants a 9-7 lead going into the final 15 minutes.

The Colts stopped the Giants on fourth-and-1 at Baltimore's 28, and Unitas took over from there. He ran 4 yards for the go-ahead touchdown 2:42 into the fourth quarter, then threw a 12-yard scoring pass to Jerry Richardson five minutes later. Cornerback Johnny Sample returned an interception 42 yards for the clinching score with 5:19 remaining.

"We beat the living hell out of them that second game," Art Donovan said. "They didn't have it. I think the only guy who was honest was [Giants guard] Roosevelt Brown. He said to me, 'You guys had a better team.'

"I didn't know this until later, but Charlie Conerly and I were in the same Marine division in the war. So we're playing and I told him at the beginning of the fourth quarter, 'Charlie, you better get the hell out of there, they're not blocking for you.'

"One time we hit him, and he rammed right into the goal post. He said to me, 'I think you're right.'

"We came on like gangbusters and blew 'em out of there."

Opposite: **By the end of the decade, the Baltimore Colts were the NFL's dominant team, and Johnny Unitas (passing) was its most coveted quarterback.**

Team *of the* Fifties

EAGLES HIT
BY BROWN OUT

For some reason, the sages who pay attention to such things usually have glossed over what might have been the greatest pro football team of all time, the early Cleveland Browns.

When we think of great upstart young teams from new leagues, we think of the New York Jets, stunning the mighty Colts in Super Bowl III. When we think of dominant teams, we think of the Green Bay Packers, rolling over the NFL in the sixties. When we think of great coaches—well, we think of Paul Brown, but probably not first. Most likely we think of George Halas or Vince Lombardi.

Let's consider these Browns for a moment, point by point:

• The Upstart New Team: The Jets, of the American Football League, beat the NFL Colts by nine points in Super Bowl III. After four seasons in the All-America Football Conference, the Browns, in their first NFL game in 1950, traveled to Philadelphia and beat the reigning NFL champions by 25 points.

• The Dominant Team: Green Bay won 73 percent of its games and five NFL championships in the sixties. The Browns, in their first 10 pro seasons beginning in 1946, won 84 percent of their games and played for the championship of their league (AAFC and NFL) every year.

Cleveland, incidentally, placed three players—quarterback Otto Graham, kicker Lou Groza, and defensive end Len Ford—on the NFL Team of the Fifties, plus another two—end Dante Lavelli and fullback Marion Motley—on the Team of the Forties. The 1950s team also included such legends as Rams receivers Tom Fears and Elroy (Crazylegs) Hirsch, plus defensive stalwarts such as linebacker Sam Huff and safety Emlen Tunnell, both of whom played on the Giants' great defense late in the decade.

• The Great Coach: Most legendary NFL coaches—Halas, Lombardi, Curly Lambeau, Don Shula, Bill Walsh—controlled their own personnel and were the focal points for every move their organizations made. They made innovations, too. Lambeau and Walsh did wonders for the passing game, and Halas helped build a long-term architecture for the league.

But it's hard to imagine a coach meaning more to his team—or the game—than Paul Brown did. He was the first to scout and sign black players on a widespread basis. He invented the playbook. He pioneered the hiring of full-time assistant coaches and the use of game film and intelligence tests. He coached his team to four consecutive AAFC titles, then to three NFL titles in the Browns' first six seasons in the senior league.

The story of the decade might have happened, just nine months into the fifties, at a ramshackle Philadelphia structure called Municipal Stadium.

Browns 35, Eagles 10.

History teaches us so much. Every new commissioner of a new league should study the success of the Browns and the AAFC, and the shortsightedness of those who pooh-poohed this team and this league. In 1949, Washington owner George Preston Marshall said of the AAFC: "The worst team in our league could beat the best team in theirs."

When the NFL took in three AAFC teams in 1950—Cleveland, Baltimore, and San Francisco—the NFL was nonplussed about the incredible record of the Browns, who'd gone 35-1-2 in their last 38 AAFC games. The Eagles pointed to their own 11-1 mark and a shutout they had scored in the 1949 NFL title game. "This is the best team ever put together," Philadelphia coach Earle (Greasy) Neale boasted. "Who is there to beat us?"

Commissioner Bert Bell gerrymandered the 1950 schedule to have Cleveland open at Philadelphia, and the game drew so much interest that he moved it from Sunday to Saturday night, and from cozy Shibe Park to cavernous Municipal Stadium to maximize the frenzy of 71,237 fans (still the fourth-largest turnout in Eagles' history).

All the while, the Browns were getting ready. Brown kept posting incendiary NFL comments about the inferior AAFC on the locker-room bulletin board. He had a member of his staff scout the Eagles through much of 1949 because he knew the merger was coming. The Eagles never scouted the Browns.

"For four years," Otto Graham said, "Coach Brown never said a word. He just kept putting the stuff on the bulletin board. We were so fired up we would have played them anywhere, anytime."

Graham had been respected but not worshipped by the NFL in the forties. He was the first player Brown signed for the Browns, and it seemed a curious choice because Graham had been a music major at Northwestern. Did the coach really know what sort of treasure he had found? "I knew that Graham would be the centerpiece of everything we did," Brown said years later. "He had poise and leadership, and he was a great ball handler."

Before the game, under the Philadelphia stands, Brown said to his team: "Remember, the worst thing you can do to an opponent is defeat him. Nothing hurts as bad as losing."

The Eagles were stunned early by the Browns' strength and quickness. On the first two plays of the game, Cleveland defensive lineman Bill Willis steam-rolled center-of-the-decade Chuck Bednarik. After the Eagles had taken a 3-0 lead, Graham went to work. Still in the first

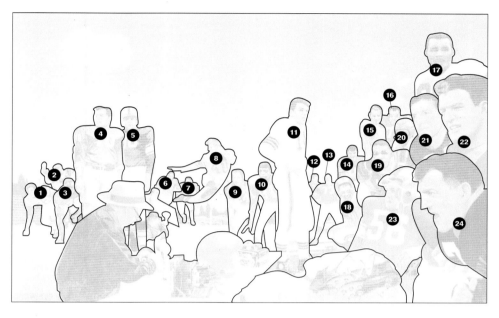

1) Raymond Berry, end; 2) Lou Groza, kicker; 3) Roosevelt Brown, tackle; 4) Sam Huff, linebacker; 5) Jack Butler, defensive halfback; 6) Emlen Tunnell, safety; 7) Joe Perry, fullback; 8) Elroy (Crazylegs) Hirsch, flanker; 9) Jack Christiansen, safety; 10) Dick (Night Train) Lane, defensive halfback; 11) Otto Graham, quarterback; 12) Bob St. Clair, tackle; 13) Leo Nomellini, defensive tackle; 14) Hugh McElhenny, halfback; 15) Gino Marchetti, defensive end; 16) Jim Parker, guard; 17) Ollie Matson, halfback; 18) Tom Fears, end; 19) Len Ford, defensive end; 20) Chuck Bednarik, center; 21) Bill George, linebacker; 22) Dick Stanfel, guard; 23) Joe Schmidt, linebacker; 24) Ernie Stautner, defensive tackle.

quarter, he hit speedy halfback Dub Jones, who beat defensive back Russ Craft for an easy 59-yard touchdown. "Trying to cover their receivers," Craft said later, "was like trying to cover three Don Hutsons."

Philadelphia came right back, plodding to the Cleveland 6-yard line. Surprise! Brown inserted Marion Motley at middle linebacker, and the Browns held. (Motley would go on to break Philadelphia's Steve Van Buren's three-year grip on the rushing title in 1950, with 810 yards.) On four straight plays, the Motley Crew stuffed Eagles runners, and the Browns took over on downs. It got ugly for the Eagles from there. Graham threw 2 more touchdown passes, and then Brown played the clock, dominating the game on the ground. Philadelphia managed just 118 total yards, one-third of Graham's passing total.

Suitably humbled, the NFL began to acknowledge the incredible talent that had

come from the AAFC. "Cleveland is the best football team I have ever seen," Bell said.

Brown and the Browns kept getting better. They followed their 10-2 debut season with a 30-28 triumph in the 1950 NFL Championship Game against the Los Angeles Rams. They beat Detroit by 46 points in the 1954 title game. They won in 1955, stopping Los Angeles again.

A 1950 postscript: Neale, bitter about the aerial show, complained afterward that the Browns couldn't slug it out toe-to-toe with the Eagles. They weren't tough enough to fight in the trenches and let the strongest men win, he blustered.

When they met in a December rematch, Brown ordered Graham not to throw a pass. Cleveland ran on every play. Every one! Motley, who averaged an astounding 5.7 yards per carry in his pro life, ran and blocked the way to a 13-7 victory.

All-Time Teams

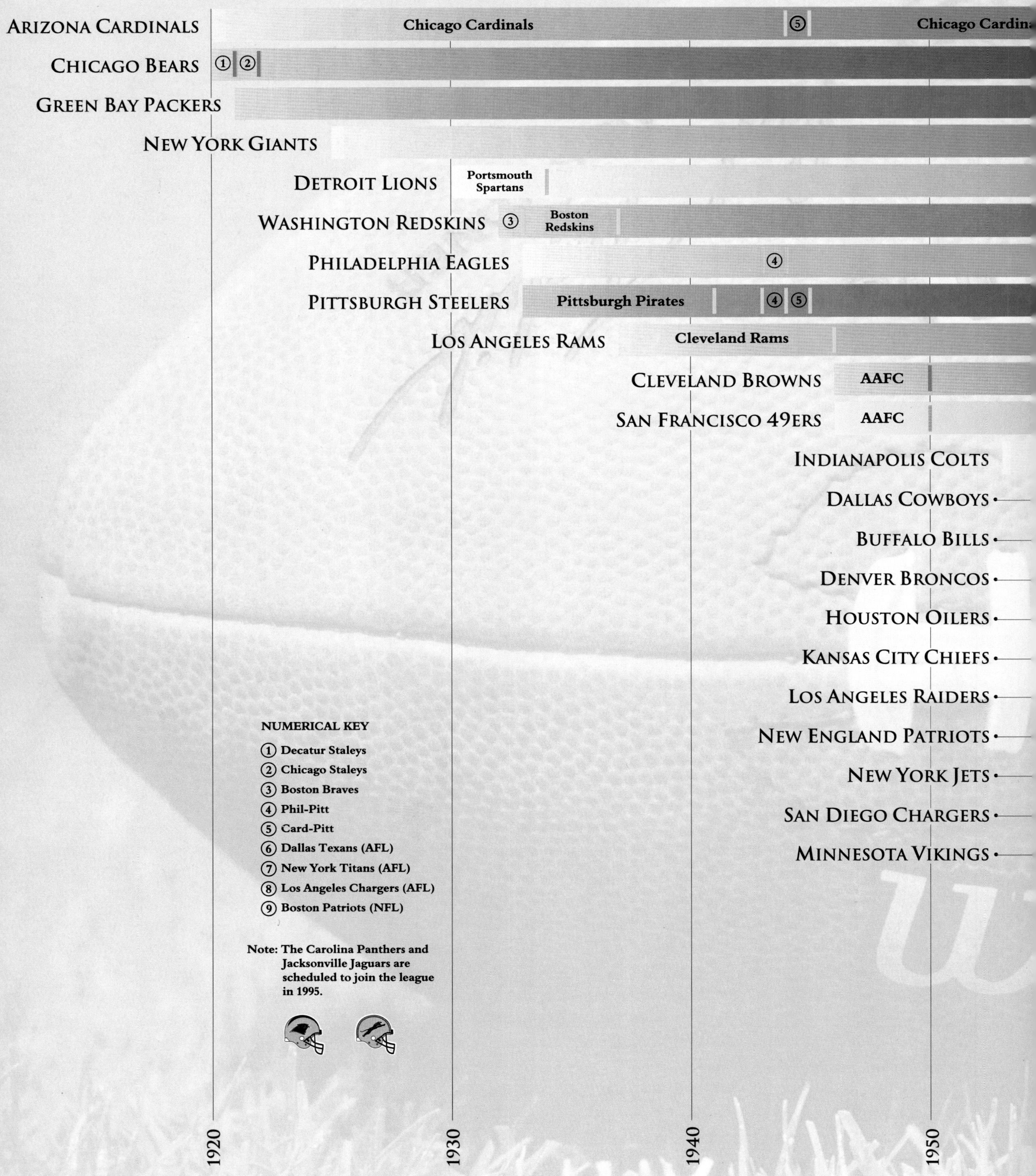

ARIZONA CARDINALS	Chicago Cardinals ⑤	Chicago Cardin...
CHICAGO BEARS ① ②		
GREEN BAY PACKERS		
NEW YORK GIANTS		
DETROIT LIONS Portsmouth Spartans		
WASHINGTON REDSKINS ③ Boston Redskins		
PHILADELPHIA EAGLES ④		
PITTSBURGH STEELERS Pittsburgh Pirates ④ ⑤		
LOS ANGELES RAMS Cleveland Rams		
CLEVELAND BROWNS AAFC		
SAN FRANCISCO 49ERS AAFC		
INDIANAPOLIS COLTS		
DALLAS COWBOYS		
BUFFALO BILLS		
DENVER BRONCOS		
HOUSTON OILERS		
KANSAS CITY CHIEFS		
LOS ANGELES RAIDERS		
NEW ENGLAND PATRIOTS		
NEW YORK JETS		
SAN DIEGO CHARGERS		
MINNESOTA VIKINGS		

NUMERICAL KEY
① Decatur Staleys
② Chicago Staleys
③ Boston Braves
④ Phil-Pitt
⑤ Card-Pitt
⑥ Dallas Texans (AFL)
⑦ New York Titans (AFL)
⑧ Los Angeles Chargers (AFL)
⑨ Boston Patriots (NFL)

Note: The Carolina Panthers and Jacksonville Jaguars are scheduled to join the league in 1995.

1920   1930   1940   1950

Origins of the 28 Active NFL Franchises

St. Louis Cardinals
Phoenix Cardinals
Baltimore Colts
American Football League
American Football League
American Football League
⑥ AFL
Oakland Raiders (AFL)
Oakland Raiders
Boston Patriots (AFL)
⑨
⑦ AFL
⑧ American Football League
Atlanta Falcons
Miami Dolphins
AFL
New Orleans Saints
Cincinnati Bengals
AFL
Seattle Seahawks
Tampa Bay Buccaneers
1960
1970
1980
1990

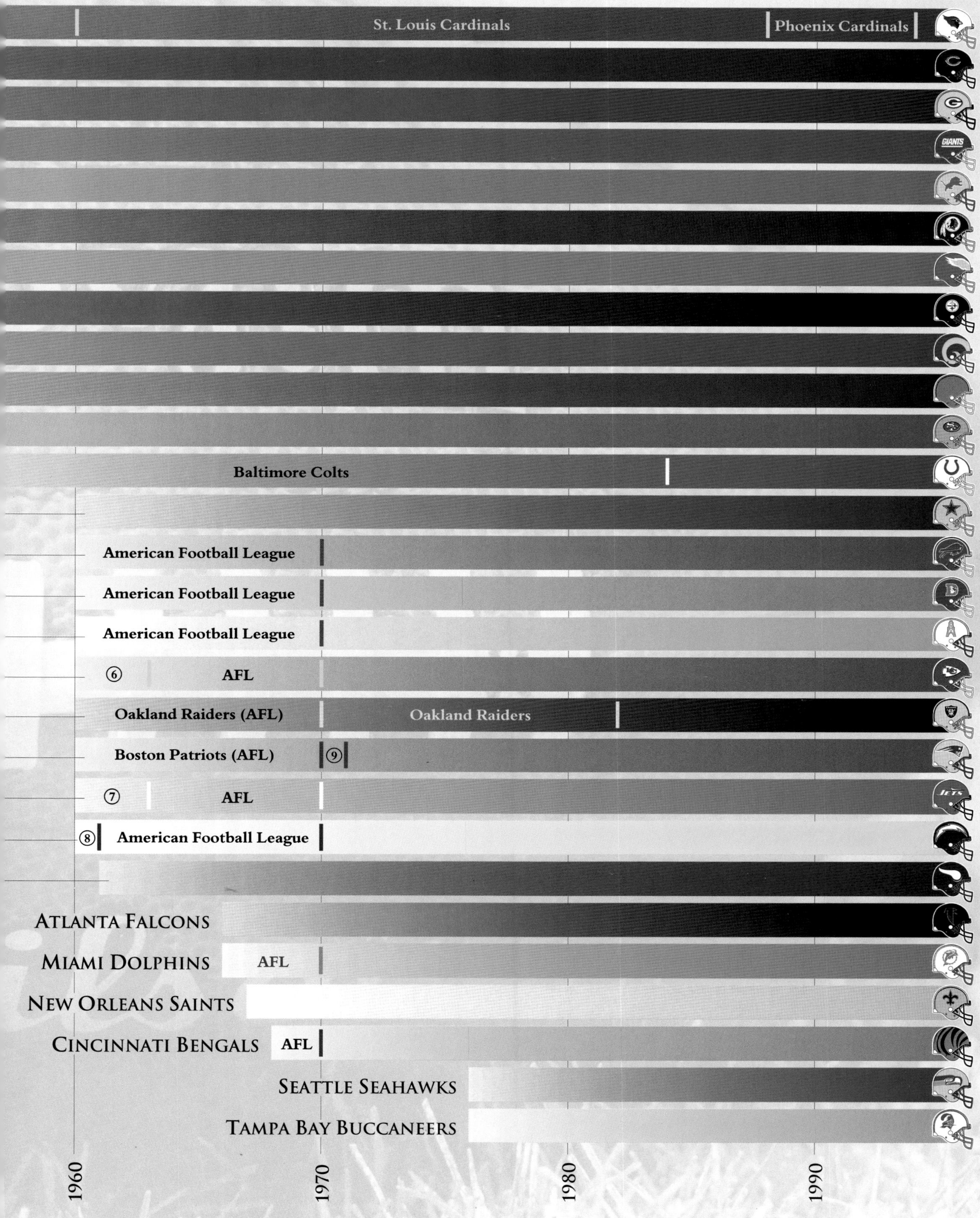

All-Time Team

	Position	Team(s)	Ht.	Wt.	College
Sammy Baugh	QB	Washington Redskins (1937-1952)	6-2	180	Texas Christian
Otto Graham	QB	Cleveland Browns (1946-1955)	6-1	195	Northwestern
Joe Montana	QB	San Francisco 49ers (1979-1992)	6-2	195	Notre Dame
		Kansas City Chiefs (1993-)			
Johnny Unitas	QB	Baltimore Colts (1956-1972)	6-1	195	Louisville
		San Diego Chargers (1973)			
Jim Brown	RB	Cleveland Browns (1957-1965)	6-2	232	Syracuse
Marion Motley	RB	Cleveland Browns (1946-1953)	6-1	238	Nevada-Reno
		Pittsburgh Steelers (1955)			
Bronko Nagurski	RB	Chicago Bears (1930-37, 1943)	6-2	225	Minnesota
Walter Payton	RB	Chicago Bears (1975-1987)	5-10	202	Jackson State
Gale Sayers	RB-KR	Chicago Bears (1965-1971)	6-0	200	Kansas
O.J. Simpson	RB	Buffalo Bills (1969-1977)	6-1	212	USC
		San Francisco 49ers (1978-79)			
Steve Van Buren	RB	Philadelphia Eagles (1944-1951)	6-1	200	Louisiana State
Lance Alworth	WR	San Diego Chargers (1962-1970)	6-0	184	Arkansas
		Dallas Cowboys (1971-72)			
Raymond Berry	WR	Baltimore Colts (1955-1967)	6-2	187	Southern Methodist
Don Hutson	WR	Green Bay Packers (1935-1945)	6-1	180	Alabama
Jerry Rice	WR	San Francisco 49ers (1985-)	6-2	200	Miss.Valley State
Mike Ditka	TE	Chicago Bears (1961-66)	6-3	225	Pittsburgh
		Philadelphia Eagles (1967-68)			
		Dallas Cowboys (1969-1972)			
Kellen Winslow	TE	San Diego Chargers (1979-1987)	6-5	250	Missouri
Roosevelt Brown	T	New York Giants (1953-1965)	6-3	255	Morgan State
Forrest Gregg	T	Green Bay Packers (1956, 1958-1970)	6-4	250	Southern Methodist
Anthony Muñoz	T	Cincinnati Bengals (1980-1992)	6-6	285	USC
John Hannah	G	New England Patriots (1973-1985)	6-3	265	Alabama
Jim Parker	G	Baltimore Colts (1957-1967)	6-3	273	Ohio State
Gene Upshaw	G	Oakland Raiders (1967-1981)	6-5	255	Texas A&I
Mel Hein	C	New York Giants (1931-1945)	6-2	225	Washington State
Mike Webster	C	Pittsburgh Steelers (1974-1988)	6-2	250	Wisconsin
		Kansas City Chiefs (1989-1990)			

Selection Committee:
Curt Gowdy, former NBC Sports announcer; Will McDonough, *Boston Globe* and NBC Sports; Peter King, *Sports Illustrated*;
Paul Zimmerman, *Sports Illustrated*; John Steadman, *Baltimore Sun*; Harold Rosenthal, former *New York Herald Tribune*; Bucko Kilroy,
New England Patriots; Jim Gallagher, Philadelphia Eagles; John Wiebusch, NFL Properties Creative Services; David Boss, former
NFL Properties Creative Services; Don Smith, Pro Football Hall of Fame; Joe Horrigan, Pro Football Hall of Fame; Joel Bussert,
National Football League; Bill Polian, National Football League; Don Weiss, National Football League.

D E F E N S E

	Position	Team(s)	Ht.	Wt.	College
David (Deacon) Jones	DE	Los Angeles Rams (1961-1971) San Diego Chargers (1972-1973) Washington Redskins (1974)	6-5	250	Miss. Vocational
Gino Marchetti	DE	Dallas Texans (1952) Baltimore Colts (1953-1964, 1966)	6-4	245	San Francisco
Reggie White	DE	Philadelphia Eagles (1985-1992) Green Bay Packers (1993-)	6-5	290	Tennessee
Joe Greene	DT	Pittsburgh Steelers (1969-1981)	6-4	260	North Texas State
Bob Lilly	DT	Dallas Cowboys (1961-1974)	6-5	260	Texas Christian
Merlin Olsen	DT	Los Angeles Rams (1962-1976)	6-5	270	Utah State
Dick Butkus	LB	Chicago Bears (1965-1973)	6-3	245	Illinois
Jack Ham	LB	Pittsburgh Steelers (1971-1982)	6-1	225	Penn State
Ted Hendricks	LB	Baltimore Colts (1969-1973) Green Bay Packers (1974) Oakland/L.A. Raiders (1975-1983)	6-7	235	Miami
Jack Lambert	LB	Pittsburgh Steelers (1974-1984)	6-4	220	Kent State
Willie Lanier	LB	Kansas City Chiefs (1967-1977)	6-1	245	Morgan State
Ray Nitschke	LB	Green Bay Packers (1958-1972)	6-3	235	Illinois
Lawrence Taylor	LB	New York Giants (1981-1993)	6-3	243	North Carolina
Mel Blount	CB	Pittsburgh Steelers (1970-1983)	6-3	205	Southern
Mike Haynes	CB	New England Patriots (1976-1982) Los Angeles Raiders (1983-89)	6-2	190	Arizona State
Dick (Night Train) Lane	CB	Los Angeles Rams (1952-53) Chicago Cardinals (1954-59) Detroit Lions (1960-65)	6-2	210	Scottsbluff JC
Rod Woodson	CB	Pittsburgh Steelers (1987-)	6-0	200	Purdue
Ken Houston	S	Houston Oilers (1967-1972) Washington Redskins (1973-1980)	6-3	198	Prairie View A&M
Ronnie Lott	S	San Francisco 49ers (1981-1990) Los Angeles Raiders (1991-92) New York Jets (1993-)	6-0	200	USC
Larry Wilson	S	St. Louis Cardinals (1960-1972)	6-0	190	Utah

S P E C I A L   T E A M S

	Position	Team(s)	Ht.	Wt.	College
Ray Guy	P	Oakland/L.A. Raiders (1973-1986)	6-3	190	Southern Miss.
Jan Stenerud	K	Kansas City Chiefs (1967-1979) Green Bay Packers (1980-83) Minnesota Vikings (1984-85)	6-2	190	Montana State
Billy (White Shoes) Johnson	PR	Houston Oilers (1974-1980) Atlanta Falcons (1982-87) Washington Redskins (1988)	5-9	170	Widener

ALL-TIME TEAM: THE HARDEST CUTS

Selecting an all-time NFL team is simple, really. Thumb through the *NFL Record & Fact Book* and the players all but jump out and tap you on the shoulder. As New England's Frank (Bucko) Kilroy, who has spent 52 years in the game as a player, coach, and administrator said, "Everybody has pretty much the same idea. You start with Sammy Baugh and go on to the next and the next."

Sure, it's easy to choose players. It's stopping that's difficult.

Baugh is a perfect example. He's an automatic at quarterback because of how he changed the game. Then you want Joe Montana, of course, and Johnny Unitas, Otto Graham, Norm Van Brocklin, Bob Waterfield, Y. A. Tittle, Terry Bradshaw, and Dan Fouts—all members of the Pro Football Hall of Fame.

It is about then that someone points out that you can't have an entire team of quarterbacks. Besides, it's time to get to work on the runners. Who do you like? Bronko Nagurski, Marion Motley, Earl Campbell,

Steve Van Buren, Jim Brown, Ernie Nevers, Barry Sanders, Jim Taylor, Walter Payton, Gale Sayers, or O. J. Simpson?

"It's tough, to be honest with you," said Harold Rosenthal, a former sportswriter with the *New York Herald Tribune*, and member of the 15-man selection committee for the NFL's 75th Anniversary Team.

Don Weiss, the league's director of planning and former NFL executive director, tried to help narrow the field by devising a rough formula for the positions.

"We kind of screened the nominees and made some suggestions," Weiss said. "We began with Joe Horrigan from the Pro Football Hall of Fame and Joel Bussert, the NFL director of personnel, and came up with credentials. It's a lot like the way the Hall prepares induction credentials."

Still, that sounds a lot more cut and dried than the way it happened. At-large selections poured in. The team swelled to 48 players. A firm decision to include just three quarterbacks was revoked so a fourth could be added. An All-Two-Way

team was created to honor the greats from the era of the 60-minute players.

And it still was tougher than fourth-and-goal. How do you deal, for example, with the fact that Green Bay tackle Forrest Gregg had to block pass rushers with his arms in against his chest while Cincinnati's Anthony Muñoz, playing 20 years later, was allowed to extend his arms after a change in the rules?

In such cases, the committee relied on the wise counsel of advisors such as Weeb Ewbank, who expressed the opinion that Muñoz was such a fine athlete he would have excelled in the 1960s just as he did in the 1980s.

As usual, it was up to Kilroy to cut through the verbiage and reduce their task to a few words. "My opinion was that we should pick the players who dominated the game," he said.

Were there disagreements? You bet.

"Some people felt very strongly," Weiss said. "Some even asked for re-votes. On two occasions we increased the number of

roster spots. A couple of times we had ties and we kind of made an arbitrary decision as to how to handle them."

One of the stickiest problems resulted from the passage of time. As Weiss said, "How do you rate a two-hundred-pound middle guard against a three-hundred-pound nose tackle?"

The committee members relied on Ewbank and veteran coaches such as Don Shula, who was glad to offer input. They also got a history lesson from Kilroy, a tackle with the Eagles in the 1940s and 1950s.

"That [weight] is a misnomer on some of those guys," Kilroy said. "The guys were big people then. The Bears would put down 240 [in the program] and they would go 280. Some of those guys were a perfect cube. They must have gone 290."

Still, the committee members were willing to admit the selection process was not an exact science. Were great players left off the list? Necessarily. Take Baltimore tight end John Mackey, who was left off the team after long, hard deliberation.

Mackey was a tough and fabulously well-rounded tight end who was selected to the All-Time All-Pro team by a Hall-of-Fame selection committee in 1969. Still, he couldn't beat out Kellen Winslow or Mike Ditka for the 75th Anniversary team. Some old-guard types have questioned Winslow's blocking abilities, but his pass-catching skills changed the position, making him a can't-miss pick for this year's selectors. "We all loved Mackey and saw him make some great plays," Weiss said. "You can assume that he was right behind Ditka and Winslow."

Or, to go to the other extreme, how can you pick Sayers when he played only 68 NFL games in his entire seven-year career? "As I recall," Weiss said, "that was the question when he came up for the Hall of Fame, too, and he got in on the first ballot."

"How about a guy who played only six years and is in the Hall of Fame?" asked Kilroy. "That's Doak Walker."

The pleasant surprise of the process was getting to know and appreciate some of the legends from the past. Almost everyone, for example, knew Mel Hein from his work as NFL supervisor of officials. But it was impressive to hear the testimonials for "Old Indestructible" from those who knew him as one of the best two-way players in the history of the game.

"I was in college when the Cleveland Browns were formed," Weiss said, "and I came into the game when [fullback] Marion Motley was a little past his peak. I knew he was in the Hall of Fame, but I never realized how highly he was regarded in the overall scheme of things. You know, he probably could have been an all-pro linebacker."

In the end, the committee members could take comfort in this fact: There may not have been enough room for every deserving player, but there is nothing but brilliance in the batch they picked.

"You can't say that anybody on that list didn't dominate the game," Kilroy said. "It's just researching when they played, how they played, and what they did."

SAMMY BAUGH

*I*n 1937, the Redskins sent poor, skinny Sammy Baugh out to face the meanest, roughest players in professional football. The kid from Texas was unawed. "I didn't even know anything about pro football," Baugh said. "At TCU [where he had led the Horned Frogs to a national championship], if it was anything east of the Mississippi we didn't know too much about it. Hell, I didn't even know who was in the league."

Baugh didn't have to get used to the league; the NFL had to adjust to him. Once he began firing passes, the game never was the same. "They had some silly damn rules," said Baugh, still sounding indignant at 80. "They thought they wanted a running game and a defensive game. Every damn rule was against making you want to throw the ball. I thought it was a very conservative game."

But Baugh wasn't easily discouraged. He completed 11 of 16 passes in the first game of his NFL career, and the 5 incompletions were dropped by receivers. The owners and coaches of the NFL may have been slow to accept Baugh's style, but they weren't foolish. "After that year, my first year," Baugh said, "more teams started passing the ball. They finally realized that people like to see scoring. You don't want to sit out there in the cold and see a 14-6 game."

"Slingin' Sam" was a sensation. He not only made the Redskins regulars in the playoffs—they won their division five times and the NFL championship twice in his first 10 years—he filled stadiums. At one point Washington had a string of 40 consecutive sellouts at a time when

professional football was just finding its way from the red side of the financial ledger to the black.

The NFL, and Washington owner George Preston Marshall, knew what they had in Baugh, so they changed some of those "silly" rules. "They had no protection for the passer," Baugh said. "They could hit him until the whistle blew. Sometimes they'd run the quarterback back twenty yards trying to put you on your back. They're out there chasing you and the ball is seventy yards away with the guy running with it."

Like most players of the time, Baugh played both ways. And he didn't lay back to avoid injuries. In 1943, Baugh led the NFL in passing, interceptions, and punting. "I really enjoyed that year more than any other," Baugh said. "I had eleven interceptions, but intercepted four passes in one ball game. That is a record that has been tied but has not been broken."

What Baugh didn't mention is that he still holds the NFL all-time records for punting average in a season and a career, as well as most seasons leading the league in passing. When he retired in 1952 after 16 seasons, he was badly missed by the fans. But as someone said at the time, all you have to do is flip through the record books. Sammy Baugh always will be there.

1946-1955
OTTO GRAHAM

The Cleveland Browns dominated the All-America Football Conference for four years, but when they joined the NFL in 1950, most people thought they would be lucky to finish with a .500 record. To make it tougher, the Browns had to play their first game against the defending NFL-champion Philadelphia Eagles.

Philadelphia realized it might be in a real contest when the first pass Cleveland quarterback Otto Graham threw went for a long touchdown to end Dante Lavelli. Then Graham threw another. For the game, he was 21 of 38 for 346 yards and 3 touchdowns. The Browns won 35-10 and became the team to beat in the NFL.

That may have been a surprise to some NFL fans, but not to anyone who had followed the career of "Otto-matic" Graham. In his 10 pro seasons, Graham led the Browns to 10 championship games (four in the AAFC, six in the NFL), winning seven times—including that first season in the NFL.

"The test of a quarterback is where his team finishes," said Graham's coach, Paul Brown. "By that standard, Otto was the best of them all."

The Browns were a superb team, of course, but there is no overestimating Graham's contribution. During his days with the team he accounted for one-third of the 3,500 points Cleveland scored.

Graham was not highly regarded after his career at Northwestern, and it is easy to see why. Not only had he not been offered a football scholarship there, he wasn't even invited to try out for the team. Graham was on the basketball team instead and was spotted throwing his trademark long, high passes in intramural football games.

Brown was coaching at Ohio State when he got a good look at Graham. The Northwestern quarterback engineered an upset victory over the Buckeyes, and Brown never forgot it. Five years later, when Brown was building his pro team, Graham was the first player he picked.

The two built an impressive record, though Graham sometimes groused that Brown would not allow him to call his own plays. It became a sore point, but Brown still was able to talk Graham into coming out of retirement in 1955 at age 34 to win the second of back-to-back championships (a 38-14 victory over Los Angeles one year after the Browns had thrashed Detroit 56-10).

Graham was a bit of a renaissance man. He played the piano, violin, and French horn. The son of two music instructors, Graham majored in music in college and found time to play French horn in the Northwestern orchestra for one year.

"Music means rhythm and rhythm means timing," Graham said. "Music has taught me everything."

1979-PRESENT

JOE MONTANA

Slender and boyish, Joe Montana impressed almost no one when he reported to San Francisco's training camp as a draft choice in 1979. Dwight Clark, who would become his best friend and favorite receiver, swore he thought Montana was a kicker looking for a tryout.

"We took him in the third round," said Tampa Bay head coach Sam Wyche, who was the 49ers' quarterbacks coach in 1979, "and that first year Steve [DeBerg] set an NFL record for completions. So when Montana walked out there the first day... no, he didn't look like much."

He wasn't much more impressive once he put on the pads. Montana's lack of tremendous arm strength was one reason he lasted until the third round, and even on short patterns he seemed unable to spin a perfect spiral. Teammates called it a tight wobble. "He had a little porpoise to it," Wyche said. "But the ball landed very softly in the receiver's hands. A lot of guys, they're throwing strikes, but people aren't catching them."

It didn't take long for the 49ers to learn what had impressed head coach Bill Walsh in an informal workout before the draft. "He would eat the words right out of your mouth," Wyche said. "He would kind of lean into you as you would talk to him."

In 1981, his first full season as a starter, Montana led the surprising 49ers to victory in Super Bowl XVI. It was the beginning of an amazing run for the 49ers in the 1980s, a decade in which the wiry quarterback from Notre Dame led them to seven NFC West championships and four Super Bowls in nine years. A Montana-led team never lost a Super Bowl.

He also had an uncanny gift for comeback victories. From the 1979 Cotton Bowl, when he hit Kris Haines in the end zone for a 35-34 Notre Dame triumph with no time on the clock, to Super Bowl XXIII in January of 1989, when he finished a 92-yard drive with a 10-yard touchdown pass to John Taylor with 34 seconds left, Montana always seemed to come up with the big play.

"He was very soft-spoken, almost shy," Wyche said. "But he'd get in that huddle and get that look in his eye. Sometimes the corner of his mouth would just turn up with a little smile. He was saying, 'This is a lock. This is going to work.'"

Montana's 49ers teammates, who idolized him, loved to tweak their quarterback about his physical limitations. "If you put Joe Montana up against guys like John Elway, Dan Marino, and Jim Kelly [in an athletic competition]," said former 49ers guard Randy Cross, "he'd come in fifth in a five-man field."

Yet, by the time Montana was traded to Kansas City in 1993, he owned NFL records for highest passer rating in a career (93.5) and a season (112.4 in 1989), and highest career completion percentage (63.67).

1956-1973
JOHNNY UNITAS

From the toe of his high-top cleats to the top of his crew cut, there was nothing flashy about Johnny Unitas. His trademark wasn't a stylish flip over the middle, it was getting off the deck and throwing a touchdown pass.

"With those slumped shoulders," said wide receiver R. C. Owens, who played with the 49ers and Colts, "you would think you had him caved in with the blitz. But he'd come back to the huddle, maybe bleeding a little, and do it again. The harder you hit him, the more he came back."

The Baltimore Colts liked to say they acquired Johnny Unitas for 80 cents, the price of a phone call from Baltimore to Pittsburgh. That's true, but the real story was what Unitas was doing in Pittsburgh, running a pile driver and playing for a semipro team called the Bloomfield Rams. He'd been cut the year before by the Pittsburgh Steelers, who waited until the ninth round of the 1955 NFL draft to choose the former walk-on at Louisville.

When the Steelers cut Unitas, team owner Art Rooney wanted to know the reason. Rooney favored local kids, and Unitas had gone to high school in Pittsburgh. "Aw," a member of the coaching brain trust told Rooney, "he's too dumb to remember the plays."

Well, the coach wasn't far off. What he probably meant was that Unitas would turn out to be arguably the greatest quarterback of all time. Unitas played in 10 Pro Bowls and was named NFL most valuable player three times. He also directed the Colts to three NFL championships, including Super Bowl V. He retired with 40,239 passing yards and 290 touchdown passes.

"He coulda been a helluva general," said Pro Football Hall-of-Fame defensive tackle Art Donovan, who played with Unitas. "He was the boss. He didn't have to holler or scream. It was just, 'Get John the ball, and he'll win.'"

Unitas was not physically imposing. In addition to his outward appearance, he never had the easy grace of a natural athlete. In fact, running to the huddle for his first professional start, he tripped and fell on his face.

What he had was savvy and guts. As Hall-of-Fame defensive tackle Merlin Olsen once said, "It isn't his arm or even his football sense. It's his courage."

Unitas had some remarkable accomplishments, including an "untouchable" streak of 47 games in which he threw a touchdown pass. But he always will be remembered for his leadership in the 1958 NFL Championship Game against the New York Giants, in which he engineered a heart-pounding drive in the final two minutes to force overtime, then completed 3 consecutive passes in the extra period to set up the game-winning touchdown run by Alan Ameche.

A lot of people still call that the greatest football game ever played. "You know," Unitas said later, "it really was just another football game as far as I'm concerned."

1 9 5 7 - 1 9 6 5

JIM BROWN

ometimes you will hear someone say that Cleveland's Jim Brown was not the greatest running back in football history. Walter Payton gained more yards or O. J. Simpson was faster, they'll say.

But their premise ruins their argument. They begin with Brown, then try to find better. That's the point. It always starts with Brown.

The 6-foot 2-inch, 232-pound former Syracuse fullback and All-America lacrosse player was big, fast, tough, and handsome. He could run away from almost anyone on the field and he could run over all of them. In nine NFL seasons he never carried the ball fewer than 200 times and never missed a game.

Brown's explosive power and intensity made stopping him next to impossible. Only the Lions' Alex Karras ever came up with a sure-fire plan. "Give each guy on the line an axe," Karras suggested.

When it came to advancing the ball downfield, Brown did it all. He averaged 5.2 yards per carry (still the NFL record), caught 262 passes for 2,499 yards, and returned kickoffs. In 1963, he carried the ball 291 times and gained a then-record 1,863 yards, averaging 6.4 yards per attempt and posting a pair of 200-yard games. For his career, he had 58 100-yard games (almost half of his total starts) and was selected to the Pro Bowl in each of his nine seasons. He led the NFL in rushing eight times (nobody else has done it more than four times) and failed to reach 1,000 yards only twice—his rookie year and in 1962, when a severely sprained wrist "limited" him to 996 yards.

When Brown retired, he had accounted for 12,312 rushing yards and 126 career touchdowns—106 on the ground, 20 on receptions—two NFL records that survived more than 20 years. Chicago's Payton eclipsed the career rushing mark in 1984, and San Francisco wide receiver Jerry Rice, the greatest scoring machine of the modern day, broke the touchdown record in 1994.

"And remember," said long-time NBC broadcaster Charlie Jones, "[Brown] set those records in twelve- and fourteen-game seasons. Now they're trying to break them with sixteen games."

Brown powered Cleveland to the NFL Championship Game in 1957, when he was named rookie of the year. The Browns also made the playoffs the following season, but they didn't reach the postseason again until 1964. After helping the team to a 27-0 victory over Baltimore for the NFL title that year, Brown played one more season, then quit the game to appear in movies. Lately he has worked to rehabilitate young gang members in Los Angeles.

Was he the greatest ever? Brown said he was. Who can argue?

MARION MOTLEY

Marion Motley had more to deal with than blitzing linebackers and big defensive linemen. At 6-1 and 240 pounds, he could handle them. But as one of the first black players in modern pro football, Motley was subjected to brutal tactics and cheap shots. It was a rare pileup in which someone didn't "accidentally" stomp on his hand or fling an elbow at his head.

"He had such vivid recollections of the first official, a guy named Tommy Hughitt, who finally said, 'That's enough,' and threw a flag," said Joe Horrigan of the Pro Football Hall of Fame. "He always remembered Hughitt's name."

Within the rules, Motley needed no help from anyone. Although he is remembered as the consummate power runner, he and Browns quarterback Otto Graham accidentally invented a play that has become one of the most common in the sport: the screen pass.

Motley, a superb blocker, was Graham's bodyguard, dropping back to pick off pass rushers. As the story goes, on one play a tackler broke through and Graham, in trouble, turned, spotted Motley, and flipped him the ball. Thus was created one of the most terrifying sights in sports.

"Marion Motley standing still was one thing," Horrigan said, "but Marion Motley with a full head of steam was something else. We have a film at the Hall where he starts with a little swing pass, goes down the sideline, knocking players out of the way, gets his helmet knocked off, and keeps on running."

Coach Paul Brown and Motley met in 1945 when Brown was coaching at the Great Lakes Naval Training Center. Brown thought he had quite a team, but the entire group was moved to Fleet City, California. "The only player they left for me was Motley," Brown said. "They didn't take him because no one knew he was a football player."

Brown didn't have much competition for Motley's services when he was putting together the Browns for the All-America Football Conference, either. Inasmuch as Motley was 26 at the time (after a stint in the Navy), it did look like a gamble.

Motley made an immediate impact, and so did the Browns. After winning the AAFC championship each of the four years that league existed, Cleveland entered the NFL in 1950. Motley, 30, led the league in rushing. He gained 188 yards on just 11 carries in one game against Pittsburgh, an average of 17.09 yards per carry that remains an NFL record. In his eight professional seasons, Motley had 828 carries for 4,720 yards, an average of 5.7 yards per carry.

"If you didn't stop him at the line of scrimmage," said Hall-of-Fame defensive tackle Art Donovan, who played for the Colts, "you were in trouble."

In 1968, Motley became the first black player to be inducted into the Hall of Fame.

BRONKO NAGURSKI

No name says leather helmets and high-top black cleats louder than Bronko Nagurski.

"His name is like Paul Bunyan," said Joe Horrigan of the Pro Football Hall of Fame. "You couldn't have played in the thirties and not mention it. It was as if you'd played against Babe Ruth."

The tall tales about Nagurski have grown over the years. There was the time he was forced out of bounds at full speed and flattened a policeman's horse. They say he once missed a tackle, slammed into a Model T, and sheared off the fender. No wonder he was nicknamed after a wild mustang.

Actually, Nagurski's parents, Ukrainian immigrants, named their son Bronislau. When one of his teachers couldn't pronounce that, it was shortened to Bronko, and it stuck.

Nagurski's championship ring has become famous at the Hall of Fame because, at size 19½, you can pass a regular-sized ring through it with ease. But Nagurski was "only" 6 feet 2 inches and 225 pounds. That's big, but no larger than many of the linemen who were tackling him.

It was Bronko's strength that was unmatched.

After Nagurski became the first, and only, college player ever to be named All-America at two positions—tackle and fullback—his coach at Minnesota, Doc Spears, was asked how he discovered Bronko.

"I was driving by a farm when I noticed this big, strong farm boy plowing a field," Spears

would say. "I stopped to ask directions and the boy picked up the plow and pointed with it."

Nagurski electrified the Bears. He powered Chicago to NFL championships in 1932, 1933, and, after five years in retirement, in 1943 at age 35.

Statistically, we can only imagine his production. Although Nagurski played nine years (1930-37, 1943) and was named all-pro six times, yardage statistics were not carefully kept in those days. The totals he is credited with: 4,301 rushing yards in 872 attempts, an average of 4.9 yards per carry.

Nagurski cashed in on his growing fame after the first NFL championship by taking up professional wrestling. Life in the ring proved to be more lucrative than football, though he tried to juggle both jobs for a while. In one three-week period in 1937 he played in five Bears games and wrestled in eight cities: Portland, Vancouver, Seattle, Phoenix, Los Angeles, Oakland, Salt Lake City, and Philadelphia.

The irony in Nagurski's larger-than-life image was that he was a rather shy, private man. After football, he opened a service station in International Falls, Minnesota, but refused to make any reference to his playing career.

138

1975-1987
WALTER PAYTON

etween 1975 and 1987 there were three givens in Chicago: The wind was blowing off the lake, the Cubs were not in the World Series, and Walter Payton was in the backfield for the Bears.

In his 13-year NFL career, Payton missed only one game. In 1984, he proved more durable than the entire depth chart at quarterback. When they all turned up injured, he took snaps.

Payton carried the ball more often (3,838 attempts) for more yards (16,726) than anyone who ever played the game. He ran the ball 842 times more than Eric Dickerson, who is in second place. The most amazing part of Payton's records is that for a large chunk of his playing days, the Bears were not a good team. As former Chargers tight end Kellen Winslow said, "For most of his career, he took on the NFL with no offensive line."

Payton earned a Super Bowl ring following the 1985 season, but during the first nine years of his career the Bears were 61-70. In those days, the opposing strategy was simple: Stop Payton, and you stop the Bears. He took a ferocious pounding in those days. For 8 of his first 10 seasons, he averaged more than 20 carries per game.

Not that the relatively small (5 feet 10 inches, 202 pounds) Payton was defenseless. "What people didn't know was how rough he was," said Matt Millen, who picked up his experience firsthand as a linebacker for the Raiders. "He didn't give straight arms, he'd punch you. Or he would lower his shoulder and kind of jump into you. He was one of the few who got personal fouls running with the ball."

Some, including legendary running back Jim Brown, felt that the only quality Payton lacked was a "passing gear" for those long, long runs. But others reply that Payton could have been a speed back had he not been asked to run inside so much.

It hardly matters. Payton simply did whatever he was asked, including exemplary blocking. He was more than willing to pick off a blitzer or catch a pass. His 492 receptions were a record among running backs when he retired, and his string of three consecutive years with 2,000 total yards from scrimmage was another NFL standard.

Still, Payton was best at taking the ball and running with it. Against Minnesota in 1977, he carried 40 times for 275 yards, an NFL single-game record. That year, after rushing for 1,852 yards, he was named the NFL's most valuable player by *Associated Press*. Payton retired with a total of 125 touchdowns, one short of all-time NFL leader Jim Brown.

"He was one of those backs," Millen said, "where in the middle of a game, you'd come to the sideline and say, 'Did you see what he did?' It was a pleasure. You felt honored to tackle him. I always did."

1 9 4 4 - 1 9 5 1

STEVE VAN BUREN

ucko Kilroy, his old teammate with the Eagles, summed up Steve Van Buren's contribution succinctly. "He was our paycheck," said Kilroy, now vice president of the Patriots. "As he went, the Eagles went."

Van Buren did everything for Philadelphia, from leading the league in rushing a then-record three consecutive seasons to playing defensive back to returning punts and kickoffs. He even punted and kicked a few extra points. The only thing Van Buren wouldn't try was throwing the football. He didn't pass and didn't want to learn.

"The fellow who threw the first pass must have been someone too tired to run with the ball," the 215-pound halfback said.

Van Buren wasn't a finesse runner. He preferred to lower his head and blast right over tacklers. And woe to those who made him angry. "One time he told me he came to the park and he'd felt lousy all weekend," said veteran Eagles public relations man Jim Gallagher. "So they told him to just take it easy. The first play of the game they handed it to Russ Craft, a little guy, and the Steelers roughed him up. Van Buren said, 'That burned me up, so I told Greasy [Neale, the coach] to let me play. I ended up with over 200 yards.'"

The 1948 NFL Championship Game against the Chicago Cardinals was a perfect stage for Van Buren. Philadelphia was hit with such a severe blizzard on game day that Commissioner Bert Bell left it up to the players to decide whether they wanted to play. They voted to suit up,

but first they had to help shovel the snow off the Shibe Park field.

Neither team was able to score until Kilroy recovered a fumble on the Cardinals' 17 late in the third quarter. With the crowd chanting, "Steve! Steve! Give it to Steve!" Van Buren scored the only touchdown of the game on a 5-yard burst. He gained 98 yards that day; the entire Chicago team managed only 96 rushing yards.

Though he left bruises all over the Eastern Division, Van Buren could get out and stride, too. Kilroy said the former LSU star could run a 9.6-second 100-yard dash and "then line up and do it again." For 50 yards, Kilroy recalled, Van Buren could outrun teammate Clyde (Smackover) Scott, a silver medalist hurdler in the 1948 Olympics who was considered the fastest man in the NFL.

Van Buren was voted the Eagles' "Greatest Player" in 1957, but he remained a shy man off the field. Gallagher said that when Van Buren appeared for speaking engagements and was asked to compare himself to another player, he had a standard reply. "Aw," he'd say, "he's better than me."

Van Buren could say it, but no Eagles fan ever would believe it.

1 9 6 2 - 1 9 7 2
LANCE ALWORTH

Lance Alworth never liked the nickname "Bambi," but what could he do? Even he admitted it was perfect for him. "Charlie Flowers, the Chargers' fullback, gave me that name the first day I reported as a rookie," Alworth said. "I looked like a kid of about fifteen. I had real short hair and brown eyes. Charlie said I looked like a deer when I ran."

The slender, swift Alworth was one of the players who established the American Football League as the real thing. There always is a certain amount of doubt about the talent of a new league, but no one who watched Alworth questioned his ability to play at the highest levels of the game.

"He is the best wide receiver I've ever seen," said veteran NBC announcer Charlie Jones, who was known as the voice of the AFL. "He had speed, quickness, and toughness. When I draw back one of those photographs of the mind, I see him airborne, like a ballet dancer, reaching back behind him for the pass. He'd be a superstar today. He'd be one of the few [from then] who would."

Alworth had great hands, and he always was a deep threat. He could catch the short pass and turn it into a long gain, or, with a trademark leap, pull down the deep throw. He averaged more than 50 catches and 1,000 yards a year during nine seasons with the Chargers. During his 11-year career, including two with Dallas, he averaged almost 19 yards per catch.

Alworth virtually wrote AFL receiving records by leading the league in touchdowns three times and posting seven consecutive 1,000-yard seasons (1963-69). He once ran up a string of nine straight games with touchdown receptions. He also broke Don Hutson's long-standing record by catching passes in 96 successive games.

Alworth almost was too successful. Traditionalists in the NFL complained that the new league was all offense and no defense, and Kansas City Chiefs owner Lamar Hunt suggested the problem was that the NFL was watching too much of Alworth. "He made it look like a wide-open game because he was always wide open," Hunt said.

With offensive mastermind Sid Gillman drawing up San Diego's plays and John Hadl throwing most of the passes, Alworth was the AFL's showcase player. In 1978, he became the first AFL player inducted into the Pro Football Hall of Fame.

Alworth's 85 career touchdown receptions do not seem as lofty as they once did, but no one ever will match his flair for those leaping, acrobatic catches. "We always kid Lance," Jones said, "because Hadl wasn't that accurate. We always say if he'd had a Joe Montana throwing to him, he wouldn't have had to be nearly as spectacular."

defenders. One version has him catching the ball with the other hand at the same time.

Hutson made a huge impact when he arrived at Green Bay. The Packers won the NFL championship in 1936, Hutson's second season, and he led them on a remarkable run that included three league titles and four Western Division championships.

"You had to be there to see Don Hutson," said New England Patriots vice president Bucko Kilroy, a former Eagles guard who faced Hutson. "He [always] made the play that determined the outcome of the game."

1955-1967
RAYMOND BERRY

*T*he usual Pro Football Hall-of-Fame wide receiver has a laundry list of important qualities: speed, size, and great ability to run with the ball. That's Raymond Berry's list, too. Those are all the things he didn't have.

Throw in poor eyesight and one leg that was shorter than the other, and you have the complete Raymond Berry package. He was drafted in the twentieth round as a future in 1954, and there were some who wondered why the Baltimore Colts bothered to pick him at all. In his entire college career he caught just 33 passes for exactly 1 touchdown.

But Berry had a full understanding of his abilities. He had excellent hands, so catching the ball was

1985-PRESENT
JERRY RICE

*A*s former 49ers coach Bill Walsh tells the story, he was on a scouting trip and had flipped on the television in his hotel room. It turned out to be a game between two NCAA Division II teams. But there was one player who looked interesting. As Walsh watched, the kid caught a touchdown pass, then another, another, and another…

By the time Jerry Rice had made his fifth touchdown reception of the game, Walsh was jotting down his name and making plans to look into the man they called "World" at Mississippi Valley State because there was "nothing in the world" he couldn't catch.

Walsh was so convinced that Rice would be a quality wide receiver in the NFL that he arranged a draft-day trade to move up in the first round. Not that Rice was every team's dream. He was the third wide receiver picked in 1985 after the Jets took Al Toon with the tenth choice and Cincinnati went for Eddie Brown with the thirteenth.

Rice did not have a smooth adjustment to the pro game. He is the first to admit that he dropped some passes he should have caught as a rookie. After one miserable half against the divisional-rival Rams, Rice burst into tears in the locker room at halftime. That may not have been the turning point, but from that year on, the defensive backs were the ones who needed handkerchiefs. Rice has become the most dominant touchdown-scoring receiver in the history of the game.

It took Green Bay's Don Hutson, a charter member of the Pro Football Hall of Fame, 11

years to catch 99 touchdown passes; Rice caught 103 in eight seasons. In 1987, he caught an NFL-record 22 in 12 games in the strike-shortened regular season.

Rice has the whole package. At 6 feet 2 inches and 200 pounds, he can take a shot from a safety and bounce off for more yardage. He has the breakaway speed to separate from a defender and take a short pass all the way to the end zone. And he has the enthusiasm of a high school freshman.

When he was working with quarterback Joe Montana, the two had their own version of mental telepathy. To the exasperation of the coaching staff, Rice would break off his pattern, put up his hand, and go deep, and Montana invariably would spot the receiver and hit him for a huge gain.

Rice is a conditioning fanatic who hired a personal coach to work him out in the offseason. In his first nine seasons, Rice did not miss a single game due to injury, and he had a streak of 127 consecutive games with a reception. That's not luck; it's a portrait of someone who wants the ball.

As quarterback Steve Young said of Rice, "I think he believes that if they covered him with eleven guys, he should still be open and win the game."

1 9 6 1 - 1 9 7 2

MIKE DITKA

he look of the tight end position changed in the 1960s, and it turned out to have the steely glare and lantern jaw of Michael Keller Ditka.

Some say Green Bay's Ron Kramer started the revolution when he went from playing the "third tackle" to a legitimate pass-catching threat in the early 1960s. But everyone agrees that Ditka defined and molded the position. At 6 feet 3 inches and a solid 230 pounds, he had the size to do some blocking, and he certainly had the demeanor. But what defenders failed to realize until they caught a look at the back of his jersey, headed goalward, was that he also could go deep. In 1961, his first season, Ditka not only caught 56 passes, he scored 12 touchdowns and gained 1,076 yards, averaging 19.2 yards per reception. For a position full of plowhorses, that was remarkable.

"He is the best rookie I have ever seen," Bears linebacker Bill George said at the time.

Ditka was named NFL rookie of the year, selected all-pro, and voted to the Pro Bowl in his first season. Although he never again would gain more than 1,000 receiving yards, he'd gotten people's attention. As Cooper Rollow of the *Chicago Tribune* said, "Ditka made people realize the importance of the tight end."

Ditka caught 58 passes in 1962, 59 in 1963, and 75 (a record for tight ends that would stand for 16 years) in 1964. In '63, he displayed another Ditka trademark—toughness. As New England executive and long-time football devotee Bucko Kilroy said, "Ditka was a fullback playing tight end."

When Chicago trailed Pittsburgh 17-14 in the third quarter that season, Ditka took a short pass over the middle and rumbled through the Steelers, breaking 6 tackles en route to a 63-yard gain that set up a game-tying field goal. That tie allowed the Bears to win the Western Conference en route to the NFL title.

"To this day, I believe that if Mike doesn't make that play, we don't win the championship," Bears defensive end Ed O'Bradovich said.

Dikta is remembered for a growling intensity, rattling blocks, and a nasty straight arm. He took that intensity to the sidelines in 1982 when George Halas hired him as Bears head coach. Ditka became an icon in Chicago as he led the team to six NFC Central titles and a victory over New England in Super Bowl XX during his 11 years at the helm.

As a player, he suited up for 12 seasons, including two with Philadelphia and four with Dallas, where he played on the Cowboys' Super Bowl VI championship team. He caught the final touchdown pass in that game, but fans left talking about his trick play, on which he gained 17 yards with a shocking end-around. Yes, Ditka was an innovator down to the last game of his career.

GUARD

1967-1981

GENE UPSHAW

Oakland's Gene Upshaw wasn't the first guard to lead a sweep. But he may have been the best. "That's my play," he used to say. "A wide receiver wants to catch a long touchdown pass. A defensive lineman wants to sack the quarterback. I get my satisfaction pulling to lead those sweeps."

Defensive backs weren't quite as enamored of the play. When the 6-foot 5-inch, 255-pound Upshaw turned the corner, they were the ones who took the punishment. "And," said NBC announcer Charlie Jones, who had watched Upshaw since his AFL days, "when they went to artificial turf, where he was faster, it should have been illegal for him to lead a sweep."

In his prime, left guard Upshaw dominated the line of scrimmage. Oakland general manager Al Davis originally drafted him to handle Buck Buchanan, Kansas City's big defensive tackle. Upshaw did that, and more, appearing in the Raiders' first three Super Bowls (II, XI, and XV) as they became virtually the only left-handed team in the NFL, running behind Upshaw and all-pro tackle Art Shell.

Upshaw's height drew attention, and his power and speed made him a force, but it was his savvy and intelligence that completed the package. One of his nicknames on the Raiders was "Gov" because Davis used to jokingly predict that with his flare for handling himself in public, Upshaw would be governor of California before he was done. He did reach the level of executive director of the NFL Players Association.

On the field, it wasn't until his later years that Upshaw proved just how wily he could be. Outside, he could run with the backs. Inside, there wasn't a guy in the league who played more mind games.

A battered veteran in his fourteenth season, Upshaw helped the Raiders to an 11-5 regular-season record and a victory over Philadelphia in Super Bowl XV, with an assortment of clever moves and sleight of hand worthy of someone who played in a club-record 24 postseason games.

He would line up with a wide split between him and Shell to convince defenders that the play was going in another direction. He also was known for bending over in the huddle and peeking back between his legs at the defense, in an attempt to figure out which defensive linemen were talking to each other about a planned stunt.

At that point in his career, Upshaw sometimes was accused of doing a little creative holding, a charge he always answered in the same way. Holding up his heavily wrapped hands and arms, he'd say, "How can I hold with all this stuff on?"

Those who knew Upshaw said he would find a way. In any case, he usually found a way to win.

1 9 3 1 - 1 9 4 5
MEL HEIN

*I*n 1938, Mel Hein was named the NFL's most valuable player. He was the only offensive lineman to win the award in its brief (nine-year) history. That a center could be MVP says something about the game in those days. It also says something about Mel Hein.

He was nicknamed "Old Indestructible" and it was said that Hein played more minutes of more games than any other man in football history. Those who would disagree are invited to match these standards: In 15 years as a pro and eight years in college and high school, Hein played both ways, offense and defense, and never missed a game. At 36, in his last pro season, he still was playing 60 minutes, although he was coaching at Union College at the time and had to make a three-hour train trip to New York for weekend games.

It was said that he called time out to treat an injury only once. That was in 1941, when he suffered a broken nose. Hein had it treated and went back in the game. "He was," said Harold Rosenthal, long-time writer for the *New York Herald Tribune*, "about as tough as they come."

At 6 feet 4 inches and 235 pounds, Hein was fairly big for the day, but no larger than the defensive linemen he faced. His greatest attribute was his agility. Unlike most centers of his era, Hein was not content to make the snap to the quarterback and hold his ground. He roamed downfield, knocking down linebackers and defensive backs. Hein was the first center ever to pull from the line to lead running plays, and he pioneered the strategy of dropping back to protect the passer.

He was so nimble and athletic that the Giants used him on a famous trick play that had him line up at the end of the line and snap the ball to quarterback Harry Newman, who surreptitiously would flip it back to him. As Newman faked handoffs to his backs, Hein would ramble down the field until someone discovered he had the ball.

In addition, he also was a full-time linebacker known for his ferocious tackling. He even dropped back into pass coverage. No wonder that when he was asked to pick an all-time Giants team, former head coach Steve Owen selected Hein, who was named all-pro eight straight seasons, as his captain.

"Hein," Owen said, "was able to carry his great playing over fifteen years, and in all that time I can count on the fingers of one hand the mistakes he made offensively and defensively."

As Hein's career drew to a close, the team put on a spectacular day at the Polo Grounds to honor him in 1942. Mayor Fiorello LaGuardia made a speech, and Hein was given a new car and a stack of gifts. Unfortunately, the Giants went out and lost 17-7 to the Dodgers. "We're sorry we didn't win for Mel," Giants halfback Hank Soar said after the game, "but, hell, every day the Giants have played in the last twelve years has been Mel Hein Day."

1974 - 1990

MIKE WEBSTER

There wasn't any mystery to Mike Webster. His occupation pitted strength against strength, and he was pretty sure who was going to win. He made it official in 1980 when he won the "NFL's Strongest Man" competition, despite weighing less than many of the participants at 260 pounds.

"Webby," former NFL linebacker and current network football analyst Matt Millen said, "was the first center to bring attention to the position. He was the first one with muscles. You noticed him because he was the first guy out of the huddle and he plopped over the ball with those big ol' arms. He was the first center, when you looked at films, you'd say, 'Let's see what Webster did here.'"

Webster was not so highly regarded coming out of Wisconsin. Although he was team MVP and a three-year starter for the Badgers, he was not an All-America choice. Drafted in the fifth round in 1974, the man from Tomahawk, Wisconsin, came to the Steelers hungry to establish himself. He was a weightlifting fanatic, and he encouraged the rest of the Pittsburgh offensive line to follow his example. Although the Steelers' blockers weren't big, they led the league in blown-up T-shirt sleeves. Every one of them had arms like sides of beef, and they made sure everyone saw them. "They were the first ones to go to cold-weather games and have their arms hanging out," Millen said.

As team captain and unquestioned leader of the Steelers' offensive line, Webster called out adjustments at the line of scrimmage for a team that had the most complicated ground strategy

since General Patton. When the ball was snapped, everyone seemed to move in a different direction.

The Steelers' traps were legendary, and it didn't hurt to have some of the most powerful men in the game springing Franco Harris and the team's other backs. Webster played 17 seasons, including the last two with Kansas City, and he credited weight training for his longevity.

Webster appeared in nine Pro Bowls and was a fixture on all-pro squads of the late 1970s and early 1980s. In 1986, he dislocated his elbow and was placed on injured reserve for the first time in his career—a run of 12 years at that point. That injury stopped his streak of consecutive games at 177. In all, he played in 245 regular-season NFL games.

Of course, while Webster was garnering individual acclaim, the Steelers were making a remarkable run in the 1970s, winning four Super Bowls beginning with Webster's rookie season.

For all the talk of his power, Webster could discuss hard-core *X's* and *O's* with anyone. "He'd recognize a defense," said Craig Wolfley, a former teammate, "and turn around and suggest an audible. You don't see that very often."

DEACON JONES

*H*e was a vision on a grainy black-and-white film. For all the two Los Angeles Rams' scouts knew, he may have been a mirage. David Jones came out of Mississippi Vocational, but to Johnny Sanders and Eddie Kotal he was heaven sent. "We were looking at a defensive back," Sanders recalled a generation later, "and suddenly we saw this huge guy catch a tackle-eligible pass and outrun the defensive back. Well, we immediately rejected the defensive back and started a file on the tackle."

Still, the Rams didn't select Jones until the fourteenth round of the 1961 draft. The rookie had tremendous tools but limited schooling as an offensive lineman, so the coaches switched him to the other side of the ball. Thus was born "Deacon" Jones, a father of invention.

He refined the head slap, a pass-rushing technique that caused severe headaches for blockers. He coined the term "sack" and collected them in unheard-of numbers, though the league did not endorse the statistic for another two decades. He even created his own image, dubbing himself Deacon "because nobody would ever remember a player named David Jones."

Given his level of performance, that wasn't particularly likely. "You can't believe Deacon's quickness and speed, even when you're playing next to him," said Merlin Olsen, the Pro Football Hall of Fame defensive tackle who lined up alongside him for the first time in 1962. "It's really quite frustrating. You'll have a good shot at the ball carrier when, all of a sudden, *whap*— Jones is sitting on him….I doubt if there's ever been a quicker big man in professional sports."

Jones had astonishing speed for a 6-4 behemoth whose weight fluctuated between 250 and 270 pounds. He once found himself chasing fleet Washington halfback Bobby Mitchell, who had caught a short sideline pass. Jones matched strides with him for 10 yards before knocking him out of bounds. "I just wanted to see if I was as fast as he was," Jones said.

But he was tough, too, starting with the head slap that finally was outlawed by the league (but not until after he retired). "You hadn't lived until you had your bell rung by Deacon a few times," said Ron Mix, the Hall-of-Fame offensive tackle.

While with the Rams, Jones anchored the "Fearsome Foursome," one of the NFL's legendary defensive lines. In 1967, a year in which Rams quarterbacks were sacked 25 times, Jones had an unofficial total of 26 in 14 games. It was altogether fitting that he specialized in the procedure he dubbed and popularized.

Why a sack? Because, he said, it was like "the devastation of a city." There was another reason. Conscious of the value of public relations, he said, "You need a short term that will fit easily into newspaper headlines."

Jones appeared in a lot of headlines himself, hailed throughout the league as the "Secretary of Defense." Along with being selected to the Hall of Fame in 1980, he was a Pro Bowl choice eight times.

1952 - 1966
GINO MARCHETTI

Surely, it ranks among the great ironies in NFL history that the most significant tackle of Gino Marchetti's career resulted in his only serious injury. In the case of the Colts' defensive end, the price of his first championship was a broken leg. His Baltimore teammates presented him with the ball from what has been called the NFL's greatest game—while he lay flat on his back in the locker room.

The occasion was the storied title match between the Colts and the New York Giants at Yankee Stadium on December 28, 1958. It was the first official overtime game in league history, and there never would have been a sudden-death period if not for Marchetti. With Frank Gifford driving for a first down that would have enabled the Giants to run out the clock for a 17-14 victory, Baltimore's defensive captain led the charge that wrestled down the running back inches short of his objective on third down.

Marchetti was carried off the field on a stretcher, but he refused to leave the sidelines until he saw quarterback Johnny Unitas lead the famous comeback. (The Colts won the game at 8:15 of overtime on a 1-yard touchdown run by Alan Ameche.) Because of the injury, Marchetti missed the Pro Bowl for the only time between 1955 and 1965.

Years earlier, when Marchetti's immigrant father reluctantly allowed his son to play high school football, he had told him, "Gino, whatever you do, stay out of the other boys' way so they no hurt you." A lot of opponents might have laughed at that suggestion, considering the havoc the 6-foot 4-inch, 245-pound Marchetti created in the NFL, but his father remained so

opposed to the sport that he didn't watch his son play until he tuned in for the telecast of the 1958 championship game. Of course, his worst fear was realized.

By then, the younger Marchetti was well on his way to professional immortality. When he retired, following two championships, long-time NFL and AFL coach Sid Gillman called him "the most valuable man ever to play his position."

While growing up in Antioch, California, Marchetti did not seem destined for a life in pro football. He enlisted in the Army as a teenager and earned medals fighting on the Siegfried Line with the 69th Infantry. Because of his heroism, his Italian-born parents were released from an internment camp.

After World War II, Marchetti resumed his football career at Modesto (California) Junior College and then earned a scholarship to the University of San Francisco, where his teammates included future NFL great Ollie Matson. Marchetti's size, speed, and toughness were perfectly suited to the NFL in the 1950s.

In 1955, he played the final four games of the season with a dislocated shoulder. "I was all taped up on one side and I could use only one arm," he recalled. "I hurt like hell, but they had no replacement for me."

1985-PRESENT
REGGIE WHITE

Unrestricted free agency wasn't created specifically for Reggie White, but he became its foremost NFL beneficiary. For several weeks during the late winter and spring of 1993, the outstanding defensive end of his era became every team's dream acquisition.

An ordained Baptist minister who had counseled countless people—particularly youngsters—from the worst neighborhoods in Philadelphia when he was playing for the Eagles, White eventually chose the small city of Green Bay. He said God told him where to play. The Packers' offer was $17 million for four years, unprecedented for a lineman.

Then again, White had enjoyed unprecedented success as a pro. In his first season with Green Bay he surpassed Lawrence Taylor's NFL record for career sacks and finished the campaign with 137 in nine years, or exactly 137 games. After a slow start both for him and his team, White dropped quarterbacks an NFC-best 13 times, helped the team into the playoffs, and earned his eighth successive trip to the Pro Bowl. "Find me the guy who says Reggie White has lost a step," said Dallas tackle Erik Williams after an early-season struggle. "Get him down on the field and I'll make him line up against Reggie so he can see for himself."

Brett Favre, the Packers' quarterback, was thrilled to welcome White to Green Bay. A year earlier, the 6-foot 5-inch, 290-pound defender had fallen on the quarterback's left shoulder, causing a slight separation. "He's a guy you definitely want on your side rather than against you," Favre said.

White, who visited Milwaukee projects on off days, returned to his ministry in the offseason. In 1992, he received the NFL Players Association's Byron (Whizzer) White Humanitarian Award for his service to team, community, and country.

Reggie White's humanitarian efforts do not extend to quarterbacks, at least not those employed in the NFL. A punishing player who spent two seasons with the Memphis Showboats of the United States Football League, White was selected by the Eagles as their first-round choice in the 1984 supplemental draft of USFL players. He joined the team in week four of that season and made a memorable debut against the Giants, collecting 2½ sacks and deflecting a pass that Herman Edwards intercepted and returned for a touchdown.

White became a starter the following week and never missed a subsequent start. In the strike-shortened 1987 season, he was credited with 21 sacks (1 short of the NFL record established by the Jets' Mark Gastineau three years earlier) despite appearing in only 12 games. "He's the most incredible player I've ever worked with in twenty-some years of coaching," said Greg Blache, the Packers' defensive line coach. "He's an amazing person and an amazing player."

line late in the first quarter and teamed with Larry Cole to chase Dolphins quarterback Bob Griese back, back, back into his own territory and tackle him for a stunning 29-yard loss.

1 9 6 9 - 1 9 8 1

JOE GREENE

1 9 6 2 - 1 9 7 6

MERLIN OLSEN

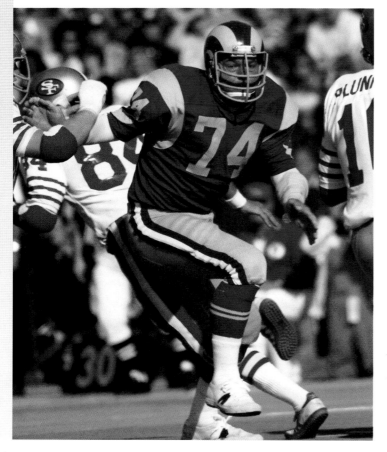

erlin Olsen had a hard time breaking into television. Before serving as a football analyst, before getting his own dramatic series, even before becoming the spokesman for a nationwide florist, he endured 15 years of brutal manual labor. Working with two padded hands, he fashioned a career unequaled in its quality and quantity of performance.

The thoughtful and erudite Olsen, a Phi Beta Kappa at Utah State University who later earned a master's degree in finance, was among the best defensive tackles in the NFL. A mainstay of the Los Angeles Rams' celebrated "Fearsome Foursome," he was selected to the Pro Bowl in 14 consecutive seasons. And despite the punishment visited on his position, he was sidelined by injury for a total of only two games. He had played in 198 consecutive games when he announced his retirement in 1976.

At 6 feet 5 inches, 270 pounds, Olsen was a natural talent. He never lifted weights. His size and strength, he said, were due to the chores he did as a youngster in Utah. "I also worked as a ranger in Yellowstone Park," he joked, "until visitors began mistaking me for a bear."

Although Utah State wasn't exactly a football power, Olsen was a first-round draft choice both of the Rams and the Denver Broncos of the fledgling AFL. Olsen signed with the established league, and by the team's third preseason game he was lining up alongside David (Deacon) Jones. For the next decade, they would form one of the most dominant duos in NFL history.

"He knew what to expect from me, and I knew what to expect from him," Olsen said. "He was quicker than I, which meant that sometimes he left some territory uncovered. So I accepted the responsibility of covering that territory."

And he lived up to that responsibility. Olsen helped the Rams win six division titles and was voted into the Hall of Fame in his first year of eligibility, following in the footsteps of Jones.

As much as his ability, it was Olsen's approach to his position that raised him above his peers. "He was calculating and collected, one of the most intelligent men ever to play the game," said George Allen, his former coach. "He knew what was going on at all times and took advantage of every weakness the opposition had and every mistake that was made."

Despite his cerebral nature, Olsen was no reluctant warrior. Agile for his size, he threw himself into the action. "They don't call the middle of the line 'the pit' for nothing," Olsen noted. "We really do get like animals, trying to claw one another apart in there.... We get so bruised and battered and tired we sometimes wind up playing in a sort of coma. By the end of the first half your instincts have taken over. By the end of the game you're an animal."

It was good preparation for a life in television.

1965 - 1973
DICK BUTKUS

*I*t stands to reason that the definitive tale of Dick Butkus is unattributed and perhaps even apocryphal. Because by the time a shredded right knee forced the middle linebacker of the Chicago Bears to retire in 1973, after only nine professional seasons, he had achieved mythological stature throughout the NFL.

According to the story, the Baltimore Colts were en route to the airport following a violent afternoon at Wrigley Field. When their bus stopped suddenly in traffic, it was rammed by a trailing vehicle. The Colts looked at each other and said, in unison, "Butkus."

The linebacker used his 6-foot 3-inch, 245-pound frame like a weapon. He brought a remarkable instinct and an all-consuming frenzy to his position. "It's like he was from another world, another planet," said Pro Bowl guard Bob Kuechenberg of the Miami Dolphins. "He didn't run a four-six forty, he wasn't a great weight lifter, but he just ate them alive—all those four-six sprinters and five-hundred-pound bench pressers."

Even Mike Ditka, Butkus's tough former teammate who later coached the Bears, was awestruck. "With the highest respect, I've got to say Dick is an animal," Ditka once said. "He works himself up to such a competitive pitch that on the day of the game he won't answer a direct question. He'll grunt."

Butkus finished his career with 25 fumble recoveries and 22 interceptions. But even those fine figures only suggest the kind of destructive force he was. "When I hit a guy," he said, "I wanted him to know who hit him without his ever having to look around and check a number. And I wanted him to know I'd be back. I wanted him to think about me instead of what he was supposed to be doing."

A Chicago native who played at the University of Illinois, Butkus was drafted by the Bears with one of their three first-round picks in 1965. Another of those selections, Gale Sayers, became a Pro Football Hall of Fame running back. Both careers were cut short by knee injuries. "My knees were so bad the last two seasons of my career that I almost never practiced," Butkus said. "It took me from one game to the next just to recover to the point where I could play effectively."

But that didn't stop him from Herculean feats. "Dick was just reckless," recalled Bob DeMarco, a center who spent time with four NFL teams. "He played with that bad knee and they'd have to tape his leg in a bent position so he could run."

Sometimes, Butkus believed, the reputation got out of hand. "You know, some people think I have to get down on all fours to eat my couple of pounds of raw meat a day," he said after his retirement. "Others think that George Halas taught me to walk upright and I have to have an agent do my reading and writing for me. But people who know me know I can read a little."

1971-1982

JACK HAM

To Jack Ham, pro football was a business and his office was a 100-yard field. Unlike some of his more celebrated peers at linebacker, his approach was cerebral and calculated. "We were sitting on the bench during a game once," recalled Andy Russell, the other outside linebacker on Pittsburgh's first two championship teams in the 1970s, "and he was telling me about some stock deal he was interested in. Then we had to go out on defense. On the first play, Jack read the pass and dropped into the zone, deflected the ball with one hand, caught it with the other, flipped it to the ref, and overtook me on the way off the field. 'Like I was telling you, this stock's really a good deal,' he said, like nothing had happened."

Ham's demeanor, like his size (6 feet 1 inch, 220 pounds), masked a major talent. The preeminent outside linebacker of his era often faced the opposition not with a snarl but with a bemused smile.

"Because he was a quiet guy who didn't like attention, no one pushed him as the greatest thing ever," said his head coach, Chuck Noll. "But he basically had no weaknesses. If you wanted to stop the run, there was no one better. If you wanted to stop the pass, there was no one better. If you needed the big defensive play to get back into a game, there was no one better."

Ham spent his early years battling misperceptions. Because he weighed only 185 pounds as a high school senior, he attracted faint interest from major colleges and was fortunate to receive Penn State's final scholarship in 1967. Although he had an outstanding career for Joe Paterno, his switch to middle linebacker in his senior season again raised questions about his physical stature. Noll was so intrigued by Ham that he wanted to draft him in the first round in 1971,

but skepticism among NFL scouts told the Steelers they could wait until the second round for his services.

Noll envisioned him on the outside, where Ham's combination of quickness, mobility, and intelligence stamped him as a potentially outstanding pass defender. In his second season, Ham finished third in the NFL with 7 interceptions, and by 1973, he was on his way to becoming a Pro Bowl fixture, earning the first of eight consecutive trips to the game.

Ham's ability to defend downfield never was more evident than in the 1974 AFC Championship Game, when, in addition to 7 solo tackles, he contributed 2 interceptions, 1 to stymie an Oakland drive and the other to set up the go-ahead touchdown in a 24-13 victory that sent the Steelers to their first Super Bowl. "I love playing pass coverage," he said. "Some people think of a linebacker only as a guy who can get to the right hole in a hurry and hit hard. To me, that's less than half of being a linebacker. You've got to do your job on pass coverage, or else you're a liability."

Ham, who finished his dozen NFL seasons with 32 interceptions and one designation as the league's defensive player of the year (in 1975), never came close to being a liability.

1969-1983
TED HENDRICKS

When John Madden announced his retirement as coach of the Oakland Raiders in 1979, the first player to ring his doorbell was Ted Hendricks. The linebacker did not arrive empty-handed. En route to Madden's house, he had decided on an appropriate token of appreciation.

"On the way over," the former coach recalled, "he saw a 'Yield' sign. He thought that would be a nice gift for me. So he knocked it over with his car, pulled it out of the ground, and brought it over."

Hendricks expressed similar spontaneity in a 15-year professional career that was filled with impromptu visits and special deliveries. Quarterbacks, running backs, receivers, punters, and kickers all fell victim to his looming presence. His unprecedented 25 blocked kicks and record-tying 4 safeties were evidence of a most unusual approach to the sport.

The uniqueness of Hendricks wasn't limited to his size, although, at 6 feet 7 inches and with a size-37 sleeve, he certainly stood out on the field. What distinguished him was an uncanny sixth sense. His ability to show up where the offense least expected him led to eight Pro Bowl appearances and a bust in the Pro Football Hall of Fame at Canton.

All the while, he added to a reputation as one of the game's blithe spirits. Hendricks once rode a horse onto the field in training camp, and he designed his own workout contraption called the "Hurricane Machine," which featured weightless weights and a beer-can holder. He occasionally affixed feathers to his practice helmet. Although he earned a Super Bowl ring in Baltimore and represented both the Colts and the Green Bay Packers in the Pro Bowl, it was with the Raiders that his personality and talents flourished.

The Raiders allowed him to free-lance, and it paid remarkable dividends. Defensive coordinator Charlie Sumner admitted that the number of blitzes he called and those called by his defensive captain "were about fifty-fifty."

Hendricks's statistics in 1980, when the Raiders became the first wild-card team to win a Super Bowl, were extraordinary for a linebacker—9 sacks, 3 interceptions, 2 blocked kicks, and a safety. "At least once a game," Sumner said, "he'd do something that I didn't know how he did it."

Hendricks, who had gained the nickname "Mad Stork" during an outstanding career at the University of Miami, intercepted 26 passes, recovered 16 fumbles, scored 3 touchdowns, and appeared in all 215 of his teams' games during his NFL career.

"He was the most dominating defensive player I've ever coached," said Tom Flores, who directed the Raiders to two Super Bowl titles as Madden's successor.

Hendricks also was perhaps the most entertaining defensive player in NFL history.

1974-1984

JACK LAMBERT

The play was over. The first half was winding down. Trailing the Dallas Cowboys 10-7 in Super Bowl X, the defending-champion Pittsburgh Steelers were preparing to jog off the field, hoping to regroup.

But one of their number, Jack Lambert, spotted an offense against sportsmanship he could not abide. Roy Gerela had missed a 36-yard field-goal attempt that would have tied the score, and Dallas safety Cliff Harris patted the Pittsburgh kicker on the helmet, then put his arm around Gerela's shoulders, thanking him for his failure. Enraged, the Steelers' middle linebacker grabbed Harris and threw him to the ground. Lambert then carried his fury to the locker room.

"When Harris did what he did to Gerela," Lambert explained, "I responded the only way I know how. I never want to see us intimidated. Never! Until then, that's exactly what Dallas was doing. It had never happened before while I'd been with the club, and I never want it to happen again. After that we went back to being the Steelers I love and respect."

And they emerged with a 21-17 victory. Lambert was in only his second season, but he was not reluctant to step forward. Jack might be nimble and might be quick—assets no other middle linebacker possessed in such abundance—but he brought an additional dimension to the sport.

"Jack didn't have to psych himself to play," teammate and Pro Football Hall of Fame defensive tackle Joe Greene said. "He lived to play."

It was no coincidence that Pittsburgh won the first of its four Super Bowl titles following

Lambert's rookie season in 1974. Nor that the suddenly complete "Steel Curtain" led the NFL in total defense and takeaways that year. Lean but mean, the 6-foot 4-inch, 218-pound youngster from Kent State became a starter during preseason, and he remained a fixture for 10 years before a severely dislocated toe forced him to miss most of the 1984 season. The Steelers' defensive captain for his last eight seasons, he played in nine consecutive Pro Bowls (1976-1984) and twice was named NFL defensive player of the year.

"Of all the great middle linebackers, what set him apart was his ability to play the pass," said Jack Ham, Pittsburgh's Hall of Fame outside linebacker. "He was the most complete middle linebacker ever to play."

Lambert intercepted 28 career passes during the regular season, and he picked off Rams quarterback Vince Ferragamo at Pittsburgh's 14-yard line late in the fourth quarter to preserve the Steelers' 31-19 victory in Super Bowl XIV.

Although Lambert was about 20 pounds lighter than most of his peers, he was a savage tackler. "I love contact," he once said. "I believe the game is designed to reward the ones who hit the hardest. If you can't take it, you shouldn't play."

1967-1977
WILLIE LANIER

Football players scream, and glare. Sometimes they even cry. Under special circumstances, if the emotion flows from a highly respected athlete, the effect can be inspirational. Such a moment occurred for the Kansas City Chiefs en route to the franchise's defining moment in Super Bowl IV.

What set off Willie Lanier was the sight of the New York Jets one yard from the Kansas City goal line in the fourth quarter of their AFL playoff game at Shea Stadium in 1969. The defending Super Bowl champions appeared to be on the verge of turning a 6-3 deficit into a 10-6 lead. Lanier, the Chiefs' second-year middle linebacker, wouldn't let that happen.

"He was crying on the goal line," cornerback Emmitt Thomas reported. "He was hysterical. He kept begging us to stop them. He said we had worked since July for this and we couldn't throw it away now."

The will preceded the way. After plunges by Matt Snell and Bill Mathis netted only inches, Joe Namath attempted a pass on third down. The play was covered. The Jets settled for a short field goal, temporarily tying the score, but the revived Chiefs struck back for a quick touchdown and a 13-6 victory that placed them one step closer to the Super Bowl.

Although coach Hank Stram's system was dubbed the "Offense of the Seventies" in the wake of Kansas City's Super Bowl IV triumph, it was defense that made it all possible. After stuffing the Jets, the Chiefs held the high-scoring Oakland Raiders to seven points in the AFL Championship Game, thwarting the home team three times inside the 25-yard line after turnovers. Then they throttled the Minnesota Vikings at Tulane Stadium, again limiting a favored opponent to a single touchdown.

At the heart of the defense, as he would be for 11 seasons, was Lanier. Although he didn't receive the publicity granted some of his peers, football people appreciated his talent and tenacity. "You hear a lot about [Chicago's] Dick Butkus and [Atlanta's] Tommy Nobis," Dallas assistant coach Ermal Allen once remarked, "but this Willie Lanier is really the best middle linebacker in pro football."

He was a starter by the fourth game of his rookie season, positioned between Bobby Bell and Jim Lynch, and while his fierce hitting earned him the nickname "Contact," Lanier was equally adept at pass defense. His 27 interceptions were a career record for a Chiefs linebacker. To his teammates, he was "Honey Bear," an emotional as well as a physical leader.

"I'm intense," Lanier explained. "You can't stay relaxed. You get as emotionally high as you can so you go beyond your limits. I can't really remember what I say or do. I just try to inspire the team."

He succeeded as well as anyone who ever played in the NFL.

LINEBACKER

1958 - 1972
RAY NITSCHKE

essed for battle, he had the kind of game face only a football coach could love. With a balding head, a snarl on his lips, and his upper front teeth on a shelf in his locker, Ray Nitschke was capable of scaring opponents and teammates alike. Yet, Vince Lombardi was so smitten with his middle linebacker that he once walked up to Nitschke after a game and kissed him on the cheek.

Nitschke was the extension of Lombardi on the football field: tough, emotional and consumed by the sport. He played with passion and he practiced with it, too, much to the chagrin of the other Green Bay Packers. "He seems incapable of letting up," guard Jerry Kramer once noted, "even against his own teammates. He's always grabbing people, hitting people, throwing elbows."

"Intensity was the only way I felt I could survive," Nitschke explained. "I practiced diligently. I came to play every day. I never went out on a football field without being ready to play."

Away from football, he was an altogether different person. "Actually, he's two completely different guys, on the field and off," Kramer said. "He loves to hit people, he loves body contact, yet out of uniform he's quite gentle, quite sensitive, almost professorial."

Bart Starr, the team's Hall of Fame quarterback, called him "a classic example of Dr. Jekyll and Mr. Hyde." Opponents could testify to the latter. Shaped by a hard life—his father died when he was 5, his mother when he was 13—Nitschke became the prototype for his position.

He was the hub of the Packers' defense through five NFL championship seasons and consecutive Super Bowl triumphs in I and II. At 6 feet 3 inches and 225 pounds, he was a ferocious hitter who also was adept at pass coverage (25 career interceptions).

And yet, surrounded by other great players, Nitschke was selected to the Pro Bowl only once during a 15-year career. He never considered individual honors as important as the respect of his peers. "You wanted them to remember who you were and what you could do," he said.

A third-round draft choice from Illinois, Nitschke credited virtually all of his success to Lombardi. The coach took control of the downtrodden Packers in 1959, the linebacker's second season in the league, and transformed them into title contenders in two years with a mixture of affection and intimidation. Nitschke was treated no better and no worse than the others.

"The guy never let up," Nitschke recalled. "But he was consistent. And I knew that he was good for me. He wanted me not only to be a good player but to be a good guy. I needed that. Before I got married, I was kind of runnin' them streets."

Under Lombardi's guidance, Nitschke reserved his wild side for the football field and helped the Packers make history.

1 9 8 1 - 1 9 9 3

LAWRENCE TAYLOR

Only at the very end did Lawrence Taylor allow himself a pang of nostalgia. The man who redefined the position of outside linebacker had spent 13 seasons erasing past achievements from his mind in order to focus on the next game. But late in the third quarter of the New York Giants' 44-3 playoff loss to the San Francisco 49ers at Candlestick Park on January 15, 1994, Taylor knew there would be no more games.

So he asked referee Bernie Kukar for a souvenir. "I wanted his flag when it was over," he acknowledged later. "The little yellow flag. He's thrown it against me often enough."

It was Taylor's little joke on the day he retired, following a career worthy of a monument. He already had coaxed an additional season out of his body. Disappointed at the direction of the Giants under head coach Ray Handley in 1992, he announced that season would be his last. But when Taylor suffered a torn Achilles tendon in the ninth game of the season, he decided he didn't want to leave the NFL on a flatbed cart. He rehabilitated himself and contributed to the team's turnaround under new coach Dan Reeves, producing a vintage L.T. game in the 1993 opener when he sacked Chicago's Jim Harbaugh twice and recovered the fumble that sealed the victory.

The Giants returned to the playoffs and scored their first postseason victory since Super Bowl XXV three years earlier, but Taylor understood he no longer could play up to his standards. No one else could, either. In his prime, Taylor was a destructive force. "If there was ever a Superman in the NFL," Joe Theismann said, "I think he wore number fifty-six for the Giants."

It was Taylor who broke Theismann's leg in 1985, thereby ending the Washington quarterback's career. "We were very close, literally," Theismann said. "He not only had great physical skills, but he had a relentlessness that was unmatched. He was the only defensive player I can remember who we had to design our game plan around. The first question at our meeting was, 'How are we going to handle Lawrence?'"

Not many teams succeeded in answering that query. Taylor concluded his career with 132½ sacks. That total did not include the 9½ he amassed as a rookie in 1981, a year before the sack became an official NFL statistic. He changed the parameters of linebacking with remarkable pass-rushing ability from the outside. "Everybody knows he's coming," former teammate Beasley Reece once said. "It's like a cop putting sirens on his car."

The Giants won two Super Bowls and reached the playoffs seven times during Taylor's career. "He was the catalyst," said Bill Parcells, his former coach. "He inspired the other players, he inspired the other coaches, he inspired me."

1 9 7 0 - 1 9 8 3

MEL BLOUNT

el Blount was so perfectly tailored to play cornerback in the NFL that he appeared to have been ordered, not born. He had the ideal size at 6 feet 3 inches and 205 pounds. Blount's speed never was a question. (He ran the 40-yard dash in 4.5 seconds in his fourteenth and final professional season.) Still, when the Pittsburgh Steelers selected him in the third round of the 1970 NFL draft, they were concerned about Blount's attitude.

As physically gifted as he was, Blount struggled for two seasons to take his place on the young, but promising, Pittsburgh defense. In a game against the Miami Dolphins in 1971, he was burned for 3 touchdowns, one of them for 86 yards, by the stylish Paul Warfield. He briefly considered a future without football.

Analyzing his play in the offseason, Blount came to the conclusion that his problem was not lack of ability, but lack of preparation. "Instead of thinking about how many times I had been beaten," he said, "I decided to think of how many lessons I had learned."

With a renewed commitment, Blount reported to training camp in 1972 and became one of the stalwarts of the team's celebrated "Steel Curtain." He wasn't beaten for a single touchdown that season. Allowed to hassle receivers down the field, he became such an intimidating presence that the league passed legislation limiting defenders to one bump in 1974 and to a five-yard "bump zone" in 1978. Blount quickly adapted and remained as effective as ever.

"A lot of cornerbacks want to be intimidating," said Jon Kolb, the Pittsburgh tackle who later

became an assistant coach. "They go through all kinds of things to be intimidating. Mel could just walk out there, look down on the [receiver], and then run side-by-side with him. That was intimidating."

In 1975, Blount enjoyed one of the greatest seasons any cornerback ever had. His 11 interceptions led the league and established a club record, he received his first of five Pro Bowl recognitions, and he was honored as the NFL's defensive player of the year. He also earned the second of his four Super Bowl rings.

"Mel was as good a cornerback as any that ever lived," said Bud Carson, formerly the Steelers' defensive backfield coach and defensive coordinator. "He was just a great athlete. He caught every ball that went into his hands."

As durable as he was talented, Blount missed only one of 201 regular-season games, and he retired with 57 career interceptions. He also made critical thefts against Minnesota in Super Bowl IX and against Dallas in Super Bowl XIII, thwarting drives in the vicinity of the end zone. "When you create a cornerback, the mold is Mel Blount," said teammate Jack Ham, the Pro Football Hall of Fame linebacker. "He was the most incredible athlete I have ever seen."

1976-1989

MIKE HAYNES

A t the time, money was no object. The Super Bowl was. So the Los Angeles Raiders made the kind of deal with the New England Patriots that other teams were loathe to complete. They surrendered first- and second-round draft choices in compensation, offered the holdout the money he was seeking, and acquired the best cornerback in the NFL in midseason. Oh, yes, the Raiders did reach Super Bowl XVIII, where they handily defeated the Washington Redskins. He contributed an interception in the 38-9 romp at Tampa Stadium.

Mike Haynes was that kind of player, the final piece to a championship puzzle. No team in pro football asked more of its cornerbacks, who were trained to play unadulterated man-for-man defense virtually from start to finish of a game, and no other team had a pair to match the Raiders' Haynes and Lester Hayes. "They dared you to beat them," recalled Washington quarterback Joe Theismann. Few succeeded.

Haynes had been a Pro Bowl player for the Patriots in six of his first seven seasons, the only exclusion coming in 1981 when he suffered a collapsed lung and was sidelined for six games. Technically a free agent, which carried little weight at the time because of the compensation issue, he was prepared to sit out the entire 1983 season if his demands were not met. New England was prepared to ignore him. Enter Raiders owner Al Davis.

In all, Haynes spent seven seasons with the Raiders, leading the league with 220 yards in interception returns in 1984 and earning three more Pro Bowl bids. Moreover, he established a standard for the position by which all are judged. His 46 career interceptions only hint at his ability—as often as not, opponents didn't even bother testing him. "Mike is like a batter you pitch around," Jim Murray once wrote, "a fortress a good general bypasses."

Haynes envisioned himself as a pass receiver in college. That changed when Arizona State coach Frank Kush recruited a youngster named John Jefferson, who later starred with the Chargers and Packers. "I wanted to play," Haynes said, "so I had to learn to run backwards."

He became so adept at the maneuver that the Patriots drafted him with the fifth pick overall in 1976. At 6 feet 2 inches and 195 pounds, Haynes was as smooth as silk and superbly constructed for the position. "What made him unique was his height and reach," Theismann said. "He could keep an arm on people and they couldn't get away. He had great hips. They gave him a wonderful ability to turn and break on the ball."

Haynes studied receivers and quarterbacks alike. One of the rarest sights at a Patriots or Raiders game during his tenure was Haynes being beaten deep.

"[The receiver] tells you where the ball is," he explained. "If the defensive back looks back and the ball's not there, he's beaten."

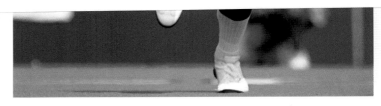

Rod's got the best physical makeup of anybody playing right now," said Tony Dungy, current Minnesota defensive coordinator and a former Steelers assistant. "Size, speed, strength, quickness, ability to play the ball—he's got everything you need there."

1 9 5 2 - 1 9 6 5

NIGHT TRAIN LANE

he story and the player belonged to a bygone era, when pro football was less

1 9 6 7 - 1 9 8 0

1 9 6 7 - 1 9 8 5

JAN STENERUD

His was one of those Only-in-America stories that no longer are in vogue. Jan Stenerud was among the first wave of Europeans and first-generation Americans who pushed the parameters of placekicking. When he started his career, the sight of an NFL player kicking a football with his instep, as if it were a soccer ball, still was so strange there was no adequate coaching and considerable resistance among full-time players. Ever-outspoken Lions defensive tackle Alex Karras had a simple solution to the sudden glut of field goals in his sport: "Tighten the immigration laws."

But Stenerud persevered and by the time he retired in 1985, the straight-ahead kicker was virtually extinct. More than any of his peers, he had withstood the test of time. Fittingly, the tall Norwegian became the first pure kicker to gain entrance to the Pro Football Hall of Fame.

Stenerud kicked more field goals (373) than any other player in NFL history and accounted for more points (1,699) than all but George Blanda. With Green Bay in 1981, Stenerud set an NFL single-season efficiency record (since surpassed) by converting 22 of 24 field-goal attempts. He kicked for three different teams in three different decades, and was so proficient that he was selected to the Pro Bowl at the age of 42. That was in 1984, when Stenerud was successful on 20 of 23 field-goal attempts for Minnesota.

"The older he got, the harder he worked," said Lynn Dickey, the former Packers quarterback, "so he never had any deterioration of his physical skills."

A back injury reduced his effectiveness in 1985 and led to his retirement after that season.

Born in Fetsund, Norway, Stenerud received a ski-jumping scholarship to Montana State. Jim Sweeney, the football coach, recruited him for the team after watching him kick some soccer balls. After only two years with the sport, Stenerud was chosen by the Kansas City Chiefs in the third round of the AFL's redshirt draft in 1966.

Before reporting to his first training camp, he went home to inform his parents of the decision, bringing along some films of his games at Montana State. "My mother was a little leery of my playing football," he said, "and my father had hoped I would jump for Norway in the Winter Olympics. When they looked at the films, nobody could understand what was happening."

Stenerud was an instant sensation as a Chiefs rookie, posting the first of his record seven seasons with 100 or more points. Kansas City advanced to Super Bowl IV at the end of his third season, and he set the tone for the Chiefs' stunning 23-7 upset of Minnesota by kicking 3 first-half field goals for a 9-0 lead. The first, from 48 yards, established a Super Bowl distance record that stood for 24 years.

"The Vikings were staring in disbelief," coach Hank Stram chortled. "They couldn't believe we didn't punt."

1974-1987
BILLY JOHNSON

*I*t wasn't his cleats, though they provided him with a memorable nickname. It wasn't the end-zone dance, though that attracted national attention. It was Billy (White Shoes) Johnson's perseverance and production with two teams in two decades that stamped him as the most distinguished punt returner in NFL history. A relatively small athlete from a relatively small college, Johnson proved to be a charismatic performer for the Houston Oilers and Atlanta Falcons. (He also played briefly with the Washington Redskins.) He overcame serious injuries to both knees to set career records for punt returns (282) and yardage (3,317), and he was a dangerous wide receiver as well.

Johnson first wore white shoes as a high school quarterback, in tribute to Joe Namath. He said they made him run faster. He took the shoes along to Widener, a Pennsylvania college more renowned for Hollywood legends Cecil B. DeMille and Humphrey Bogart than for football stars. Switched to running back in college, Johnson surpassed nine NCAA records and added the touchdown dance on one of his frequent trips to the end zone.

This new form of expression was unleashed upon the NFL during a game at the Astrodome in 1974. Johnson, a fifteenth-round pick, scored on an end-around against the Pittsburgh Steelers and reverted to his college celebration. "It was truly spontaneous," he said. "I found myself in the end zone and thought, 'Man, looka here.'"

He later checked with O.A. (Bum) Phillips, the defensive coordinator who would succeed Sid Gillman as head coach the following season. "I said, 'Bum, do you mind me doing that?'" Johnson recalled. "He said, 'You didn't hurt anybody, did you?'"

In 1975, Johnson's routine became a regular feature when he returned 4 kicks (3 punts and 1 kickoff) for touchdowns, tying the NFL single-season record. He was denied sole possession of the mark when a punt return for 75 yards was stopped at the 1-yard line. After leading the league with a 15.3-yard punt-return average, he received the first of three Pro Bowl nominations and was voted MVP of the game after scoring on a 90-yard punt return.

"He was even more exciting in practice," Phillips said. "We didn't have anyone who could tackle him. He was so elusive. And he could see everybody in the stadium."

Surgery to Johnson's left knee and then his right knee virtually wiped out the 1978 and 1979 seasons, and he didn't return a single kick in 1980, prompting him to leave for the Canadian Football League. He joined the Falcons in 1982, and in 1983, after leading the team with 64 receptions and returning punts for 489 yards, he was honored as the NFL's comeback player of the year.

By the time he retired in 1988, the 5-foot 9-inch, 170-pound Johnson had gained the reputation of a giant.

The 12 NFL club owners who convened for a winter meeting in Miami Beach, Florida, in January, 1960, might have been mistaken for mourners at a wake. Certainly, the death of Commissioner Bert Bell three months earlier still was on their minds. But the furrowed brows and pained expressions in the meeting room were the products of other concerns.

Battles seemed to loom on every front, first and foremost with the upstart American Football League, which brashly had announced its intention to put franchises in eight U.S. cities, including two that created direct competition between leagues. Another struggle was unfolding within the NFL fraternity, where the Bears and Cardinals waged an unspoken, but heated, feud over rights to the rich football market of Chicago. Plus, an argument lay in wait over a proposal for expansion, a budding issue that already had stirred friction.

And still to be resolved was perhaps the most important decision of all: Who would succeed Bert Bell? The owners ordered coffee and settled deep into their seats. They knew their meetings would last a while.

Opposing factions already had aligned themselves when the selection process for commissioner began. The old-guard owners, led by the Redskins' George Preston Marshall, stood firmly behind Austin Gunsel, a former FBI agent and acting NFL treasurer who had been interim commissioner since Bell's death at an Eagles-Steelers game in October. Gunsel was content to keep the league office in Philadelphia, where traditionalists wished it to remain.

On the other side was a solid bloc of seven owners who endorsed Marshall Leahy, attorney for the San Francisco 49ers. A husky, forceful personality, Leahy had no marriage to tradition. His vision placed the league office in San Francisco. If that notion ranked with blasphemy for some, it was non-negotiable for Leahy.

Because approval required a three-fourths majority (9 of 12 votes), both candidates were blocked—and the two factions were unflinching in their support. Across seven days and 22 ballots, the battle raged.

The lone disinterested spectator was Bears owner George Halas, who had a different agenda. Troubled by the specter of the AFL claiming new cities—Halas still had vivid recollections of the havoc caused by the birth of the old All-America Football Conference in the late 1940s—Papa Bear was intent on cementing NFL expansion plans, and he refused to do anything that might endanger them. Rather than alienate potential expansion allies by backing the wrong candidate, Halas steadfastly withheld his vote for commissioner.

Leahy was one vote shy of victory on three occasions, but Halas never blinked. If the commissioner's election was war, Halas was Switzerland.

The balloting seemed destined to go on without end. Leahy's opponents twice proposed "compromise" candidates—Lions president Edwin J. Anderson and Colts general manager Donald S. Kellett—but with no success. The deadlock continued.

Unable to contain his frustration, Colts owner Carroll Rosenbloom finally exploded, "You people are being ridiculous.

ixties

Pete Rozelle (center) with George Halas (far left) and George Marshall (second from right).

You don't want to compromise. If God Almighty came down from Heaven and agreed to serve as commissioner, you'd vote for Leahy."

Wearied and worried that the matter might never be resolved, two of the league's most respected figures—Wellington Mara of the Giants and Paul Brown of the Browns—hit upon another idea. They approached Rams general manager Pete Rozelle, a fresh-faced 33-year-old who had gained widespread respect for restoring order to the troubled West Coast franchise.

From a strictly political standpoint, Rozelle was an inspired choice. He owed no allegiance to old-guard owners, but he had been a personal favorite of former Commissioner Bell's. Rozelle was a native Californian, but he had expressed no reservations about moving out east to Philadelphia.

From a practical standpoint, the case for Rozelle was not quite as clear. He, like everyone, was aware that, despite his clear

intelligence, his youth and lack of experience worked against him. When told that he might be a candidate everyone could agree on, he had a blunt response. "That," he said, "is the most ludicrous thing I've ever heard."

On the twenty-third ballot, nearly a week after the session had begun, a haggard group of owners elected Alvin (Pete) Rozelle as the third NFL Commissioner. That same day, Dallas Texans founder Lamar Hunt was elected as the AFL's first president.

Rozelle received the news in the hotel men's room, where he had taken retreat to

avoid the probing eyes of the media during the owners' closed-door vote. Rosenbloom said only two words when he found Rozelle at a wash basin: "You're it."

The more prophetic words belonged to Brown, who sought to quell any doubts the new commissioner might have about his readiness for the job. Said the grizzled football pioneer, who had tasted so many victories, to the man who would become the most successful commissioner in the history of professional sports: "You can grow into the job."

Once again, Paul Brown was ahead of the game.

FOOTBALL IN THE EYE OF THE STORM

A touchdown still was worth 6 points, and the playing field still measured 100 yards, but virtually every other aspect of professional football changed in the 1960s.

The era of two-way players who played every down on both offense and defense became a romantic footnote in the game's history as soon as Chuck Bednarik of the Eagles made the game-saving tackle and trudged off Philadelphia's Franklin Field after the 1960 NFL Championship Game.

The Cardinals, a charter NFL franchise that had operated in Chicago for 62 years, responded to slumping gate receipts by conceding the market to the more popular Bears and relocating to St. Louis in 1960. The decade marked the addition of four NFL expansion teams—Dallas, Minnesota, Atlanta, and New Orleans—a dramatic departure for a league whose membership had not changed since 1951.

The 12-game NFL schedule, a fixture for 14 seasons, was increased to 14 games in 1961, and before the decade had ended, the Eastern and Western Conferences were subdivided, leading to a new round of playoff games.

The television industry became an invaluable ally in the game's success. Increased exposure broadened the fan base, which bolstered popularity, and, like a snowball gathering momentum as it rolled, pro football's impact expanded dramatically. NFL players became household names.

The Green Bay Packers' Paul Hornung, a golden-haired running back from Notre Dame, gained notice for his versatility, but his "Golden Boy" nickname referred equally to his popularity among female fans. Cleveland Browns running back Jim Brown, who electrified fans with his slashing, tackle-breaking style, enjoyed such a high profile that he jumped directly from his last game to a starring role in motion pictures. Even the name of an

Coach Vince Lombardi is swept from the field after the 1966 NFL Championship Game (opposite). Lombardi's Green Bay Packers changed the face of pro football.

Houston's George Blanda (with ball) was one of several castoff NFL quarterbacks who found glory in the fledgling AFL. Blanda led the Oilers to victories over the Chargers in the first two AFL Championship Games.

obscure offensive lineman, Green Bay guard Jerry Kramer, was mentioned in living rooms throughout the nation because of one key block in a frozen moment of a televised championship game.

This Means War

Pro football came of age in the 1960s. But none of the changes that marked the decade had a greater impact than the birth of an NFL rival: the American Football League. Its arrival set into motion a chain of events that helped pro football make an indelible imprint on the consciousness of the nation.

With investors in place in the summer of 1959, AFL founder Lamar Hunt contacted NFL Commissioner Bert Bell and asked if Bell would consider serving as commissioner of both leagues. Bell had no immediate response, but he obviously took the proposal seriously. The first public mention of the new league came in newspaper quotes attributed to Bell when he appeared before a Congressional committee investigating monopolistic practices in pro football. "I want to tell you fellows about this new league," he said.

That was the first hint of cooperation between the old and new leagues, and it would be the last until 1966. NFL owners were less than enthusiastic about cutting their pie into six new pieces. When Bell died of a heart attack on October 11, 1959, the last hope for a peaceful settlement disappeared.

The war was on.

The Foolish Rush In

The cast of characters changed in the intervening months, but the AFL remained on schedule for a 1960 kickoff. Max Winter's Minneapolis group pulled out when it was offered an NFL expansion franchise, and at the behest of Hilton, a franchise was placed in Oakland and awarded to an eight-man syndicate. The addition of two new owners—Ralph Wilson, Jr., in Buffalo and William H. Sullivan, Jr., in Boston—brought the number of franchises to eight.

Considering the sizable hurdle they faced, the owners seemed to merit the name that Oakland's Wayne Valley gleefully pinned on them: "The Foolish Club." As the charter AFL members knew, they were challenging a 40-year-old institution, and they had no experience in the business and little time for preparation.

The AFL owners took to their task like a whirlwind. Undeterred by their lack of detailed scouting information, they conducted a draft of college players. Then they named a commissioner—Joe Foss, the former governor of South Dakota and a much-decorated World War II fighter pilot.

If AFL draft selections evoked cynicism from the older league, the mirth was short-lived. Whatever the AFL lacked in football expertise, it made up in cash reserves. Signing battles for top draft choices began immediately.

The most celebrated of those involved running back Billy Cannon, the 1959 Heisman Trophy winner from Louisiana State. A two-time All-America with blinding speed, Cannon deserved the tag of "super athlete" that his college coach, Paul Dietzel, had placed on him.

While still general manager of the Los Angeles Rams, Pete Rozelle had persuaded Cannon to sign an undated NFL contract. It called for a $10,000 bonus and a $10,000 salary the first year, followed by two years at $15,000 each. Although the signing occurred on November 29, 1959, the date had been left blank so as not to endanger Cannon's eligibility for the Sugar Bowl.

It was easy to understand the NFL's shock when moments after the game had ended, Cannon was in the end zone with Houston Oilers lawyer Adrian Burk, signing his name to a three-year AFL contract that guaranteed $100,000, plus a $10,000 gift for Cannon's mother.

The Rams filed suit, but a judge ruled the Oilers' contract valid. The first shot had been fired in a war that would witness countless signing collisions.

It was a bitter confrontation featuring outrageous subversions—secret drafts of college players and raids of established rosters—that served to raise owners' blood pressures and players' salaries.

Continued clashes ultimately would lead to a merger of the two leagues and the creation of the Super Bowl. But that is getting ahead of the story.

Help Wanted

To a large extent, the first AFL rosters were populated with NFL castoffs, most of whom found new life against lesser competition. George Blanda, who had been released by the Chicago Bears in 1958, became a star in the AFL. He passed for 24 touchdowns in 1960 as the Oilers posted a 10-4 record and defeated the Los Angeles Chargers in the first AFL Championship Game. Blanda's championship-game counterpart, the same Jack Kemp who later would pursue a political career, became a member of the Chargers after spending the 1959 season on the taxi squad of a Canadian Football League team. His sum of previous pro football experience was four games with the NFL's Pittsburgh Steelers. In his first year in the AFL, Kemp was the league's leading passer.

Jack Kemp was a successful AFL passer long before he pursued a political career.

Though quality of play sometimes lagged, the AFL was a league of innovation and excitement. The option of a 2-point conversion after touchdowns added an element of suspense. Bombs-away game plans and unskilled defensive secondaries provided a formula for predictably high-scoring games. ABC-TV, which agreed to a five-year contract at $2 million per year, was not unhappy with the debut season of the new venture.

But the NFL clearly commanded the spotlight in 1960, thanks to a daunting array of talent. Even in his final season, flamboyant quarterback Norm Van Brocklin of the Philadelphia Eagles captured the public's fancy with a passing attack that featured flanker Tommy McDonald, tight end Pete Retzlaff, and nearly 9 yards per passing attempt. At 34, in his twelfth NFL season and several years past his prime, Van Brocklin passed for 24 touchdowns and 2,471 yards in leading the Eagles to a 10-2 record. After directing a 17-13 victory over Green Bay in the championship game, he pulled off shoulder pads that were destined for the Pro Football Hall of Fame.

More would be heard from the Packers. The tough running of fullback Jim Taylor and multiple-threat scoring of Hornung would become recognizable trademarks of a team molded by Vince Lombardi, the stocky, animated coach who spent Sundays screaming and gesturing on the sidelines.

Hornung scored an NFL-record 176 points (the record still stands) on 15 touchdowns, 15 field goals, and 41 extra points in the final 12-game NFL season. Taylor ground out 1,101 yards on 230 punishing carries, the first of seven successive seasons he would lead the team.

Only Cleveland's Brown gained more yards (1,257), marked by a trail of bruised defenders left in his wake. Along with backfield mate Bobby Mitchell and quarterback Milt Plum, the NFL's leading passer, Brown helped make Cleveland the league's highest-scoring team.

One item of note that went largely unappreciated in 1960 was the birth of the NFL's newest team. The Dallas Cowboys were baptized at the Cotton Bowl on September 24 with a 35-28 loss to the Pittsburgh Steelers. It was a game that featured 345 passing yards from diminutive Cowboys quarterback Eddie LeBaron.

Although the Cowboys struggled through an agonizing first season (0-11-1) that included losses by 34, 38, and 41 points, they had begun a remarkable journey. Head coach Tom Landry and general manager Tex Schramm eventually would transform a conference cellar dweller into one with the exalted title of "America's Team."

Rozelle's Tele-Vision

If Commissioner Pete Rozelle seemed content to remain in the

Versatile Paul Hornung (in flight) led the NFL in scoring three consecutive seasons.

background during his first year on the job, he clearly made his presence felt in 1961. The successful lobbying effort that he waged in paving the way for television negotiations hinted at his insight into the future of the game.

Rozelle sensed pro football's rising popularity, and he recognized the disparity of its markets. He believed it was self-destructive for NFL franchises to sell television rights individually. As a package, the rights were greater than the sum of the parts. Divided equally, revenues would enable small-market teams to compete with large ones.

Rozelle first had to sell the long-term benefits of his plan to clubs that already had profitable local TV packages. They figured to earn less, not more, in the early years of this arrangement. The situation tested the commissioner's powers of persuasion and diplomacy, two of his biggest strengths.

"Pete does his best to leave the other fellow his dignity," Rams owner Dan Reeves explained. "He's a guide, not a dictator. But it must drive him nuts. He knows the answer all the time."

Next, the plan had to clear legal hurdles posed by antitrust regulations. When a two-year contract calling for more than $9 million was negotiated with CBS, a Federal Court ruled it void and forced teams to return to the individual contract plan.

Rozelle was nothing if not persistent. He soon made the acquaintance of U.S. Representative Emanuel Celler (D-New York), who by year's end had introduced a bill legalizing single-network package sales by professional sports leagues. President John F. Kennedy signed it into law on September 30, and, by the end of 1961, the NFL and CBS had agreed to a two-year contract calling for $4.65 million annually.

One of the most interesting facets of the 1961 NFL season was the Shotgun offense of 49ers coach Red Hickey, which not only posed strategic problems for defenses but also precipitated the year's most memorable player trade. Unlike the standard Slot-T formation of the time, the Shotgun placed the quarterback several yards behind the line of scrimmage. In theory, it presented versatility and a better view of the defense. In practice, it required a nimble quarterback.

Because Hickey felt that incumbent 49ers quarterback Y.A. Tittle was ill-equipped for the role, he traded the 11-year veteran to the New York Giants for second-year offensive lineman Lou Cordileone. Tittle, the 49ers' starter since 1952, was not the only player surprised by the trade. "Me for Tittle?" asked Cordileone. "Just me?"

From the 49ers' perspective, the trade looked no better in years to come, after Tittle had led the Giants to three Eastern Conference championships and been named the league's MVP. But in early 1961, all eyes were focused on San Francisco, where Hickey's revolutionary offense quickly struck gold.

With quarterbacks John Brodie, Bill Kilmer, and Bobby Waters alternating on successive downs, the 49ers exploited every advantage of the formation. Brodie was a talented passer, Kilmer a gifted runner, and Waters was comfortable in either role. The 49ers won four of their first five games, including a 49-0 victory over Detroit and a 35-0 win over Los Angeles.

"You start to get one quarterback figured out," Lions linebacker Joe Schmidt lamented, "and another guy comes in who does something else."

Hickey's hopes for lasting acclaim faded in the sixth game of the season

GOING 60 IN '60

In the mid-1980s, Chuck Bednarik, Hall of Fame center and linebacker, participated in a roast of Frank Gifford. Bednarik of the Philadelphia Eagles and Gifford of the New York Giants forever will be linked by a collision during the 1960 season that knocked Gifford unconscious.

"So I get this idea," Bednarik said. "I get to the hotel and I tell the guy in charge, 'When they introduce me, turn the lights down for ten seconds.' So they do that, and when they turn the lights up I say, 'Frank, does that ring a bell?' When you roast, you gotta roast hard."

Bednarik, who also played hard, is remembered as the last of the NFL's 60-minute men, guys who played on offense and defense. He earned the distinction in 1960, when he filled in for injured linebacker Bob Pellegrini, starting in midseason.

With Bednarik going both ways, Philadelphia advanced to the championship. Besides the hit on Gifford, his crowning moment came when he stopped Green Bay fullback Jim Taylor near the goal line as time ran out in the Eagles' 17-13 victory.

"That championship game, above all, was the one that says it all for me," Bednarik said. "I was in for every play, at thirty-five years old. It took me twenty years to realize what I did."

VINCE AND TOM...AND SID

The NFL was fat in 1959. Attendance was at an all-time high. Player salaries were low and there were only 12 teams to share the wealth. They couldn't accommodate the overload of talent. The time was ripe for a new league, and so along came the American Football League in 1960.

Taking the lead of the old All-America Football Conference of the late 1940s, the AFL strategists pushed for razzle-dazzle. They threw the ball like mad, passing more often than anyone ever had seen, for more yards and more touchdowns.

In a much quieter way, Tom Landry was accomplishing equally amazing things for the Dallas Cowboys, an expansion team in 1960. Landry and Lombardi had been assistants with the Giants in the 1950s. When Lombardi took his Run to Daylight idea to Green Bay in 1959, Landry, still in New York, came up with a package to stop it.

The 4-3 Outside positioned the defensive tackles on the outside shoulders of their men, assigning middle linebacker Sam Huff inside responsibility. The 4-3 Inside, designed especially for Lom-

cated set of pick routes for his receivers. He had some success with it, first at St. Louis, then with Houston of the AFL. The San Francisco 49ers shocked everyone—briefly—with their Shotgun, which had the quarterback playing deep and the linemen screening, or brush-blocking, a modification of Glenn (Pop) Warner's ancient Double-Wing.

And in San Diego, an influential system was born. Sid Gillman, with an offense as explosive as the lightning bolts on the sides of his players' helmets, had created a passing attack that stretched defenses to the limit. The Chargers ran deep posts, corner routes, and seam routes, then threw to the backs underneath, or threw to the wide receivers on precisely timed patterns, the ball delivered to a spot, on the break. "We don't take what they give us," Gillman said. "We make them take what we give them."

Al Davis, who had been Gillman's ends coach, took the philosophy with him to Oakland, and was fond of repeating the phrase. Gillman assistants Chuck Noll and Jack Faulkner took it with them to Pittsburgh and Denver, respectively. Don Klosterman took it to the Los Angeles Rams. San Diego State coach Don Coryell, a frequent visitor to Gillman's practices, used it as the basis of Air Coryell. Joe Gibbs, Coryell's assistant, brought it to Washington.

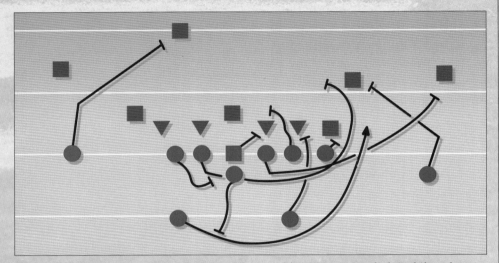

Vince Lombardi's power sweep (above) complemented his "Run to Daylight" philosophy.

The NFL was passing, too, but it stressed quality. Its overall completion percentage in the 10 years the two leagues coexisted (1960-69) never dipped below 50 percent; the AFL, with its emphasis on long passes, never reached it.

In Green Bay, of course, there was Vince Lombardi, whose inspirational qualities have been well-documented. As a strategist, though, he never got his full due.

Lombardi introduced option blocking —taking the opponent in whichever direction he's going—to combat the immense middle guards of the 1950s and the equally huge defensive tackles of the '60s. The back would read the block and make his cut accordingly. "Run to Daylight" was Lombardi's philosophy.

bardi's power sweeps and option running, plus Cleveland's Jim Brown, had the tackles pinching and occupying their men, leaving Huff free to go with the flow.

Lombardi reacted with traps and weakside counters; Landry parried by dropping the strongside defensive end and weakside tackle off the line, into a reading, or "flex" position. It became the basis of the Dallas Flex defense.

The 1960s produced a few innovations here and there. George Halas's Bears introduced a two-tight end alignment, with one of them positioned as a slotback. Frank (Pop) Ivy came down from Canada ("Where everything is second-and-ten," said ex-Eagle Bucko Kilroy) with a flashy four-wide receiver package and a compli-

In 1969, Hank Stram filled up his bag of tricks in Kansas City: the moving pocket, in which his passer did a half-roll behind a couple of pulling linemen; the odd-man defensive front, with tackle Curley Culp facing a center head-on; the Stack, which hid one or more linebackers directly behind a lineman.

In January, 1970, the Chiefs caught the heavily favored Minnesota Vikings unprepared. The result was a second consecutive Super Bowl victory for the AFL. "Football of the Seventies," Stram called it. The world was waiting.

when the 49ers collided with the Chicago Bears and were handed a 31-0 defeat. Bears assistant coach Clark Shaughnessy revamped his defensive alignment, moving middle linebacker Bill George to nose guard, directly over the ball. When the center lowered his head to see where he was snapping the ball, George capitalized on an unobstructed path into the backfield.

"Bill got to the tailback almost as fast as the ball did," said teammate Abe Gibron.

Thirty-Six Stiffs

The NFL arrived in Minnesota in 1961, and it was difficult not to notice. The franchise's first coach was Norm Van Brocklin, who greeted a roster of modest talent with demanding workouts and a hair-trigger temper.

It was a roster composed of unproven rookies and unwanted veterans claimed from established clubs. Van Brocklin, never one to mince words, called them his "thirty-six stiffs." At least one among the 36 merited loftier praise. Quarterback Fran Tarkenton, a third-round draft choice from Georgia, was about to launch an 18-year career in which he would establish NFL passing records for attempts, completions, yards, and touchdowns.

A skitterbug with quick feet and natural instincts, Tarkenton offered a glimpse of the future in his first game, a 37-13 victory over Chicago, when he passed for 4 touchdowns and ran for another. If his hair-raising scrambles exasperated Bears coach and owner George Halas, who watched from the other side of the field, they tormented Van Brocklin nearly as much. In Van Brocklin's book, quarterbacks were to stay in the pocket, *dammit*.

There was little question about the quarterback of the year in the AFL, where Blanda enjoyed the most prolific season of his career. His 3,330 passing yards and 36 touchdowns easily led the league, as the Oilers scored a resounding 513 points—an average of nearly 37 per game. In the championship game, Houston coughed up 7 turnovers and still managed to defeat the Chargers 10-3.

The 1961 NFL season belonged to Green Bay. Lombardi's unrelenting insistence on fundamentals and his demand for execution were the hallmarks of a machine that pounded out an 11-3 record and obliterated Tittle and the New York Giants 37-0 in the championship game.

The Lombardi philosophy was simple, as receiver Max McGee recalled from the coach's first speech to his players: "Anybody who doesn't want to play winning football, get the hell out of here right now."

"He told us that the people who were members of this organization must be willing to submit their own desires to the good of the team," quarterback Bart Starr said.

The power sweep became the Packers' calling card, and Taylor was a relentless tank who rambled for 1,307 yards and 15 touchdowns in '61. Hornung led the league in scoring for a third straight year with 146 points. Starr was a

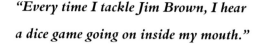

The Minnesota Vikings cheer their victory over Chicago in their first game.

flawless technician who passed for 2,418 yards and 16 touchdowns.

The Packers sent eight players to the Pro Bowl. They would do the same in 1962. There was little question about which was the best team in pro football.

Burn, Baby, Burn

In 1962, the AFL had no illusions of grandeur. Its next goal was the same as its last: survival. The Chargers had relocated from Los Angeles to San Diego in 1961. Both the Broncos and Raiders had changed principal owners. A U.S. District Court in Baltimore had ruled against the league in its antitrust suit against the NFL.

Still, the AFL would not go away.

For all its shortcomings, the new league was cultivating a growing stable of star players—Billy Cannon in Houston, end Lionel Taylor in Denver, flanker Don Maynard in New York, and running back Paul Lowe in San Diego were prime examples. Thanks to regular network television exposure, they attracted a loyal following.

But not every aspect of the AFL was serious enterprise, as best illustrated by the preseason antics of the 1962 Denver Broncos. In a promotional gimmick that doubled as a waste-disposal project, the Broncos scheduled a public burning of their socks, the vertically striped, brown-and-yellow eyesores that accented the garish uniforms they wore.

Buoyed by this smoky sendoff—8,000 fans attended the bonfire—the Broncos won six of their first seven games, recorded the club's first non-losing (7-7) season, and played to an average home attendance of more than 25,000 fans.

More far-reaching developments occurred elsewhere in the league, among them the arrival of thundering running back Carlton (Cookie) Gilchrist in Buffalo after eight seasons in the Canadian Football League, and quarterback Len Dawson in Dallas after five uneventful years in the NFL.

Gilchrist arrived with a boom, packing 240 pounds on a 6-foot, 2-inch frame. His 1,096 yards in 1962 led the AFL. Gilchrist, along with Abner Haynes of Dallas (1,049 yards) and Charlie Tolar of Houston (1,012), posted the league's first 1,000-yard seasons. Gilchrist helped turn the Bills into contenders.

"He didn't have the speed of Jim Brown, but he ran almost as hard," said Tom Bass, an assistant coach with the Chargers for four seasons. "If he broke through the line, the free safety would take a long, deep breath."

Dawson's impact was even more profound. In five seasons as a backup for the Steelers and Browns, he had strapped on his helmet only often enough to complete 21 passes in 45 attempts. But in the Texans' offensive system, under old friend and former college coach Hank Stram, Dawson averaged nearly 9 yards per passing attempt, threw for a league-leading 29 touchdowns, and guided Dallas to the AFL title.

On December 23, 1962, in a game that required two overtime periods and spanned 77 minutes 54 seconds—the longest game in pro football history at the time—Dawson and Dallas defeated Houston 20-17.

It was the last game for the Texans, who took their AFL trophy to Kansas City two months later and changed their name to Chiefs, in honor of Kansas City mayor H. Roe (Chief) Bartle, a political ally in the relocation.

Taylor Measures Up

The most startling development in the 1962 NFL season was the interruption of Jim Brown's five-year reign as the rushing champion. The Packers' Jim Taylor put his head down 272 times, gained 1,474 yards, and scored a league-leading 19 touchdowns. Defenders who had been dazzled by Brown were knocked dizzy by Taylor, who firmly believed that the shortest path between two points was a straight line.

Giants linebacker Sam Huff, who often stood in that path, offered a vivid description: "He ran hard and he loved to kick you in the head with those knees. I loved playing against him because I never had to go far to find him. He'd try to find you so he could run over you."

Guards Jerry Kramer (64) and Fuzzy Thurston (63) pull to make room for fullback Jim Taylor on one of the Packers' feared sweeps. Taylor was a five-time 1,000-yard rusher.

On a cold, blustery day at Yankee Stadium, Green Bay defeated the Giants 16-7 in the 1962 NFL Championship Game.

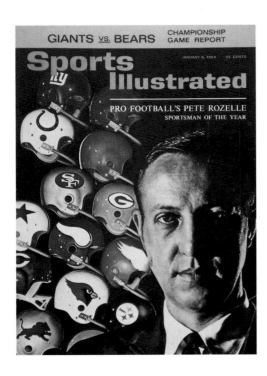

Pete Rozelle was named 1963 Sportsman of the Year by *Sports Illustrated*.

No two teams belonged together more than the Packers and Giants, who for the second year in a row had the two best records in the NFL. The 13-1 Packers led the league in scoring with 415 points, and the 12-2 Giants were second with 398. The Packers had six starters for the West in the Pro Bowl, and the Giants had six starters for the East.

They collided in the NFL title game on December 30, 1962, with the temperature at 13 degrees and winds whipping through Yankee Stadium at up to 40 miles per hour. What followed was one of the game's great defensive battles. Fumble recoveries set up Green Bay's only touchdown and 1 of its 3 field goals. A blocked punt accounted for the Giants' only touchdown. Frozen turf and ferocious tackling left players on both sides bruised and battered, but the Packers were the ones with smiles on their faces after a 16-7 victory.

What had pulled the Packers through? A veteran player explained: "We were afraid to lose and have to face Lombardi afterward."

Before 1962 ended, the same NFL owners who had found it so difficult to agree on a commissioner only two years earlier were unanimous in awarding Rozelle a new five-year, $50,000-per-season deal. He could bask in the knowledge that NFL attendance was steadily on the rise. The league had enjoyed four successive years in which the gate exceeded 3 million.

Three days later, the AFL responded by extending the contract of its commissioner, Joe Foss. Never mind that they played on separate fields. In all other ways, the two leagues were competing.

'Most Difficult Decision'

Of all the decisions in which Rozelle participated during his 30-year tenure as commissioner, none was more profound than the one announced on April 17, 1963.

He arose at 5:15 that Wednesday morning, after a long, sleepless night, and anxiously walked the 15 blocks from his apartment to the NFL office at Rockefeller Plaza. After notifying the parties involved, he announced that Packers running back Paul Hornung and Lions defensive tackle Alex Karras were suspended from the NFL indefinitely for gambling on football games.

Unsubstantiated rumors previously had linked Hornung to gambling figures, but as months passed without action, suspicions faded. In Rozelle's announcement, he explained that he had wanted to be certain of all the facts before acting. An investigation that spanned 10 months and involved 52 interview sessions left little doubt. Both Hornung and Karras had made "significant bets" on NFL games between 1958 and 1961.

Rozelle handed down the NFL's harshest penalty in 17 years—since Frank Filchock and Merle Hapes of the Giants were expelled in 1946 for failure to report a bribe attempt—and in so doing took some risks. The suspension of Hornung, one of the game's glamour players, meant the loss of a powerful drawing card, and the acknowledgement of wrongdoing cast a cloud of suspicion over the league.

"It is the most difficult decision I've ever had to make," the commissioner said. It also may have been his most important. In no uncertain terms, it defined the penalty for endangering the integrity of the NFL.

Five Lions players received lesser penalties—John Gordy, Gary Lowe, Joe Schmidt, Wayne Walker, and Sam Williams were fined $2,000 apiece—for making $50 bets on one game, and the Detroit franchise was fined $4,000 for failure to report questionable "associations" by players and for allowing unauthorized persons on the sidelines during games.

The significance of the moment was not lost on Hornung, who contritely acknowledged his guilt. "I made a terrible mistake," he said. "I realize this now. I am truly sorry. What else is there to say?"

Karras, who vowed to fight his suspension, announced that "this isn't over yet." But it was. Both players sat out the 1963 season before being reinstated in 1964.

Largely because of his handling of the crisis, Rozelle was named 1963 Sportsman of the Year by *Sports Illustrated*—the first non-athlete to receive the prestigious award. But if 1963 was the year in which the commissioner most distinguished himself, it also was when he was most harshly criticized.

Critics arose in force when Rozelle announced that regular-season games would be played as scheduled on November 24, two days after the assassination of President John F. Kennedy. Although it was a measured decision—Rozelle conferred with White House press secretary Pierre Salinger, who thought the games would be a healthy diversion at a time of tragedy—Rozelle's detractors were no less angered at the perceived insensitivity.

Eagles owner Frank McNamee refused to attend his team's home game against the Washington Redskins. "Simply and flatly, the game is being played by order of the commissioner," McNamee said. "I'm going to a memorial service at Independence Hall for President Kennedy."

"I guess I feel like everyone else. I've lost a brother," said Redskins flanker Bobby Mitchell. "I really didn't want to play."

"It was hard to think about football before the game," Cardinals quarterback Charley Johnson said.

CBS broadcast none of the games. The AFL postponed its schedule. Public opinion seemed to weigh against Rozelle. But the size of the crowds at

THE FLIP FLOP

The date: December 23, 1962. The teams: The Dallas Texans and the Houston Oilers. At stake: The championship of the American Football League.

With the teams tied 17-17 at the end of regulation, Dallas coach Hank Stram was instructing his captain, Abner Haynes, on what to do during the overtime coin toss. Concerned about the strong wind howling through Houston's Jeppesen Stadium, his offense's inability to move the ball since halftime, and the Texans' shaky kicking game, Stram told Haynes: "If we win the toss, we don't want to receive. We want the wind. If they win the toss [and choose to receive], we want to kick to the clock [with the wind]. We want the wind."

Haynes, an NBC microphone poised at his left shoulder (inset), stood across from Houston captain Al Jamison. Referee Mike Bourne tossed the coin. Haynes called heads. It landed heads.

Haynes knew his line: "We'll kick to the clock."

Bourne told Haynes his only choice was to receive or defend. "We'll kick," Haynes said.

"Soon as he said the word *kick*, the Oilers automatically had their choice of which side of the field they wanted," Stram said.

Fortunately for Haynes, his blunder didn't cost his team in the end. In the second overtime, the Texans' Tommy Brooker ended the 77-minute, 54-second game with a 25-yard field goal. Dallas 20, Houston 17 was the final score.

DENVER IS BURNING

Before the student protests of the 1960s, before anyone thought of burning a bra or a draft card, a football coach set fire to the objects of the Denver Broncos' wrath—the team's socks.

Never has there been such a burning hate for a football team's uniforms, particularly the Broncos' offensive, vertically striped socks. Denver had worn the uniforms in 1961, but when Jack Faulkner became their head coach in 1962, he refused to let his players near them.

"They had brown pants and yellow jerseys and those ugly socks," Faulkner said. "No way was I going to put that on the players. I got sick of looking at them. Before our first preseason game, I brought out a big tub and we burned the socks and some of the other stuff. I put in new colors—orange, blue, and white."

The Broncos still wear those colors, and many other NFL uniforms of today owe their identities to the 1960s. It was the decade in which the American Football League was born with its colorful logos and uniforms, the decade in which television fell in love with the pro game.

Team logos sprouted onto virtually every helmet. The New York Giants first displayed the initials "ny," and the Pittsburgh Steelers used the steel industry

The Denver Broncos' vertically striped socks invited drastic action by coach Jack Faulkner.

logo—but only on the right side of their helmet. The Green Bay Packers' "G" became the most famous monogram in pro football.

Most players switched to low-cut shoes, and quarterback Joe Namath of the New York Jets stunned the old football guard (not to mention old tackles) by wearing white shoes. Artificial turf

first appeared in the sixties, prompting experimentation with shoes to wear on the new surface. And numerals on jersey sleeves came into widespread use to aid the growing pack of television viewers.

For the first time since 1941, a football other than the official Wilson "Duke" appeared in an NFL game when the AFL met the older league in the first Super Bowl in January, 1967. When the NFL's Packers were on offense, they used the Duke. When the Kansas City Chiefs had it, they used the official AFL ball, the Spalding J5-V. Though they were equal in length and weight, the AFL ball was tapered more.

"The NFL ball appears to be a little fatter," said quarterback George Blanda, who played in both leagues. "However, I've always felt that the NFL ball is easier to throw because its contour is molded more to the hand."

Stronger plastic was developed in the 1960s for use in helmets, but other than graphic alterations, the NFL uniform changed little during the decade.

The Spalding J5-V was more tapered than its NFL counterpart, though they weighed the same.

NFL games—nearly 63,000 watched the Cardinals upset the Giants, and more than 60,000 saw the Redskins defeat the Eagles—suggested that fewer fans were offended by the decision to play.

Years later, however, Rozelle said it was the one decision in his tenure that he would have changed if he had the chance.

Passing the Torch

The 1963 season marked a changing of the guard. The legendary Paul Brown, the only coach the Cleveland Browns had known in their 17 years, was dismissed by owner Art Modell and replaced by Blanton Collier before the season.

Weeb Ewbank, who had directed the Baltimore Colts to NFL titles in 1958 and 1959, was fired by owner Carroll Rosenbloom, as a *Los Angeles Times* sports headline reported on page 3: "Colts Dismiss Ewbank; Detroit Aide Named."

The Detroit assistant coach to whom the headline referred was a 33-year-old unknown by the name of Don Shula. He was about to embark on a coaching career that would be the winningest in NFL history. But this wasn't the last the Colts would hear of Ewbank, who would return to face Shula as the New York Jets' coach in Super Bowl III.

The Los Angeles Rams made an acquisition that paid immediate dividends. In a trade with the New York Giants, at the cost of defensive tackle John LoVetere and a draft choice, they acquired Roosevelt (Rosey) Grier, the final brick in construction of a defensive line known as the Fearsome Foursome. Rams coach Harland Svare spoke a mouthful when he said of Grier, "A player of his caliber, together with the men we already have, will give us one of the best defensive lines in the league." The players the Rams already had were David (Deacon) Jones, Lamar Lundy, and Merlin Olsen.

Before the 1963 calendar could be retired, the NFL had visited lofty peaks and deep ravines. One of the darkest days was May 10, when celebrated defensive lineman Gene (Big Daddy) Lipscomb (who played with three teams) died of a drug overdose. At 6-6 and 288 pounds, enormous dimensions at the time, Lipscomb had tickled admirers with a playful explanation of his football technique ("I just grab me an armful of men, pick 'em over until I find the one with the ball, then I throw him down"). Almost unbelievably, football's most powerful warrior was dead.

The sun shone brightest on September 7, in a special ceremony in Canton, Ohio, where the birthplace of the sport became home to the Pro Football Hall of Fame. Eleven of the hall's 17 charter members attended ceremonies: Mel Hein, Curly Lambeau, Red Grange, Cal Hubbard, Earl (Dutch) Clark, Don Hutson, Johnny Blood (McNally), Sammy Baugh, George Halas, Ernie Nevers, and Bronko Nagurski. Ailing Redskins owner

The Los Angeles Rams' "Fearsome Foursome," from left to right: Lamar Lundy, Roosevelt Grier, Merlin Olsen, and Deacon Jones

"To me, football is a contest in embarrassments. The quarterback is out there to embarrass me in front of my friends, my teammates, my coaches, my wife, and my three boys. The quarterback doesn't leave me any choice. I've got to embarrass him instead."

—ALEX KARRAS, DETROIT LIONS DEFENSIVE TACKLE

George Preston Marshall sent his regrets. Inducted posthumously were Joe Carr, Bert Bell, Tim Mara, Jim Thorpe, and Pete (Fats) Henry.

Lost among the headlines in 1963 was the creation of NFL Properties, which would handle the league's licensing and, later, its marketing and publishing. It was another example of the sport's growth in the sixties.

The Pro Football Hall of Fame induction was not the only celebration for Halas, who subsequently directed the Bears to their eighth NFL championship. A defense spearheaded by linebacker Larry Morris led Chicago to a 14-10 victory over the New York Giants and their battered quarterback, Y.A. Tittle, who still was throwing deep as the clock ran out.

The AFL championship went to Sid Gillman's San Diego Chargers, who rode the 329 yards (206 rushing and 123 receiving) of Keith Lincoln to a 51-10 demolition of the Boston Patriots. The moment moved Gillman to issue a challenge: "The only way to settle the argument about NFL football and the AFL is to play. I definitely feel it would be a match."

Rozelle responded bluntly: "We have no plans for such a game."

The NFL on CBS

The surest measure of pro football's rise in stature came at the television bargaining table in 1964. The NFL and CBS agreed to a two-year contract on January 24 that called for $28.2 million—an average of more than $1 million per club per season. Only two years earlier, under the terms of a two-year, $9.3-million deal with CBS, each club had received $332,000 per season.

"We regard the NFL games as the finest sports package on television," CBS vice president William McPhail said, "which is why we bid what we did. No other sports package can compare to it in interest."

But the AFL came pretty close, at least according to NBC. The network signed a five-year, $36-million deal (beginning in 1965) that guaranteed each of the AFL's eight teams an average of $900,000 per season.

Football was a healthy business, with growing legions of fans. There were more than enough stars to light up the nation's television screens. The Chargers' fleet-footed Lance Alworth, running under rainbows from John Hadl, terrorized the AFL with an average of 20 yards per catch. Houston's Charley Hennigan latched on to 101 receptions, a record that would stand for 20 seasons. Boston receiver Gino Cappelletti, the AFL's answer to Hornung, had 155 points—7 touchdowns, 25 field goals, and 38 extra points. After five college drafts, the AFL talent pool finally had deepened.

Veteran players propelled the NFL, and none more than Baltimore's Lenny Moore, a versatile running back who produced a record-setting 20 touchdowns by rushing and receiving. Colts quarterback Johnny Unitas, still in his prime at 31, passed for 2,824 yards and 19 touchdowns for the Western Conference champions. Jim Brown won his seventh rushing title, and quarterback Frank Ryan threw 25 touchdown passes, including 9 to rookie receiver Paul Warfield, as the Browns won the Eastern Conference.

Lodged among the memories of the 1964 season was a game in San Francisco attended by only 31,845 but remembered by all who treasure football lore. On October 25, with the Vikings leading the 49ers 27-17, defensive end Jim Marshall recovered a fumble by San Francisco's Bill Kilmer and galloped 66 yards…in the wrong direction.

WE REPEAT…

Vince Lombardi's Packers joined an exclusive club when they won their third consecutive NFL title in 1967—the Packers of Curly Lambeau (1929-1931) were the only other team to accomplish the feat. In fact, since the Canton Bulldogs of 1922-23 established themselves as the league's first powerhouse, only a handful of franchises have won back-to-back championships. The teams that have successfully defended NFL titles:

FRANCHISE	CONSECUTIVE TITLES
Canton Bulldogs	1922-23
Green Bay Packers	1929-1931
Chicago Bears	1932-33
Chicago Bears	1940-41
Philadelphia Eagles	1948-49
Detroit Lions	1952-53
Cleveland Browns	1954-55
Baltimore Colts	1958-59
Green Bay Packers	1961-62
Green Bay Packers	1965-67
Miami Dolphins	1972-73
Pittsburgh Steelers	1974-75
Pittsburgh Steelers	1978-79
San Francisco 49ers	1988-89
Dallas Cowboys	1992-93

"I was rushing up to get Kilmer when I saw the ball lying there on the ground," Marshall said. "So I picked it up and just started running. I saw everybody waving their arms and yelling at me, but I thought they were cheering me on."

After reaching the end zone for what he thought was a touchdown, Marshall tossed the football out of play, which translated to a safety for the 49ers. San Francisco lineman Bruce Bosley, who had been trailing the play, came over to shake Marshall's hand. "That," said Marshall, "was the first inkling I had that something had gone wrong."

But the season's biggest story unfolded in the NFL Championship Game, where the underdog Cleveland Browns stunned Baltimore 27-0. Brown shredded the Colts' defense for 114 yards on 27 carries, and Ryan threw 3 touchdown passes to Gary Collins as Cleveland, under Blanton Collier, won its first NFL championship without Paul Brown as coach.

There were no surprises in the AFL, where the 12-2 Buffalo Bills won their first league title. Cookie Gilchrist gained 122 yards in a 20-7 championship-game victory over the Chargers, who were without injured offensive stars Keith Lincoln and Lance Alworth. The winning locker room echoed with a familiar challenge. "We could hold our own against the NFL," Gilchrist said.

Behind the running of Jim Brown and the passing of Frank Ryan (above), Cleveland shocked the powerful Colts 27-0 in the 1964 NFL title game.

"I've always considered myself a group therapist for sixty-thousand people. Every Sunday I hold group therapy and the people come and take out their frustrations on me. If I fail, it magnifies their failures, and if I succeed, it minimizes them."

—SONNY JURGENSEN,
WASHINGTON REDSKINS QUARTERBACK

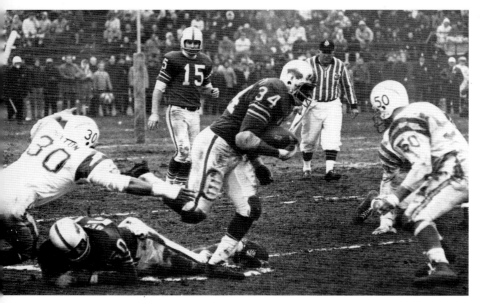

Powerful fullback Cookie Gilchrist (34) led Buffalo to the 1964 AFL title with 122 yards against San Diego.

GALE SAYERS
CHICAGO BEARS   HALFBACK

As a rookie in 1965, Chicago's Gale Sayers set an NFL record with 22 touchdowns.

Broadway Joe

For all of the bravado the AFL had displayed in five years of verbal sniping, it had failed to land a damaging blow to the image of the older league. That changed on New Year's Day, 1965. At the end of a fierce bidding war, the New York Jets were winners and the St. Louis Cardinals were losers in the courtship of Alabama quarterback Joe Namath.

The terms of Namath's contract commanded headlines across the nation. Pro football had its first $400,000 player.

Sonny Werblin, who two years earlier had acquired controlling interest of the club and changed its name from Titans to Jets, beamed with pride: "I'm sure this contract pays the largest amount ever given to a young athlete in any sport. We feel that in getting Joe we get the number-one college football player in America."

And, just as important, the NFL did not.

It was easy to see why the Jets liked Namath, whom coach Weeb Ewbank likened to another player he had tutored. "I see in this young man the same qualities that are found in Unitas," Ewbank said. But why, reporters wondered, with the bids nearly equal, would Namath prefer the Jets over the Cardinals?

"I wanted more than money," he said. "I was interested in the coach and the organization. Weeb Ewbank is an outstanding coach."

The explanation must have surprised St. Louis coach Wally Lemm, whose Cardinals were coming off seasons of 9-5 and 9-3-2. In losing seven of their final nine games, Ewbank's Jets had finished 5-8-1 for the second year in a row in 1964.

Not even the most perceptive of AFL supporters could have foretold the long-term impact of Namath's decision. Four years later, with the league's credibility perched on his shoulders, Namath would slay the NFL champion in Super Bowl III.

The NFL was reminded almost weekly of the quarterback who got away. The AFL's rookie of the year, playing in the media capital of the world, Namath generated press clippings that exceeded even his performance. His glibness made him popular with reporters, and his fast lifestyle earned him a nickname. This was no ordinary Joe. This was Broadway Joe.

Warning! Beware of Bears

If no NFL rookie could match Namath's flair, there were a couple who could match his talent. Linebacker Dick Butkus and running back Gale Sayers, both first-round picks of the Bears, quickly demonstrated their aptitude for the professional game.

Butkus, who seemed even larger than the 245 pounds he carried on a 6-foot 3-inch frame, delivered thundering tackles, chased down ball carriers from behind, and intercepted 5 passes in his rookie year. He would be the hub of the Bears' defense for the next nine years.

Sayers was lightning on cleats. His 22 touchdowns established an NFL record that stood for 10 years—and a rookie record that remains unequaled. He scored 14 touchdowns on the ground, 6 on pass receptions, 1 by kickoff return, and 1 by punt return. He gained an average of 9.8 yards every time he touched the ball, and he drove defenders batty.

His most memorable game was played December 12, against the San Francisco 49ers. In the first quarter, Sayers scored from 80 yards on a screen pass; in the second quarter, on runs of 21 and 7 yards; in the third quarter, on an off-tackle run of 50 yards and a dive play from the 1; and in the fourth quarter, on a punt return of 85 yards. His 6 touchdowns tied an NFL record.

"The greatest exhibition I have ever seen by one man in one game," said George Halas, who had seen a lot of them.

The grittiest performance of 1965 belonged to Baltimore halfback Tom Matte, who was forced to fill in at quarterback when John Unitas and Gary Cuozzo were injured. Matte, who had completed only 1 regular-season pass, faced the Green Bay Packers in a playoff game for the Western Conference title on December 26. He came armed with a hand-written list of plays strapped to his wrist, and he spent much of the game calling his own number as he rushed for 57 yards.

"When Cookie [Gilchrist] came out of the blocks, you just heard this rumbling, like an earthquake. The quarterback handed off to him and got the hell out of the way. We were in as much danger as the defensive linemen."

—AL DOROW,
BUFFALO BILLS QUARTERBACK

Sayers's most memorable performance was a 6-touchdown game against the 49ers. He scored on 4 runs, a pass, and a punt return.

APPLE OF THE ELECTRONIC EYE

His dream was to be a sportswriter, but Alvin Pete Rozelle never realized it. Instead, he went on to write the formula that would turn the National Football League into the greatest sports entity in the nation.

By his admission, he wasn't much of a writer. But he had vision and a keen sense of business. He was public relations director of the Los Angeles Rams, then the club's general manager, but by the dawn of the 1960s, Rozelle was at the forefront of key NFL decisions. He became commissioner in 1960 and pro football was on the fast track, soon surpassing baseball as the nation's most popular sport.

"Before Pete Rozelle," said basketball legend Red Auerbach, who built the Boston Celtics into a sports dynasty, "the National Football League was minor league. He's the guy who brought it to the top. To me, he's the greatest commissioner of all time, in any sport."

Rozelle's ascension coincided with the television boom, but it really was no coincidence. Rozelle saw TV as a necessary vehicle. "Television was ready to explode and pro football was ready to explode," said long-time Dallas Cowboys general manager Tex Schramm, "so the two exploded together. Football went right past baseball, which no one ever would have believed possible."

Two key moves were orchestrated early in Rozelle's reign. In 1961, the NFL commissioner petitioned Congress for antitrust exemption so the NFL could negotiate single-network television contracts, which would allow the league greater access to network television. "It was critical," Rozelle said. "To this point, teams had their individual TV deals in their regions, and some didn't have any at all. It was not balanced. But to get the deal done with Congress, we agreed that we would not televise our games on Fridays and Saturdays during the season when high school and college games were being played. They didn't want us to hurt high schools and colleges and, of course, neither did we."

With Congressional help in hand, Rozelle went to CBS and worked out a two-year, $9.3-million package. On January 10, 1962, the 14 NFL club owners were told the league would split this TV money evenly.

"They were happy," Rozelle said, "but beyond the money the legislation was important. It just didn't make good business sense to have some clubs with TV deals and others without them. It would have destroyed competition and, in my mind, the greatest thing about the NFL is the competition on the field."

"I wouldn't ever set out to hurt anybody deliberately unless it was, you know, important—like a league game or something."

—DICK BUTKUS,
CHICAGO BEARS LINEBACKER

By the margin of a disputed field goal by Don Chandler—did the kick sail wide of the upright?—Green Bay extended the game into overtime. Another field goal by Chandler, after 13:39 of the extra period, secured a 13-10 victory.

One week later, in classic Green Bay weather, the Packers had less difficulty subduing Cleveland 23-12 for the NFL championship. A four-inch morning snowfall was cleared from the field, barely in time for a steady, misting rain that made 33 degrees feel like 15. While Cleveland's Jim Brown, a nifty cut-back runner, struggled to gain his footing and 50 yards, the Packers' power sweep plowed relentlessly through the muck. Paul Hornung gained 105 yards and Jim Taylor had 96.

Some classic coaching strategy highlighted the AFL Championship Game, in which Lou Saban's Bills met Sid Gillman's Chargers. The explosive Chargers had led the AFL in scoring, thanks largely to Lance Alworth, who led the league with 1,602 receiving yards and tied for the league lead with 14 touchdown receptions.

But Saban kept the Chargers off balance by switching defensive fronts and he suffocated Alworth with double-coverage on every play. ("One guy was always knocking me off the line," Alworth said.) The Bills' 23-0 victory secured their second straight AFL title. That was satisfaction enough for Saban, who had grown weary of the pressure. He resigned in the offseason and took a college coaching job at Maryland.

Houston, Do You Read Me?

The battle for college talent had reached a new plateau as the 1966 season approached. So had interest among fans. It was clear the signing wars commanded attention when astronaut Frank Borman, circling the earth aboard Gemini 7, radioed this message back to mission control: "Tell Nobis to sign with the Oilers."

Tommy Nobis, the Outland Trophy winner from Texas, was a can't-miss linebacker prospect whom both the NFL's Falcons and AFL's Oilers had made the number-one overall pick. Prestige was at stake for both leagues.

"I remember I was on campus when a young coed ran up to me and said that one of the astronauts had asked me to sign with the Oilers," Nobis said. "That was one of the most flattering aspects of the whole ordeal. The world was listening to every word those astronauts spoke, and they took time to recognize me. I was proud of that."

For several weeks, the football world orbited around Nobis, with the rival owners dangling six-figure bonus checks—and incentives. The Oilers' Bud Adams, a successful oilman, offered Nobis a Phillips 66 dealership and a herd of registered Hereford cattle. The Falcons' Rankin Smith traveled by private jet to San Antonio, Texas, to whisk Nobis's parents off to Atlanta for a stay in a luxury hotel and a personal tour of the community.

"My family and I weren't used to that kind of treatment," Nobis said. "All of a sudden, we were somebody, and it was because of football."

The Falcons prevailed after Smith conducted a tour of new Atlanta Fulton County Stadium, including a ride in his golf cart to the center of the newly installed field. "Here I was looking up at all these brightly colored seats in a brand-new empty stadium," Nobis said, "and Mr. Smith says to me, 'This is going to be your home for the next few years.' Well, that was my dream. I'd always wanted to play in the NFL."

It was the tip of the iceberg in the signing wars, which soon extended also to veteran players. The shot heard around both leagues came on May 17, when the Giants signed Buffalo kicker Pete Gogolak, pro football's first soccer-style kicker. Gogolak had played out his option, but that didn't make the Bills any less annoyed.

New AFL Commissioner Al Davis, the former Raiders general manager and coach who succeeded Foss, encouraged club owners to retaliate. Soon, the Oilers agreed with 49ers quarterback John Brodie on a five-year contract that called for $750,000 to be paid over 10 years, to take effect after his option year. The Raiders signed the Rams' Roman Gabriel to a four-year contract that included a $100,000 signing bonus. Houston began talk-

THE SIXTIES

YEAR AFTER YEAR

In 1966, the Dallas Cowboys made the playoffs for the first of eight consecutive seasons. After a one-year hiatus in 1974, Dallas ran off a string of nine years in postseason play, a record that still stands. Here are the clubs that have put together the most consecutive playoff seasons:

SEASONS	TEAM	
9	Dallas Cowboys	1975-1983
8	Dallas Cowboys	1966-1973
8	Pittsburgh Steelers	1972-79
8	Los Angeles Rams	1973-1980
8	San Francisco 49ers	1983-1990

Tom Matte, Baltimore's makeshift quarterback in a 1965 playoff game.

201

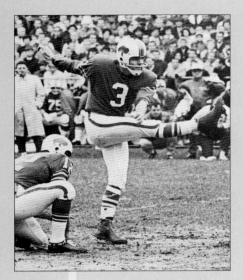

SIDESHOW

Pete Gogolak remembers kicking tryouts during his junior year at Ogdensburg (New York) Free Academy. A couple of his teammates lined up and took their shots, kicking straight-on. What other way was there? Then Gogolak volunteered, unwittingly introducing to his Blue Devils teammates the fine art of soccer-style kicking.

"I'll never forget the expression on the holder's face," he recalled. "He said, 'Either line up straight or you're going to kick me in the butt.'

"But I kicked from the side and hit a low line drive that got about six feet off the ground. It went under the crossbar and everybody started laughing and saying, 'Send this kid back to Europe.' But I knew I had a lot of power."

After playing at Cornell, Gogolak was drafted in the twelfth round by the Buffalo Bills. In 1966, he broke tradition again, becoming the first player to jump from the AFL to the NFL. Having played out his option with the Bills, he signed with the New York Giants.

Gogolak, who escaped Hungary at age 14 during the 1956 uprising, remembered an early bout with culture shock. "When I got to the U.S.," he said "I watched a few American football games and wondered why the kickers came at the ball straight-on. Kicking soccer-style, you can get more of your foot on the ball and hit more surface area."

ing to Mike Ditka, and the Dolphins sounded out Alex Karras. Clearly, competition was turning to madness.

At Last, a Truce

The notion of an NFL-AFL merger had been discussed casually among representatives of the rival leagues for six years. But the first meaningful exchange began in the spring of 1966 when Cowboys general manager Tex Schramm arranged a secret meeting with Chiefs owner Lamar Hunt.

From April 4 through June 7, the two exchanged phone calls, proposals, and counterproposals. Acting on behalf of the commissioner, Schramm sounded out NFL owners—especially those who shared cities with AFL teams. Hunt performed the same duties in the AFL.

On June 8, 1966, after the basic issues had been resolved, the two leagues announced an agreement in which: (1) the nine AFL clubs would pay a total of $18 million (over 20 years) to join the NFL; (2) Rozelle would serve as commissioner; (3) the two leagues would play a world championship game after the 1966 season; (4) existing franchises would remain at present sites; (5) a common draft would be held beginning in January, 1967; (6) two new franchises would be added by 1968, one in each league, but both franchise fees would be paid to the NFL; and (7) interleague preseason games would be played in 1967, and a common schedule would begin in 1970. Players such as Brodie and Gabriel remained with their NFL teams.

A new door opened for pro football just as an old one was about to close. A week before he was scheduled to report to training camp, eight-time NFL rushing leader Jim Brown shocked the sports community by retiring.

Only 30 years old, Brown still was in his prime—he had rushed for 17 touchdowns and 1,544 yards the previous season—but he also was in demand for motion pictures. When faced with suspension by Browns owner Art Modell if he failed to report to training camp on time, Brown said his football farewells from the movie set of *The Dirty Dozen*.

"There is a time for everything," Brown said. "This is my time to turn to other things."

The NFL-AFL merger received Congressional approval on October 21, when an antitrust exemption was added as a rider to an anti-inflation tax bill. President Lyndon Johnson signed the bill into law, and the last legal hurdle had been cleared in preparation for the first "AFL-NFL World Championship Game," later to become known as the Super Bowl.

The Packers represented the NFL, hardly a surprise. A 12-2 record was the club's eighth consecutive winning season under Lombardi. A thrilling 34-27 victory over Dallas in the title game secured Lombardi's fourth league championship.

What the Packers lacked in youth and speed they more than compensated for in skill and savvy. Bart Starr, Lombardi's "push-button" quarterback, threw only 3 interceptions as he led the league in passing. Tackle Forrest Gregg and guard Jerry Kramer gave blocking demonstrations in dismantling defensive lines. Linebacker Ray Nitschke anchored a defense that included Pro Bowl performers such as end Willie Davis, tackle Henry Jordan, cornerback Herb Adderley, and safety Willie Wood. The Packers were a formidable foe, not easily awed.

The Kansas City Chiefs won the AFL title, arriving in Los Angeles for the long-awaited challenge with their own assortment of stories. Quarterback Len Dawson was an NFL castoff who had blossomed with the Chiefs as the AFL passing leader. Running back Mike Garrett, a rookie from USC, had spurned the Rams to play in the AFL. Defensive back Fred (The Hammer) Williamson was known for both big hits and big talk. He promised to devastate Green Bay ball carriers with his bone-crushing tackles.

In a game that proved to be a mismatch—Max McGee made 2 touchdown receptions, and Green Bay runners ground out 3 scores—the play that best symbolized the day came in the fourth quarter when Williamson attempted to tackle Green Bay running back Donny Anderson. Anderson's knee slammed into The Hammer's helmet, knocking the defender unconscious. When linebacker Sherrill Headrick fell on top of the pile, Williamson's arm was broken. As the Chiefs' cornerback, now silent, was carried off the field on a stretcher, Green Bay guard Fred (Fuzzy) Thurston could be heard humming the tune "If I Had a Hammer."

The Super Bowl, as it had been dubbed by the media was super only for the Packers: Green Bay 35, Kansas City 10.

"Make no mistake about it," Hunt said. "We met a superior team."

"I felt like one of the losers at Pompeii. I was overwhelmed by the feeling that there would never be another chance, that there would never be another Super Bowl game or another football season. It was like being on a deathbed. Everything you've accomplished up to that point didn't mean a damn thing."

—CURTIS MCCLINTON, KANSAS CITY CHIEFS RUNNING BACK, AFTER HIS TEAM LOST TO THE PACKERS IN SUPER BOWL I

Quarterbacks, Anyone?

The addition of the New Orleans Saints in 1967 increased the number of NFL clubs to 16, and realignment subdivided the Eastern and Western Conferences into four four-team divisions. But the most interesting changes in both leagues involved playing personnel, in particular, quarterbacks.

In a little-noticed trade with the Buffalo Bills, the AFL's Oakland Raiders acquired the strong right arm that would propel them to Super Bowl II. Oakland gave up quarterback Tom Flores (who later gained fame as the Raiders' head coach), end Art Powell, and two draft choices for end Glenn Bass, a draft choice, and quarterback Daryle Lamonica. Lamonica had been a backup at Buffalo (150 completions in four seasons), but in his first season with Oakland, he led the AFL in passing.

The Raiders also acquired a backup quarterback/kicker, 40-year-old George Blanda, a 17-season veteran who arrived via trade from Houston. Blanda's heroics in pressure-packed situations would become the stuff of legends before he retired—eight seasons later.

The most publicized of all transactions occurred in Minnesota, where

Colts linebacker Mike Curtis and Rams quarterback Roman Gabriel meet violently.

a long-simmering spat between coach Norm Van Brocklin and quarterback Fran Tarkenton ended with both parties leaving the Vikings.

Because coach and quarterback repeatedly were at odds over play calling and execution, Tarkenton announced on February 10 that "under no circumstances" would he play for the Vikings in 1967. One day later, with four years remaining on his contract, Van Brocklin announced his retirement from coaching. Tarkenton's response? "In no way does it affect my decision."

Within a month, Tarkenton had been traded to the Giants for three draft choices, and Bud Grant had been hired to coach the Vikings. Van Brocklin, Tarkenton, and Grant eventually would wind up on the same team—as members of the Pro Football Hall of Fame.

Baltimore's selection of Michigan State defensive end Bubba Smith ushered in the first combined NFL-AFL draft on March 14, but it was a selection made three picks later that produced a greater impact on the pro game. The AFL's Miami Dolphins, entering only their second season, selected Purdue's Bob Griese, a quarterback who would help them to three Super Bowl appearances.

By every statistical measure, the two quarterbacks who owned 1967 were the Jets' Joe Namath in the AFL and the Washington Redskins' Sonny Jurgensen in the NFL. Namath passed for 4,007 yards and 26 touchdowns in helping New York (8-5-1) to its first winning season. Jurgensen set NFL records for completions (288) and passing yards (3,747) as three Washington receivers (Charley Taylor, Bobby Mitchell, and tight end Jerry Smith) ranked among the top four in the league, but a leaky defense doomed the Redskins to a 5-6-3 season.

The Rams and the Colts were the talk of the NFL, each with an 11-1-2 regular-season record, but it was Green Bay that excelled under the glare of the playoff spotlight. The Packers avenged a regular-season loss to Los Angeles with a 28-7 conference-playoff victory, then defeated the Cowboys 21-17 in one of the NFL's most memorable title games.

On the coldest recorded New Year's Eve in Green Bay history—the temperature was minus-13 and the wind chill minus-40—the Packers won the last of Lombardi's five NFL championships. The victory came by the margin of Starr's quarterback sneak with 13 seconds remaining and no time outs left. With the Packers less than a yard from the end zone, Starr had told Lombardi that a sneak would work. "Then do it, and let's get the hell out of here," Lombardi said. Jerry Kramer threw the key block on Jethro Pugh, opening a hole through which the Packers advanced to the Super Bowl.

Super Bowl II offered an intriguing matchup: a veteran Packers team that thrived on defense and fundamentals against the explosive Raiders, who specialized in lighting up scoreboards (no other team in either league matched the 468 points of the 1967 Raiders). But from the time the Packers arrived in Miami, the game was almost secondary to the rumor that preceded it: Vince Lombardi would retire.

> *"You go with the pain because you know you have a job to do. It's going to hurt you but you know your playing can help the team, and you find yourself in there doing what you are supposed to do. As football players, we have something more important to us than our own selves."*
>
> —CARL (SPIDER) LOCKHART,
> NEW YORK GIANTS SAFETY

GOOD POINTS

The wide-open play of the AFL in the 1960s produced an abundance of high-scoring offenses, most notably those of the Houston Oilers and Oakland Raiders. In 1961, the Oilers scored 513 points over a 14-game schedule, a whopping 36.6 points per game. The only team to top that was the 1950 Los Angeles Rams, who averaged 38.8 points over a 12-game NFL schedule. The top 10:

TEAM	YEAR	PTS.	GAMES	AVG.
1. Los Angeles Rams	1950	466	12	38.8
2. Houston Oilers	1961	513	14	36.6
3. Chicago Bears	1941	396	11	36.0
4. Chicago Bears	1942	376	11	34.2
5. Washington Redskins	1983	541	16	33.8
6. Oakland Raiders	1967	468	14	33.4
7. Chicago Cardinals	1948	395	12	32.9
8. Los Angeles Rams	1951	392	12	32.7
9. Oakland Raiders	1968	453	14	32.4
10. Miami Dolphins	1984	513	16	32.1

Rumor became reality for the players when Lombardi addressed them the Thursday before the game, and the gruff disciplinarian had to fight to keep his voice from cracking. "I want to tell you," he said, "...how very proud I am...of all of you." Silence settled over the room.

The 1967 Packers were not Lombardi's best team. Age had eroded the group's athletic edge. But when the players took the field for the last time under Lombardi, there was no question about their motivation. The defense forced 3 turnovers. The offense committed none. The Packers had the ball for 11 minutes more than the Raiders and never trailed. The victory was more lopsided than the 33-14 score.

Lombardi rode into the history books on the shoulders of his players. "This," he said, with a broad grin, "is the best way to leave a football field."

Who Wants the Throne?

The Packers had been such a dominant force under Lombardi—five NFL championships in seven years and two consecutive Super Bowls—that his

Bart Starr's (15) 1-yard plunge with 13 seconds left gave Green Bay a 21-17 win over Dallas in the "Ice Bowl," a game played under a wind-chill factor of minus-40 degrees.

departure from the sidelines created an air of anticipation. Who would claim the NFL throne?

The Cowboys, twice runners-up to Green Bay, seemed logical successors. Riding the arm of Don Meredith, in what would be his last season, along with the sure hands of receivers Lance Rentzel and Bob Hayes, the Cowboys ran off six straight victories en route to a 12-2 season.

The Vikings emerged as surprising contenders behind a defensive line led by tackle Alan Page and ends Carl Eller and Jim Marshall. The "Purple People Eaters" brought Minnesota its first winning season at 8-6—good enough to win the Central Division.

The Browns, who found a successor to Jim Brown in NFL rushing leader Leroy Kelly, and the Cardinals, behind third-year quarterback Jim Hart, engaged in the wackiest of all the division races. The Cardinals won both head-to-head matchups against the Browns, 27-21 and 27-16, but managed only a tie with the 2-11-1 Steelers, and Cleveland took the Century Division title with a 10-4 record to St. Louis's 9-4-1.

In the end, there was little doubt that the NFL's best team was the Baltimore Colts. The Colts lost only to the Browns in a 13-1 season and finished with 10 consecutive victories, including a conference playoff game against Minnesota and a title showdown with Cleveland. The Colts-Browns rematch was no match as Baltimore romped 34-0.

The Colts were worthy successors to the Packers. They posted four shutouts, going 15-1 (counting playoffs), and defeated opponents by an average score of 29-10. Not even an injury to all-pro quarterback Johnny Unitas slowed them down. Veteran backup Earl Morrall led the league in passing with 2,909 yards and 26 touchdowns.

The AFL hardly had changed in a year—with one notable exception. Legendary coach Paul Brown breathed life into the league's newest franchise when he returned to football as coach and part owner of the Cincinnati Bengals. It hardly mattered that the Bengals finished last in the Western Division at 3-11. Just two years later, they would be division champions.

The AFL powers were familiar, especially in the West, where the Chiefs and Raiders were oil and water, bitter rivals with contrasting strengths. Led by future Hall of Fame players Buck Buchanan (defensive tackle) and Bobby Bell (linebacker), the Chiefs were a defensive force that allowed a league-low 170 points in a 12-2 season. The Raiders featured a high-powered offense, with Lamonica hurling rainbows to Fred Biletnikoff and Warren Wells, in a season that produced a league-high 453 points and an identical 12-2 mark.

When the Raiders blasted the Chiefs 41-6 in a playoff for the Western Division crown, it was widely assumed that they could make Super Bowl reservations. The assumption was wrong.

Six weeks earlier, the Raiders had rallied furiously to defeat the New York Jets 43-32. The game made headlines when the decisive final two minutes were preempted by the NBC tele-

Opposite: **The Jets' Joe Namath unloads a pass despite heavy pressure from Raiders defensive end Ben Davidson.**

"The only perfect man who ever lived had a beard and long hair and didn't wear shoes and slept in barns and didn't hold a regular job and never put on a tie. I'm not comparing myself to Him—I'm in enough trouble trying to stack up against Bart Starr—but I'm just saying that you don't judge a man by the way he cuts his hair."

—JOE NAMATH,
NEW YORK JETS QUARTERBACK

The Vikings' "Purple People Eaters" rise up to block a kick attempt.

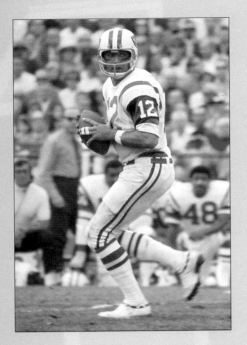

New 16, Old 7

It was January, 1969, and Western society was in upheaval. So naturally, millions turned on (their TV sets, of course), tuned in, and although they didn't exactly drop out, they did get to see a condensed version of the past decade.

New York Jets quarterback Joe Namath may not have been a bead-wearing flower child, but he was the closest thing pro football had to an alternative lifestyle in high profile. Broadway Joe closed out the 1968 season by telling a banquet audience that the Jets would beat the heavily favored Baltimore Colts in Super Bowl III, adding, "I guarantee it." When Namath and the Jets won 16-7, the NFL's sixties time capsule received its most telling entry.

Wide receiver Don Maynard recalled the mood among his teammates: "During the week, we watched a film of Baltimore versus Cleveland. [Tight end] Pete Lammons said to [head coach] Weeb [Ewbank], 'If you don't stop showing us this film, we're going to get cocky.'

So it wasn't just Joe who guaranteed it.

Some would argue that Matt Snell's running (121 yards) set up Namath in the game, others that Namath's passing opened up the running lanes. Sort of an old-school theory versus a free-wheeling interpretation, no? Sort of like the sixties.

cast of "Heidi," a made-for-television movie. But the 11-3 Jets, who had won the Eastern Division by four games, were well rested and playing at home. They had forgotten all about the "Heidi" game.

With a little more than two minutes left in a thrilling shootout that would see Namath pass for 3 touchdowns and Lamonica for 401 yards, the Raiders trailed by only 4 points and had a first down on the Jets' 24-yard line. It was a day when Biletnikoff would haul in 7 passes for 190 yards. But Lamonica chose this play to throw a swing pass to rookie running back Charlie Smith, who hadn't had a reception all day.

As soon as Lamonica released the ball, he knew it was a lateral, not a forward pass. "It was the kind of pass you'd like to pull back," he said.

The pass sailed wildly behind Smith, who made no effort to cover the ball. "I thought it was a forward pass," he said.

Jets linebacker Ralph Baker made the recovery, and the Jets' 27-23 victory had been saved. By that slim margin, New York advanced to Super Bowl III …and a date with destiny.

When Joe Namath brashly promised—and delivered—a stunning 16-7 victory over the heavily favored Baltimore Colts in a game that officially became known as the Super Bowl, the stature of the AFL suddenly rivaled the older league. The Super Bowl, a mismatch in its first two years, never would be the same.

One irony of the moment went largely unnoticed: Sonny Werblin, who had spent more than $400,000 to sign Namath four years before, was not a part of the celebration. He had sold his interest in the team before the season.

Out With the Old

In the new order of pro football in 1969, the operative word was "change." New stars emerged, coaches moved, and the balance of power was rearranged.

Vince Lombardi, out of coaching since Super Bowl II, stepped down as Packers general manager to join the Washington Redskins in a busy role: part-owner, executive vice president, and head coach. In his last autumn in football, he directed the Redskins to their first winning record (7-5-2) in 14 seasons. He died of cancer the next year.

John Rauch, head coach of the AFL runner-up Raiders, suddenly left to coach the Buffalo Bills—and just as suddenly discovered the limits of his magic in a 4-10 year. A little-known Raiders assistant, affable linebackers coach John Madden, continued where Rauch had left off with a 12-1-1 season.

A personality clash with owner Dan Reeves led to the firing of Rams coach George Allen. After the players protested, however, Reeves reversed his decision. The Rams went on to win a division title with an 11-3 record.

A caustic headline proclaimed the arrival of a new coach in Pittsburgh, where the Steelers were coming off a 2-11-1 season: "Noll to Coach Pittsburgh Losers." Chuck Noll's name would re-emerge in subsequent years when his "losers" would win four Super Bowls in six years.

Pro football's life cycle was in full spin, new names replacing old. Quarterback Don Meredith retired in Dallas, and Roger Staubach, fresh from naval duty, arrived there. Number-one draft choice O.J. Simpson joined the

Buffalo Bills on August 9, the same day Redskins owner and founder George Preston Marshall died.

By pro football's typically staid standards, it was an evolutionary time. In preparation for the merger, NFL and AFL club owners met to hammer out a realignment plan. After 36 hours behind closed doors, they announced the creation of two 13-team conferences. Three NFL teams—the Steelers, Colts, and Browns—would join the AFL clubs in the American Conference, and the remaining NFL clubs would compose the National Conference.

The last season of the old NFL-AFL format produced the fourth different world championship pairing: the Kansas City Chiefs against the Minnesota Vikings in Super Bow IV.

If a 12-2 season by the Vikings was a surprise, it was less so than the Super Bowl appearance by the 11-3 Chiefs, who finished only second best in their own division.

In order to equalize the length of NFL and AFL postseasons, a special provision in 1969 created an extra playoff round in the AFL. Under a crossover format, first-place finishers in East and West faced second-place finishers in the opposite division, with winners advancing to the title game. After beating the Eastern Division-champion Jets 13-6, the Chiefs scored a 17-7 victory over Oakland, the team that had topped them in the Western Division. The Chiefs, it might be said, arrived at Super Bowl IV through a side door.

Almost immediately, the spotlight glared on Chiefs quarterback Len Dawson, whose name suddenly—and erroneously—had been linked with gambling figures under federal investigation. Rumor and innuendo accompanied Dawson throughout his stay in New Orleans.

"It was, beyond a doubt, the toughest week of my life," Dawson said. "I don't know what the public would have thought if I'd had a really bad game. What if I had fumbled or thrown an interception with the game on the line?"

No one ever will know. The Chiefs rolled over the Vikings, grinding out a 16-0 halftime lead as Jan Stenerud made 3 field goals and Mike Garrett scored on a 5-yard run. When the Vikings later narrowed the margin to 16-7, the Chiefs struck on a short hitch pass that Otis Taylor turned into a 46-yard touchdown that broke open the game.

Dawson was named the game's most valuable player in a 23-7 victory. Chiefs head coach Hank Stram, a loser in Super Bowl I, beamed an ear-to-ear grin. And the NFL-AFL wars ended in a stalemate, two Super Bowls apiece, as the two leagues prepared to become one.

With the merger approaching, Len Dawson and the Kansas City Chiefs put the AFL on equal footing with a 23-7 victory over Minnesota in Super Bowl IV.

ONE MAN'S WORD

The United States, you may recall, was spinning in circles at about the time the Green Bay Packers came to power. We were undergoing social revolution, and it was painful.

Someone assassinated a President, and the Packers produced the most inspiring and domineering leader the game has seen. The Vietnam War divided us, and nowhere in football have we seen the teamwork we saw on those Packers (teamwork Richard Nixon often acknowledged in speeches and personal calls to the team). Crewcuts met longhairs in the philosophical clash of the century, and the Packers—black ones, white ones, religious ones, agnostic ones—united to be the most dominant team we ever saw.

It was a strange time, and an incredible team.

When the all-pro squad of the sixties was named by the Pro Football Hall of Fame, the Packers accomplished something that no other team from any other decade in NFL history ever had, and none has done since. They put at least one player from every position group on the squad. (Most, but not all, of those players were selected to the combined AFL-NFL '60s team.)

Receiver: Boyd Dowler; offensive line: Forrest Gregg, Jerry Kramer, Jim Ringo; quarterback: Bart Starr; running back: Paul Hornung, Jim Taylor; defensive line: Willie Davis; linebacker: Ray Nitschke, Dave Robinson; cornerback: Herb Adderley; safety: Willie Wood; special teams: Don Chandler (punter).

Here's the most interesting thing about it: The personnel of the Packers didn't change in a wholesale way from 1958, when they went 1-10-1 and allowed an NFL-worst 32 points per game, to 1961, when they won the first of five titles in seven years. Fourteen of the twenty-two starters in 1961 were on that dismal team in 1958. Which means we simply have to shake our heads in reverence for the job the new coach in 1959, Vince Lombardi, did with his team. During a period in America when up was down, he was the steely leader no one could knock.

Lombardi's locker-room sayings have been adopted by a whole generation of coaches. If summer practice got a little shoddy, he'd yell: "Fatigue makes cowards of us all."

If he saw a player take a conditioning short cut, he'd prod him with: "The harder you work, the harder it is to surrender."

When the Packers were on a roll, he'd preach: "Confidence is contagious. So is lack of confidence."

Lombardi never said, "Winning isn't everything—it's the only thing," which still, 24 years after he died of cancer, gets his memory skewered. He said: "Winning isn't everything. Trying to win is."

In essence, that is everything Lombardi was about.

To understand why so many button-down Americans loved the man, one only had to hear one of his speeches. He didn't give many of them, but the ones he delivered were keepers. And his words live on.

In 1967, he said this to the American Management Association in Manhattan: "Football is a symbol, I think, of this country's greatest attributes—namely, courage, stamina, and coordinated efficiency. It requires Spartanlike qualities to play.

"It's a game very much like life in that it demands that a man's personal commitment must be to excellence and to victory, and yet complete victory can never be completely won. Yet it must be pursued, it must be wooed with all of one's might. Each week there is a new encounter, each year there is a new challenge. The spirit, the will to excel, the will to win—they endure, they last forever."

Can't you see Old Glory waving in the breeze? Football, hot dogs, and apple pie?

One more point about this speech: Lombardi also gave these management guys his secret to leadership success. "Man responds to leadership in a most remarkable way," he said, "and once you have won his heart, he will follow you anywhere. Leadership is based on a spiritual quality, the power to inspire others to follow."

It was this sort of blind devotion that allowed the Packers to come back and win games they had no business winning, that helped them become the only team in the last 60 years to win three consecutive NFL championships.

The third title might have been the toughest. In the famous Ice Bowl—the 1967 NFL Championship Game against Dallas, in minus-13-degree cold at Green Bay—Dan Reeves threw a 50-yard halfback option pass for a touchdown to give the Cowboys a 17-14 lead in the fourth quarter. With 5:04 to play, the Packers took the ball at their 32-yard line, needing a field goal to send the game into overtime and, of course, a touchdown to win.

Two days before the game, Lombardi had told his players how he really felt about them. Some of them were beginning to think this might be the old man's last season with the team, that the pressure of winning and winning, and then winning more impressively than ever, had gotten to him. And when he spoke on the Friday before the game, they began to be convinced that this was it.

"Lots of better ball players than you have gone through here," Lombardi told them. "But you're the type of ball players I want. You've got character. You've got heart. You've got guts."

Even the players who grew to loathe the training camps and the practices and the brutal way Lombardi ripped into them had a deep and abiding respect for the way he got them to play at their best when times were toughest.

The Packers drove down the field, struggling to within two feet of the goal line with 16 seconds remaining. This was

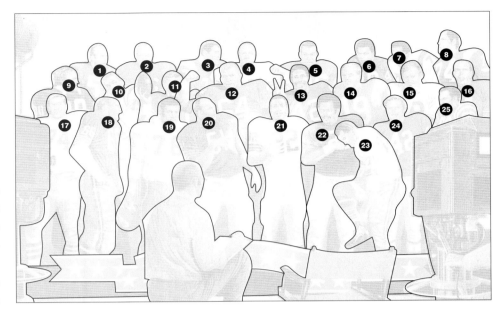

1) Paul Hornung, halfback; 2) Billy Shaw, guard; 3) Ron Mix, tackle; 4) Willie Davis, defensive end; 5) Herb Adderley, cornerback; 6) Gale Sayers, halfback; 7) Deacon Jones, defensive end; 8) Merlin Olsen, defensive tackle; 9) Jim Otto, center; 10) John Unitas, quarterback; 11) Jim Bakken, kicker; 12) Jerry Kramer, guard; 13) Charley Taylor, wide receiver; 14) Lance Alworth, wide receiver; 15) Larry Wilson, safety; 16) Don Chandler, punter; 17) Bob Lilly, defensive tackle; 18) Ray Nitschke, linebacker; 19) Bobby Bell, linebacker; 20) Dick Butkus, linebacker; 21) Jim Brown, fullback; 22) Willie Brown, cornerback; 23) Forrest Gregg, tackle; 24) Johnny Robinson, safety; 25) John Mackey, tight end.

going to be either the trademark drive of the Lombardi Era, or the most bitter end to a game Lombardi ever coached. It was third down. Green Bay called its final time out.

The safe call would have been a riskless pass into the end zone, because an incompletion still would allow the Packers a chip-shot field goal and an invitation to overtime against the offensively struggling, ice-cubed Cowboys. If Lombardi called a run, the Packers might get only one play. Lombardi said later he couldn't bear to think of the fans sitting through an overtime period at Lambeau Field, it was so sickeningly cold.

"I can sneak it in," Starr told Lombardi on the sidelines.

Lombardi said okay.

Starr saw an opening behind Kramer, the right guard, when he got to the line of scrimmage. So he burrowed behind

Kramer for about 25 inches and landed on the tundra just beyond the white stripe of the goal line.

Perfect. A dive play. Brute force. Guts. Lose if you fail, win if you make it. The Packers won. Two weeks later, they won their second straight Super Bowl, and soon after that, Lombardi, a true burnout victim, left the coaching wars. He had a brief comeback, with Washington in 1969, before a fast-moving cancer conquered him in 1970.

The legacy of the man and the team haven't died. In the years since, we thought the Dolphins, the Steelers, and the 49ers were dominant teams. They were, but none of them could win three in a row.

That is why the Packers, with society's turbulence all around them, are such an admirable group of men in retrospect—and why their leader is such a legend.

What better way to kick off the two-hundredth anniversary of the United States than to have representatives of football conferences called American and National meet to decide the championship of the NFL? After all, hadn't the Super Bowl, by January of 1976, become America's most cherished secular holiday?

The AFC's Pittsburgh Steelers and the NFC's Dallas Cowboys were fine standard-bearers, too. Pittsburgh was the defending champion and had finished in a tie for the NFL's best record (12-2) in 1975. Dallas hadn't had a losing record in a decade. The only problem with these two particular teams wearing Bicentennial patches and serving as examples of national unity was that they, well…they pretty much hated each other.

Tom Landry's Cowboys treated football like an academic discipline. Their massive playbook required attention to detail and submission to authority. The Flex defense. The Shotgun formation. They were the "well-oiled machine." To the Steelers, they were a troupe of tricksters who were afraid to play like men.

Chuck Noll's Steelers, by comparison, were as rough and sturdy as the hills of western Pennsylvania. Everything about them spoke of wrought-iron toughness. Defensive tackle Ernie Holmes cropped his hair in the shape of an arrow. The scary part was, so did his girlfriend.

To their fans, the Steelers were throwbacks to a simpler, more honorable age. To the Cowboys, they were thugs.

"Our teachings [for playing] the Cowboys were to hit 'em, and hit 'em, and hit 'em," said Pittsburgh quarterback Terry Bradshaw. "And our offensive approach was simple. Chuck would say, 'Don't worry about high-percentage completions because you're not going to have 'em against this team. But you can beat 'em deep.'"

Surprisingly, it was the Cowboys who tried to plant the seeds of intimidation before Super Bowl X. Lynn Swann, the Steelers' acrobatic wide receiver, had gone to the hospital with a concussion suffered against the Raiders in the AFC Championship Game. Dallas safety Cliff Harris wanted the injury to be the one thing that Swann did not forget.

"Getting hit really hard again has to be in the back of his mind," Harris told reporters during Super Bowl week.

"He can't scare me," Swann responded. "I'm playing."

"It suddenly became very emotional," Cowboys safety Charlie Waters said. "By game time, we were feeling pretty ornery."

The Cowboys got the first big break of the game when Steelers punter Bobby Walden muffed a center snap and was swamped at Pittsburgh's 29-yard line. Moments later, a pass from Roger Staubach to his favorite receiver, Drew Pearson, gave Dallas a 7-0 lead.

"We're getting it taken to us," linebacker Jack Lambert roared on the sidelines. "We're supposed to be the tough guys. We'd better damn well start playing like it."

The Steelers soon tied the game at 7-7. The key play on the drive was a long pass by Bradshaw. The throw went into tight coverage, but Swann, dispelling all doubt about his condition, made a fine, leaping catch along the sideline for a 32-yard gain.

The Steelers, however, wouldn't score for another 40 minutes. The Flex seemed to confuse them. Of course, Dallas was having similar problems moving against the Steelers. "They had the big defensive

enties

Lynn Swann's acrobatics were the difference in the heated confrontation of Super Bowl X.

cornerbacks, [J.T.] Thomas and [Mel] Blount," Staubach said. "They just would not let you get downfield."

Toni Fritsch's second-quarter field goal gave the Cowboys a 10-7 lead, and that's how it stood going into the fourth quarter.

The next turning point belonged to Pittsburgh. Reggie Harrison, as unlikely a Super Bowl hero as you'll ever find, blew past Cowboys blockers to block a punt—with his face. The ball bounded out of the end zone for a safety and shaved the Dallas lead to 10-9.

"That was a shocker," Bradshaw said. "And in a game that was so even, it would take something like that."

The Steelers quickly tacked on 2 field goals to post a 15-10 lead. Facing third-and-4 with a little more than three minutes left, they went for broke. Bradshaw called a deep post to Swann. The Cowboys sent an all-out blitz. Bradshaw eluded linebacker D.D. Lewis, fired the ball downfield, and was decked by defensive tackle Larry Cole. He never saw Swann's third fabulous

catch. (Swann had made an uncanny, floating reception in the third quarter.)

While the receiver was beating single coverage on a 64-yard touchdown pass play that sent the Steelers ahead 21-10, the quarterback lay spread out on the turf of the Orange Bowl in Miami.

"Man, I don't remember anything [about the end of the game]," Bradshaw said. "I mean, not a thing. The only thing I remember is waking up in the locker room. My family was around me, and the locker room was pretty much cleared out. And I had a headache like you wouldn't believe."

The rest of us watching at the time, many

of us sprawled out on beanbag chairs, sipping Tabs, never will forget the play. Or the Cowboys' frantic comeback effort that cut the lead to 21-17 with 1:48 left, on a pass from Staubach to Percy Howard. Or safety Glen Edwards's end-zone interception on the last play of the game.

The Steelers were Super Bowl champions for a second time—and it wouldn't be the last. In the locker room afterward, Noll was asked if his team was shaping up as an NFL dynasty. "I leave those judgments to the historians," he said.

Historians rarely are afforded such easy judgments.

A BULLY LOITERING ON EVERY CORNER

very player who ever got his uniform dirty on an NFL field likes to think his era represented the high-water mark of pro football, and most can present the when-men-were-men arguments to make their case.

Of course, if that player's era was the 1970s, he just might be right. The same decade that brought you the Ford Pinto and Three Mile Island and *Saturday Night Fever* also gave you great pro football.

When a committee assembled in 1988 by the Pro Football Hall of Fame chose the top 40 games in NFL history, 14 of those games were selected from the seventies, more than any other decade. When the Seventy-Fifth Anniversary Selection Committee voted on the all-time NFL team for this book, 29 of the 48 players chosen were active for some part of the '70s, another best.

Clearly, there was an abundance of great games and great players during the decade. Even more than that, there were great teams. Every decade has had a dominant team, or two or three, but the seventies had a bully loitering on every corner. Pick an NFL division in the '70s and you've got a team of lasting success.

The AFC East had the Miami Dolphins, the AFC Central had the Pittsburgh Steelers, and the AFC West had the Oakland Raiders. In the NFC, the Dallas Cowboys owned the East, the Minnesota Vikings the Central, and the Los Angeles Rams the West.

How strong were these teams? The Steelers, victors in an unprecedented four Super Bowls, were 99-44-1 in the decade. Yet, their winning percentage, .691, ranked below each of the other five teams. (The leader was Dallas, at .729, with a record of 105-39.) Miami won 5 of 10 division titles, and that was the *worst* showing of the six teams. Minnesota took 8 of 10.

Miami Dolphins fullback Larry Csonka (opposite) turns upfield. The 1970s were a decade of straight-ahead running, imposing defense...and great teams.

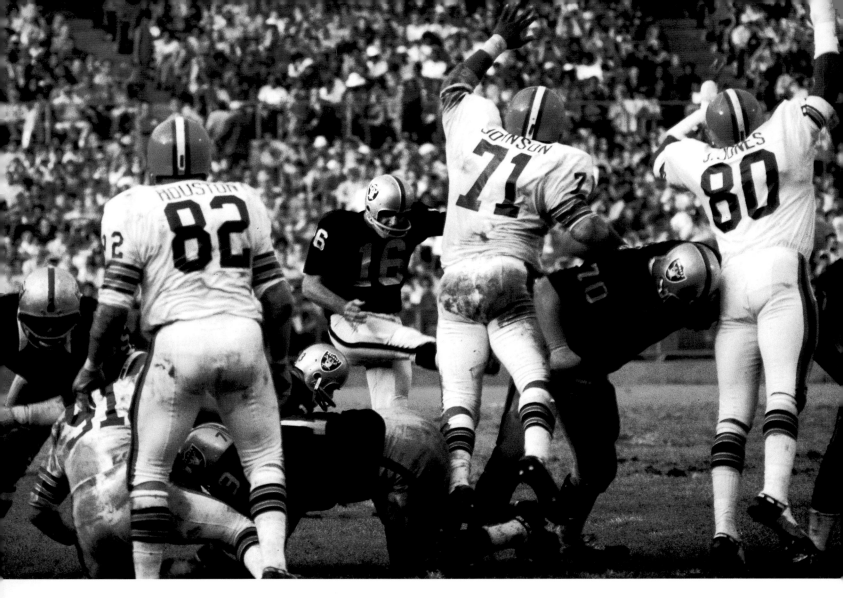

George Blanda's 52-yard field goal puts away Cleveland with three seconds left. Blanda, the Oakland Raiders' 43-year-old wonder, had a miraculous string of late-game heroics, both kicking and quarterbacking, in 1970.

It's not that other clubs had nothing to brag about during the decade. It's just that when you discuss the NFL of the 1970s, you can't wander too far without bumping into one of the Big Six.

Behind Closed Doors

When the final gun sounded at Super Bowl IV in January, 1970, it might as well have fired a bullet, for it put to rest a bold idea called the American Football League. The merger of America's two major football leagues announced four years earlier, now was put into effect.

Of course, a few knots had yet to be loosened. The NFL of 1969 had 16 teams, the AFL only 10. If the redefined NFL was to be balanced, three old NFL teams would have to join the newly created American Football Conference. Not surprisingly, clubs didn't exactly elbow one another in their haste to volunteer.

At a meeting in mid-May, 1969, Commissioner Pete Rozelle sent NFL owners behind closed doors for a marathon bargaining session that lasted 35 hours and 45 minutes.

"Those rooms were something to behold," Cincinnati Bengals owner Paul Brown wrote in his autobiography. "People slept on chairs and on the floor, no one shaved, collars rumpled, ties went askew or were discarded altogether, and tempers got shorter as each exhausting hour passed....My most vivid memory of that time was of [Kansas City Chiefs owner] Lamar Hunt sleeping on the hallway couch—a white flower across his chest that someone had placed there."

Finally, the Baltimore Colts, the Pittsburgh Steelers, and the Cleveland Browns—three franchises with a combined 74 years of NFL experience—agreed to jump to the AFC ship, for a tidy relocation fee of $3 million each. Next, the NFL was divided into six divisions (three in each conference).

Head coach Don Shula was moving to the AFC, but it wouldn't be with the Colts, the club he had guided to a 73-26-4 record in seven years. He was hired by the Miami Dolphins, who had struggled through a 3-10-1 season in 1969. Shula, however, did not go quietly.

Colts owner Carroll Rosenbloom had been out of the country when Shula asked permission to talk with the Dolphins. Shula received that permission from Steve Rosenbloom, administrative aide and owner's son, and when Carroll got back in the United States, he was livid.

The bombastic owner charged deceit and conspiracy, and his persistence was rewarded with Miami's first-round draft choice in 1971, which turned out to be running back Don McCauley. In the long run, the Dolphins would be happy with their end of the transaction.

"Our relationship came apart because of our loss to the Jets in the Super Bowl [III]," Shula said. "He [Rosenbloom] really took it hard. He lived in New York and took a lot of heat—and he passed it along to me."

Chicago Bears running back Brian Piccolo, in his prime at 26, died in June. His battle with cancer was described in Gale Sayers's book, *I Am Third,* and later turned into a movie, *Brian's Song,* at which even grown men are known to cry. The losses mounted as two legendary coaches, Vince Lombardi and Jimmy Conzelman, died in late summer. Conzelman, a pioneer of the game, was 72. But Lombardi was only 57, and his premature fall to cancer left a void not only in the hierarchy of the Washington Redskins, the team he had coached and presided over in 1969, but in the NFL's very identity.

Toward the end, Lombardi was fairly disgusted with all of the league's players. They threatened a strike until early August of 1970, when the Players Association and the owners signed a four-year agreement.

The most talked-about development of the 1970 season was the birth of "Monday Night Football." Even ABC must have been stunned by the popularity of its new week-night ritual, which in its inaugural season featured commentary by Howard Cosell and Don Meredith and play-by-play by Keith Jackson. (Jackson would be replaced by Frank Gifford a year later.) Its popularity would continue to grow through the years.

One memorable game that was not on "Monday Night Football" was a slow-paced affair pitting the Lions and the lowly Saints. New Orleans would win only two games all year, and this one required a superhuman 63-yard field goal by Tom Dempsey on the last play of the game. The kick by Dempsey, who wore a specially fitted half-shoe on his congenitally deformed kicking foot, still stands as the longest in NFL history.

ON ANY GIVEN MONDAY

For the record, the Browns beat the New York Jets 31-21 before 85,703 fans at Cleveland's Municipal Stadium on September 21, 1970. That was the regular-season debut of "Monday Night Football," ABC's popular series that has lasted a generation and become a national institution. Among prime-time shows, in fact, only "Walt Disney" and "60 Minutes" have enjoyed longer runs than "Monday Night Football."

Longest-running Prime-Time Series in TV History

PROGRAM	NETWORK	YEARS
Walt Disney	ABC, NBC, CBS	29 (1954-1982)
60 Minutes	CBS	27 (1968-current)
NFL Monday Night Football	ABC	25 (1970-current)
Ed Sullivan	CBS	24 (1948-1971)
Gunsmoke	CBS	20 (1955-1975)
Red Skelton	NBC, CBS	20 (1951-1971)

ABC's "Monday Night Football" crew of Don Meredith, Howard Cosell, and Frank Gifford, who replaced Keith Jackson.

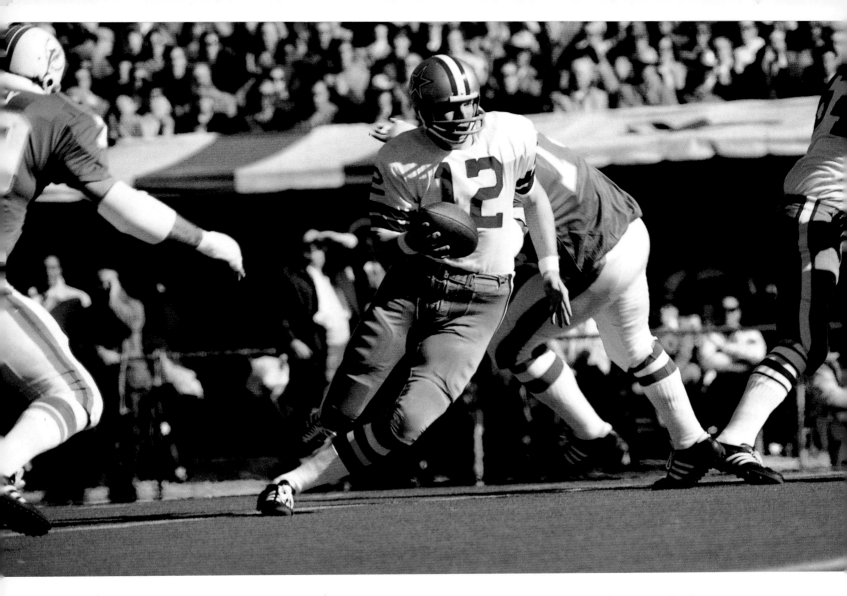

Agile, brainy quarterback Roger Staubach directed Dallas to a convincing 24-3 victory over the young Miami Dolphins in Super Bowl VI.

"If a nuclear bomb ever dropped on this country, the only things I'm certain will survive are AstroTurf and Don Shula."

—BUBBA SMITH,
LONG-TIME NFL DEFENSIVE END

safety Charlie Waters and cornerback Mark Washington, signing anonymous free-agent safety Cliff Harris from tiny Ouachita Baptist College, and trading for respected Green Bay Packers cornerback Herb Adderley.

The early portion of Dallas's '71 season, however, was consumed by a quarterback quandary. Incumbent Craig Morton was being pushed by Roger Staubach, the former Navy star who, at 29, felt he was running out of time to be a full-time starter.

"Patience isn't one of my overwhelming qualities," Staubach said. "Tom [Landry], as good a coach as he was—and I think he's the best—didn't yet understand the importance of leadership at quarterback. We were losing a lot of continuity and players were taking sides. So I was frustrated. The team was floundering. Whether it was me or Morton, we needed to have one leader."

After alternating his quarterbacks—in one game they switched after each offensive play—Landry chose Staubach, who led the NFC in passing and helped the Cowboys score an NFL-high 406 points. Dallas, which also boasted a powerful ground game and a defense that went 23 quarters without yielding a touchdown, won its last seven regular-season games to finish 11-3, then defeated Minnesota and San Francisco in the postseason.

The Longest Christmas

In the AFC playoffs, Miami and Kansas City met on Christmas Day and presented the viewers with a nicely wrapped package: an 82-minute,

DEFENSIVE POSTURE

Kansas City coach Hank Stram's "Football of the '70s" concept, triggered by his 23-7 victory over Minnesota in Super Bowl IV in January, 1970, made its mark, all right—but not the way Stram expected it. It was his defense that really took hold—the odd four-man line, with a tackle stationed over the nose, the stacked linebackers—plus the idea of a soccer-style kicker, such as Jan Stenerud.

according to Redskins head coach George Allen. In 1973, New England coach Chuck Fairbanks introduced the 3-4 defense to combat the run.

Because pro football had become a running game by the 1970s. Quarterbacks were drafted 1-2-3 in 1971: Jim Plunkett, Archie Manning, and Dan Pastorini. They reported to terrible teams and proceeded to get hammered. Meanwhile,

In 1973, more field goals were attempted per game than in any other year in history. The rules people had the answer in 1974: They moved the goal posts back 10 yards, from the goal line to the end line, and the onslaught subsided.

Pittsburgh won four Super Bowls, and there was no offensive counterpart to the type of players the Steelers put on the field, defensive ends such as Dwight White and L.C. Greenwood, who could run 40 yards in the 4.7- to 4.8-second range, and massive, cat-quick tackles such as Joe Greene and Ernie Holmes. There was no one on offense to handle the linebackers with 4.5-to-4.6 speed who were appearing everywhere.

The running game still was getting its yards, but so what? Defensive line coaches such as Floyd Peters, who built the Gold Rush in San Francisco and the Silver Rush at Detroit, had one philosophy: Rush upfield. Go after the passer and pick up the run on the go. And the athletes were good enough to pull it off.

There had been a few offensive innovations, such as Don Coryell's two-tight end, one-back set at St. Louis, but the wide-open passing attacks of the past were gone. And attendance was falling off. The league set a per-game high in 1973—and didn't top it for seven years. So the rules makers stepped in again.

In 1977, the defensive lineman's head-slap was outlawed and only one bump was allowed on a receiver. It hardly made a dent. Scoring was the lowest it had been since 1942, offensive touchdowns the lowest since 1938.

In 1978, 5-yard bump zones were established, and offensive linemen were given undreamed-of freedom, allowing open hands and extended arms on pass blocks.

For two years, passing and scoring numbers inched up sluggishly. It was as if the coaches couldn't really believe what they had. It would take the decade of the 1980s to get the ball fully inflated again.

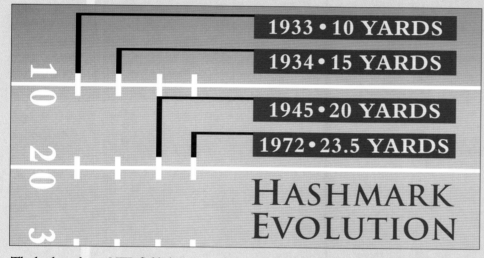

1933 • 10 YARDS
1934 • 15 YARDS
1945 • 20 YARDS
1972 • 23.5 YARDS

HASHMARK EVOLUTION

The hashmarks on NFL fields have moved three times since they were established in 1933.

Stram's offense, with its mobile quarterback and moving pocket? Forget it. The Chiefs finished next-to-last in the AFC in total offense the season following Super Bowl IV, and statistics in general plummeted throughout the NFL—fewest points and yards per game since 1946, fewest offensive touchdowns since 1938. It was the springboard to an era of defense.

It was a time of great front fours with catchy nicknames: Doomsday in Dallas, the Purple People Eaters in Minnesota, the Steel Curtain in Pittsburgh. Most of the innovative thinking was on defense. In 1971, the Oakland Raiders drafted Jack Tatum in the first round and introduced the concept of the "killer free safety," a ferocious hitter who would stake out a territory and knock any receiver stiff who ventured into it. Dallas had the NFC's counterpart in Cliff Harris, "a rolling ball of butcher knives,"

rookie first-round runners such as the Jets' John Riggins and Green Bay's John Brockington were making names for themselves. In 1971 NFL teams called the most running plays per game in 11 years, and threw the fewest passes in 12. Bring in the hashmarks, the rules makers said. Give 'em more room to throw.

It worked in reverse. The move just boosted the running game even higher. Rushing statistics went up in 1972, passing statistics down. For the first time in history, 10 NFL runners gained more than 1,000 yards. Two of them belonged to the Miami Dolphins, who built an unbeaten season and a Super Bowl victory with an ungodly run-pass overload. They had 52 runs to 10 passes against Buffalo and 52-16 against Baltimore.

The soccer-style kickers, working on fields that were going from grass to synthetic, were also putting up big numbers.

40-second war of attrition—the longest game in NFL history. Running back Ed Podolak had 350 all-purpose yards for the Chiefs, but it wasn't enough. Garo Yepremian won the game for the Dolphins 27-24 with a 37-yard field goal midway through the second overtime.

"I really thought that team was our best team," said Kansas City coach Hank Stram, expressing his frustration over the outcome.

Stram shook his head while remembering one particular play. Doing his homework, he had noticed the Dolphins' proficiency at blocking kicks. If the attempt was from a hashmark, they usually overloaded the line on the short side. So the Chiefs added sweeps to their playbook, with the ball snapped directly to kicker Jan Stenerud and guards Ed Budde and Mo Moorman out in front.

"So we're on a hashmark, and we're all excited," Stram remembered. "It's perfect. So Lenny [Dawson, quarterback and holder] calls, 'two-two.' That means the ball's coming to Jan—and nobody knew how fast Jan was, especially with somebody chasing him. He ran about four-five, four-six [for 40 yards].

"So Jan is doing such a good job of acting that Bobby Bell, as he looks through his legs, sees Jan looking down at the spot. He thought he blew the automatic. So he snaps the ball to Dawson, who is totally surprised.

"Both guards pulled on the play. They're standing out to the right side, about ten yards downfield, looking back to see where Stenerud is. He would have gone right in for the touchdown. That would have put us up seventeen-nothing in the first quarter."

As it was, the Dolphins advanced to Super Bowl VI in New Orleans,

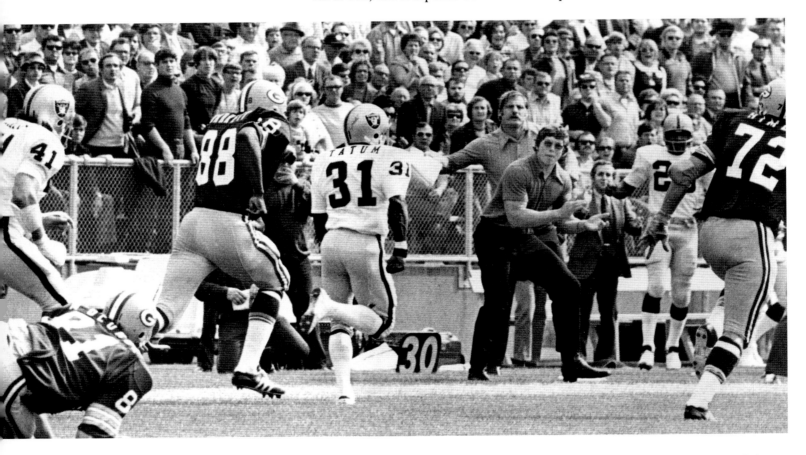

The Raiders' Jack Tatum scooped up a Green Bay fumble in the end zone and raced 104 yards for a record-setting touchdown.

where they got a little free advice from President Nixon. "I think you can hit [wide receiver Paul] Warfield on that down-and-in pattern," he told Coach Shula.

But Dallas, after years of finishing as runner-up, was too much for Shula's young team. The Cowboys played a near-flawless game and breezed to a 24-3 victory. No Super Bowl team has scored fewer points than the Dolphins in VI. "It was just the successful conclusion of our twelve-year plan," Cowboys owner Clint Murchison deadpanned.

Back Attack

The trade winds were blowing in the summer of 1972. The Giants sent quarterback Fran Tarkenton to the Minnesota Vikings—with whom he had gotten his NFL start in 1961—after a five-year stint in New York; the Houston Oilers shipped quarterback Charley Johnson to the Denver Broncos; and Dallas finally tired of pouty star Duane Thomas and unloaded him on San Diego.

Early in the season, two of the game's best-known quarterbacks, the Jets' Namath and Baltimore's Johnny Unitas, engaged in an old-fashioned shootout. Unitas passed for 376 yards; Namath was even better armed, passing for 496 yards and 6 touchdowns on just 15 completions in the Jets' 44-34 victory. Later that season, Namath's favorite target, Don Maynard, became the NFL's all-time leading receiver when he eclipsed ex-Colt Raymond Berry's 631 catches.

Sometime in between the Jets' feats, Raiders safety Jack Tatum scooped up a fumble by Green Bay's MacArthur Lane in the Oakland end zone and returned it 104 yards, outrunning the NFL record of 98 yards set by George Halas against the Oorang Indians in 1923.

But most of the standout statistical accomplishments involved rushing yards. A record 10 running backs ran for more than 1,000 yards in 1972, including Miami's Larry Csonka and Eugene (Mercury) Morris, who became the first duo ever to do it for the same team in the same season. Chicago's Bobby Douglass didn't make it to 1,000—he finished with 968—but it was a record-setting feat for a quarterback.

And pity the plight of Dave Hampton, running back for the Atlanta Falcons. Hampton went over 1,000 yards against Kansas City in the final game of the season. Unfortunately, he was tossed for a 6-yard loss on his next and last carry. He finished with 995 yards and had to wait three more seasons before he again surpassed the runners' magic number.

Csonka and Morris were only a small part of the unbelievable story unfolding in Miami. With 38-year-old quarterback Earl Morrall stepping in to replace an injured Bob Griese and engineer a methodical, error-free offense, and middle linebacker Nick Buoniconti anchoring a vastly underrated defense, the Dolphins defied the odds and finished the season with a 14-0 record. In the process, Shula became the first NFL coach to win 100 games in his first 10 seasons.

But if Miami was the most successful team in the AFC, Pittsburgh was the most surprising. Coach Chuck Noll quietly had assembled a formidable lineup since taking command in 1969. By 1972 he had Terry Bradshaw at quarterback, rookie Franco Harris in the backfield, and defensive tackle Joe Greene at the forefront of a suddenly ferocious defense.

ART
SHELL

TACKLE
RAIDERS

Art Shell received the first of his eight Pro Bowl nominations after the 1972 season. Shell teamed with guard Gene Upshaw to make the left side of the Oakland offensive line dominant.

"If Richard Nixon had had Pete Rozelle's publicity staff, he still would be president."

—AL DAVIS,
OAKLAND RAIDERS OWNER

Terry Bradshaw hands off to Franco Harris in 1972. The two young offensive players were vital to the football renaissance in Pittsburgh.

"Humility is always one play away."

—TIM FOLEY,
MIAMI DOLPHINS SAFETY

The Steelers, long known as the NFL's lovable losers, finished 11-3, won their first division title, and participated in a playoff game for the first time since 1947. In the process, they took the city of Pittsburgh by storm.

"The town caught on fire, and they gave everybody nicknames," Bradshaw said. "That was kind of neat. You know, 'Franco's Italian Army,' 'Gerela's Gorillas,' 'The Steel Curtain.' It really kind of gave the team its identity."

Bay Area Nightmare

Fittingly, the Steelers' playoff venture was anything but ordinary. Hosting a strong Oakland team, they trailed 7-6 on fourth-and-10 with 22 seconds remaining. Bradshaw heaved a desperation pass intended for running back John (Frenchy) Fuqua.

"I was trying to make sure I was between [Tatum] and the ball," Fuqua said. "If I could catch the ball, maybe we'd be able to try a field goal. Hell, I might even break the tackle and go all the way, win the game, and be on Johnny Carson as the first black king of Pennsylvania."

But Tatum slammed into Fuqua, sending the ball ricocheting through the air. While Tatum celebrated and the Three Rivers crowd fell silent, Harris plucked the ball off his shoetops in full stride and sped 60 yards for the winning touchdown.

"The worst part about being a quarterback is that you don't see a lot of stuff," Bradshaw said in reference to the critical play. "You hear the roar of the crowd, and you get up and try to gather information. But quarterbacks don't see a lot of great plays because most of the times they get knocked down."

On the same day the Raiders were cursed by the "Immaculate Reception," December 23, their Bay Area brethren, the 49ers, met a similar fate against Dallas. San Francisco led the Cowboys 28-13 in the fourth quarter, but Staubach came off the bench to spark the sort of come-from-behind victory that put him on a par with Sam Houston among Texas legends. Staubach drove the visitors to 17 points in the fourth-quarter, including a 10-yard pass to wide receiver Ron Sellers that gave the Cowboys a 30-28 victory.

"I felt so sorry for those guys that when it was over, I couldn't even look at them," Dallas guard Blaine Nye said.

A week later, Pittsburgh and Dallas ran short of miracles. It was the still-perfect Dolphins and Allen's Redskins who advanced to Super Bowl VII at the Los Angeles Memorial Coliseum. When that game was over, Miami's record was a spotless 17-0—the only unbeaten, untied season in NFL history. Griese, making his first start since the fifth game of the regular season, implemented a game plan more precise than the refrigerator-sized computers of the day, completing 8 of 11 passes in Miami's 14-7 victory.

The league's all-star game made an abrupt turn in January, 1973. The AFC-NFC Pro Bowl, and before it, the NFL Pro Bowl, had been played in Los Angeles since 1951. But the show went on the road beginning with an appearance at Texas Stadium in '73. Future stops would include Kansas City, Miami, New Orleans, Seattle, and Tampa before the game returned to Los Angeles in 1979.

Two future Pro Football Hall of Fame inductees called it quits after the 1972 season: St. Louis Cardinals safety Larry Wilson and Bears running back Gale Sayers, who, though only 30, never had fully recovered from a knee injury in 1970.

Turn on the Juice

The popular lexicon absorbed a new entry in 1973: "no-show." Congress ordered hometown television blackouts lifted if NFL games were sold out 72 hours in advance. Ticket sales were unaffected, though less-adventurous seat-holders sometimes opted for the comforts of the living room.

It also was in '73 that the league formed NFL Charities, a nonprofit foundation dedicated to a variety of educational and charitable causes, as well as financial support for former players in need. By 1993, NFL Charities would make contributions in excess of $14 million to more than 145 charitable organizations.

Running back John Brockington of the Packers became the first pro player to rush for 1,000 yards in each of his first three seasons, but his pursuit of the record was lost in the shadow of Orenthal James Simpson, more commonly known as O.J. The former Heisman Trophy winner from USC had led the league with 1,251 rushing yards in 1972, a small indication of the numbers to come. Simpson opened the 1973 season with an NFL-record 250 yards against New England, and he never looked back on the way to an unprecedented 2,003-yard campaign that made "The Juice" a household name. Simpson's offensive line, with guards Joe DeLamielleure and Reggie McKenzie, became known as "The Electric Company."

In addition to his record total, the smooth-running Simpson set single-season marks for rushing attempts (332), 100-yard games (11), and 200-yard games (3).

The Chargers were a dismal 2-11-1 in 1973, despite a roster that included quarterbacks Johnny Unitas and Dan Fouts. Unitas was well past his prime, and Fouts was too green to do much damage. "It was a dream come true," Fouts said, "because Johnny Unitas was my favorite quarterback growing up. I wish that he were younger and I were older and we could have spent six years together."

Ron Sellers's scoring catch completed Dallas's comeback over the 49ers in '72.

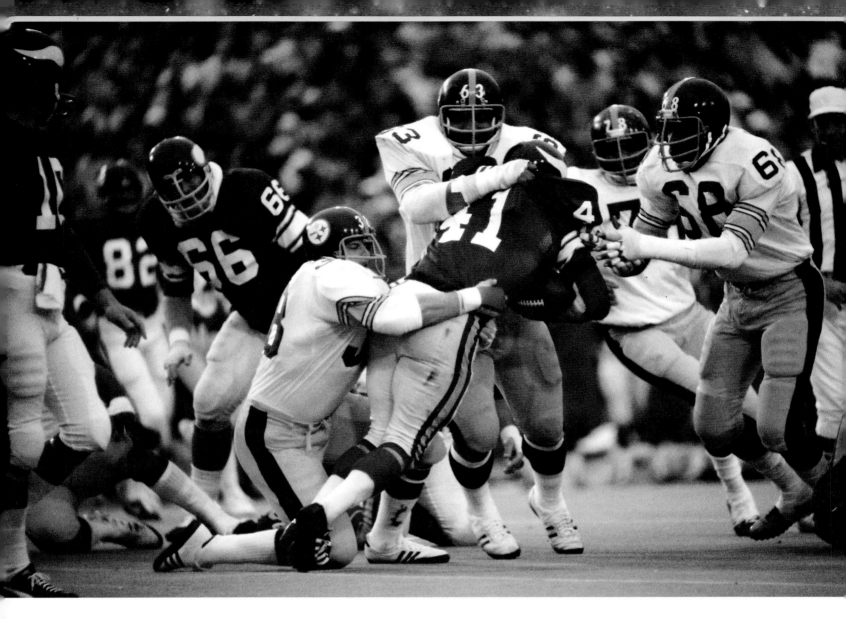

The Steel Curtain came down hard on Minnesota in Super Bowl IX, limiting the Vikings to 119 total yards.

"I had pro offers from the Detroit Lions and Green Bay Packers, who were pretty hard up for linemen in those days. If I had gone into professional football, the name Jerry Ford might have been a household word today."

—GERALD FORD,
THIRTY-EIGHTH PRESIDENT
OF THE UNITED STATES AND FORMER CENTER
AT THE UNIVERSITY OF MICHIGAN

They couldn't get past the Steelers, though. And the Rams couldn't get past the Vikings, largely because of a 98-yard Los Angeles drive—from 1-yard line to 1-yard line—that came up empty. Thus was set up the Super Bowl IX confrontation between Pittsburgh and Minnesota.

It was billed as a game pitting two great defenses. The Vikings were solid at all 11 positions, and Alan Page, in particular, was nearly impossible to neutralize.

Rams coach Chuck Knox once described preparing for a game against Minnesota. "I watched this film," Knox said, "and I kept running one play over and over. Page made three definite mistakes after the ball was snapped, and still made the tackle for no gain."

Pittsburgh had its own credentials, especially after a bountiful 1974 draft that produced wide receivers Lynn Swann and John Stallworth, linebacker Jack Lambert, and center Mike Webster, not to mention safety Donnie Shell, a free-agent pickup. In all, the five would gain 29 Pro Bowl berths.

In Super Bowl IX, only one defense lived up to its press clippings. That was the Steel Curtain of Pittsburgh, which limited the harried Vikings to 119 total yards, including a paltry 17 on the ground. Franco Harris, meanwhile, rushed for 158 yards as the Steelers won 16-6. The Vikings trailed only 9-6 after recovering a blocked punt in the end zone with 10 minutes left in the game, but they never threatened again.

After 42 seasons, only 11 of which had resulted in winning records, beloved Steelers owner Art Rooney finally owned an NFL championship trophy.

After the season, freewheeling Washington quarterback Sonny Jurgensen (who also had played for Philadelphia) and rock-solid Raiders center Jim Otto retired. So did Bengals defensive tackle Mike Reid, who left at the height of his athletic career to pursue a career in music. A gifted pianist, Reid later would write a number of country-music hits.

No Place Like Home?

Since reaching the playoffs in 1971, the Baltimore Colts had developed a serious case of vertigo. The once-dominant franchise muddled through successive seasons of 5-9, 4-10, and an NFL-worst 2-12. More of the same seemed in store in 1975 as the Colts found themselves at 1-4, but they rallied under enthusiastic new head coach Ted Marchibroda, a long-time assistant to George Allen, to win nine consecutive games and capture the AFC East title.

"At that time, they were just like any other two-and-twelve football team, I suppose," Marchibroda said. "They weren't sure of themselves. They didn't know how to win yet."

Marchibroda's emphasis was on offense. Quarterback Bert Jones (2,483 passing yards, 18 touchdowns) and running back Lydell Mitchell (1,193 rushing yards, 60 receptions) kept opponents off-balance during the team's playoff run.

"Bert did for the Baltimore Colts in those years what John Elway did for the Denver Broncos later," Marchibroda said. "Bert was the key factor to the Colts' winning."

Baltimore wasn't the only upwardly mobile team in 1975. The Oilers found sudden self-respect under new head coach O.A. (Bum) Phillips, an offseason rancher who admitted to enjoying a plug-and-a-half of White Natural Tinsley chewing tobacco every day since 1937.

Phillips delighted the press corps with his cornpone witticisms, but his Oilers had to be taken seriously. They had suffered through consecutive 1-13 seasons in 1972-73, the years before Phillips was hired as offensive coordinator. In 1975, his first season as head coach, they rose to 10-4 behind the passing of Dan Pastorini, the defensive-line play of Elvin Bethea and Curley Culp, and the electrifying kick returns of Billy (White Shoes) Johnson.

Two running backs, Buffalo's O.J. Simpson and Minnesota's Chuck Foreman, lit up NFL scoreboards. Foreman, who led the league with 73 receptions, finished the season with 22 touchdowns. That would have earned a share of the single-season record had it not been for Simpson, who posted 23. Each led his conference in scoring.

The Cardinals' Terry Metcalf didn't find the end zone as often, but he scored in a greater variety of ways. Metcalf, an explosive offensive weapon, recorded touchdowns rushing, receiving, returning kickoffs, and returning punts. He also set an NFL record for all-purpose yards with 2,462 and even threw a touchdown pass. Metcalf's offensive line—tackles Dan Dierdorf and Roger Finnie, guards Conrad Dobler and Bob Young, and center Tom Banks—allowed only 8 sacks for St. Louis (11-3).

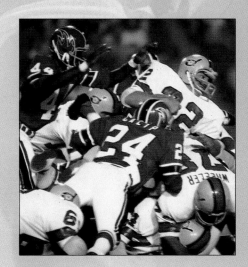

MAD WORLD

In 1974, an odd lot of owners convened the first meeting of the World Football League in Los Angeles. Restaurant owners, engineers, lawyers, and owners of sports franchises in other leagues launched a 12-team confederation that included the Chicago Fire, the Philadelphia Bell, the Portland Storm, the Southern California Sun, and eight franchises with plural nicknames.

In mid-July, the WFL kicked off its 20-game schedule of midweek contests. There were new wrinkles in the rules, such as touchdowns counting seven points with a play from scrimmage (an "action point") to follow, goal posts at the end lines, and a first-down measuring device called the "Dickerrod."

Two months into the season, one-third of the WFL's teams were in major financial trouble. The Detroit Wheels and Jacksonville Sharks both were taken over by the league and soon folded. The Houston Texans moved east to Shreveport, Louisiana, and became the Steamer, and the New York Stars went south to become the Charlotte Hornets.

Philadelphia typified the league's misery. The Bell lost 58-39 to the Sun one night, in a game televised by WTAF in Philadelphia. But with 10 minutes to play and the clock showing 1:30 A.M. on the East Coast, the station played the National Anthem and went off the air.

By December of 1975, the World Football League was extinct.

HAIL MARY

With 1:51 remaining in their 1975 NFC Divisional Playoff Game at Minnesota's Metropolitan Stadium, the Dallas Cowboys took possession on their 15-yard line, trailing the Vikings 14-10. Nine plays later came one of the best-known passes in NFL history.

Roger Staubach, his sore ribs aching in the Minnesota cold, took the Shotgun snap, pump faked to his left, then turned to his right, and let go a wobbly pass.

Downfield, both wide receiver Drew Pearson and Vikings cornerback Nate Wright decelerated to position themselves under the pass. Pearson cut inside Wright, who lost his balance and fell.

Pearson caught the ball, then trapped it against his hip at the 5-yard line, drew it to his chest, and carried it into the end zone for the winning touchdown. The Cowboys were on their way to the NFC Championship Game.

Armen Terzian, the field judge following the play, made no call and for his efforts was struck on the head (without serious injury) by a whiskey bottle thrown from the stands. An orange whizzed by Pearson as he scored.

In a postgame interview, someone described the play to Staubach. "You mean he caught the ball and ran in for the touchdown?" Staubach asked. "It was just a Hail Mary pass...a very, very lucky play."

When the playoffs got underway, they did so under a revised format. Home-field advantage, formerly rotated among division winners, now was awarded to the team with the best record. The new system had differing effects in the two conferences.

In the AFC, Oakland and Pittsburgh, which had defeated Marchibroda's Colts in a divisional playoff game, resumed their rivalry in the AFC Championship Game. Because the Steelers' 12-2 record outshone the Raiders' 11-3, the game was played at Three Rivers Stadium.

That proved to be significant as the temperature dropped to 18 degrees and ice covered the artificial turf, frustrating the Raiders' explosive offense. Pittsburgh won 16-10 when the clock ran out on Oakland at the Steelers' 15-yard line.

It was a tough way for a career to end, especially the 26-year career of the Raiders' George Blanda, who decided to retire at age 48. Blanda left with more games (340) and more points (2,002) under his belt than anyone in NFL history.

In the NFC, the new home-field method proved to be inconsequential. Dallas, which finished 10-4, took to the road and knocked off Minnesota (12-2) and Los Angeles (12-2) in succession.

At Super Bowl X in Miami, Steelers wide receiver Lynn Swann contributed a 64-yard touchdown reception, a 32-yard sideline catch, and an acrobatic 53-yard reception to lead Pittsburgh over Dallas 21-17. The game wasn't decided until safety Glen Edwards made an interception in the end zone on the final play.

Expanding Opportunity

The NFL grew to 28 teams as the Seattle Seahawks and Tampa Bay Buccaneers began play in opposite corners of the nation in 1976. Tampa Bay selected prized defensive end Lee Roy Selmon of Oklahoma after winning the first pick of the draft in a coin toss. It would be about the only thing the Buccaneers won all season—they staggered to an 0-14 mark.

Seattle won two games, including a 13-10 victory over the Buccaneers in the "Expansion Bowl," a sloppy affair that included 35 penalties. One notable player on the Seattle roster was Steve Largent. A rookie free agent who had been cut by the Oilers, Largent would advance to great heights.

The IN and OUT doors of NFL teams got heavy use during the 1976 off-season. New England, unhappy with former number-one draft choice Jim Plunkett, traded the quarterback to San Francisco. Houston and Green Bay swapped passers, with Lynn Dickey going to the Packers and the well-traveled John Hadl heading for the Oilers.

Meanwhile, the World Football League had lost its solvency—and its dignity. After playing a game in Louisiana, the Charlotte Hornets had their equipment confiscated by the Caddo Parish sheriff in compliance with a lawsuit over a $26,216 debt. The WFL's demise in 1975 brought a wave of free-agent refugees to the NFL in 1976. Larry Csonka returned with the Giants, Paul Warfield with the Browns, Calvin Hill with the Redskins, and wide receiver John Gilliam with the Falcons. Some NFL veterans also moved. Running back John Riggins and tight end Jean Fugett joined the Redskins.

But as this wealth of talent returned to the NFL playing fields, one of the game's most respected names left it. Paul Brown, who had guided high school, college, military, and pro teams for 41 years, stepped down as Bengals head coach, though he remained as the club's general manager, vice president, and owner.

"The entire [1975] season had been a happy, wonderful experience for me," Brown wrote of Cincinnati's 11-3 autumn in his autobiography, "and I had always thought that when I did finish coaching, I wanted to go out on a high C."

Brown made his announcement on New Year's Day. Flash-forward to Thanksgiving Day, 1976, when O. J. Simpson ran through, past, and around the host Lions. By the time pumpkin pie had been served, Simpson had gained 273 yards, an NFL record but not enough to bring the Bills a victory. True to form in a miserable 2-12 season that included a trade demand by Simpson, a midseason coaching change, and an injury to starting quarterback Joe Ferguson, they lost to Detroit 27-14.

Score One for the Renegades

After staggering to a 1-4 start in 1976, Pittsburgh rallied for nine consecutive victories behind an intimidating defense that recorded five shutouts. It might have been the height of the Steel Curtain. In those final nine victories, Houston was the only team to extract more than six points from the Steelers, who advanced to the AFC Championship Game and seemed poised for their third straight Super Bowl appearance. They had defeated Baltimore 40-14 in their first playoff game, running their winning streak to 10 in a row.

Standing in their way was Oakland, which had survived a tense AFC Divisional Playoff Game against New England, the NFL's most surprising team. The Patriots, going from 3-11 to 11-3 under coach Chuck Fairbanks, had handed the Raiders their only loss of the regular season. In the playoffs,

Quarterback/kicker George Blanda, the NFL's ultimate iron man, retired at age 48 in 1975, concluding a career that touched four decades and spanned 26 years. A rookie with the Bears in 1949, Blanda began the 1950 season with the Colts before rejoining Chicago later that year and remaining with the team through 1958. Released by the Bears, he sat out the 1959 season, then resurrected his career in the AFL, playing seven years with Houston before joining the Raiders in 1967. He remains the NFL's all-time scoring leader.

The league's career leaders in games played:

PLAYER	YEARS	GAMES
George Blanda	26	340
Jim Marshall	20	282
Jan Stenerud	19	263
Earl Morrall	21	255
Pat Leahy	18	250
Jackie Slater	18	246
Fran Tarkenton	18	246
Jeff Van Note	18	245
Mike Webster	17	245
Ed White	17	241

The NFL's newest teams, Tampa Bay and Seattle, went head-to-head in the 1976 "Expansion Bowl." The Seahawks won the penalty-filled game 13-10.

New England took a 21-10 lead into the fourth quarter, but Oakland,
helped by critical roughing-the-passer call against the Patriots, rallied for a

Bill Johnson in Cincinnati after five games; Chargers coach Tommy Prothro resigned after four games and was replaced by Don Coryell; and New England's Chuck Fairbanks, his team with an 11-3 record and on its way to the AFC playoffs, was fired with one game remaining after he signed a contract to coach the University of Colorado in 1979.

But the big coaching news came after the season, when Oakland's John Madden announced his retirement. His regular-season winning percentage of .750 (103-32-7 over 10 years) still is the best in NFL history among coaches with at least 100 victories. A severe ulcer forced the bombastic Madden into a less-stressful line of work.

The Steelers, now relying on offense as much as defense, sprang back to championship form and finished 14-2, the best record in the league. Terry Bradshaw won his only AFC passing title as he threw for 2,915 yards and 28 touchdowns, 11 of them to Lynn Swann.

Campbell's Super Debut

But Pittsburgh suddenly had some competition in the AFC Central. Houston, already solid, took a long step forward with the addition of one player: running back Earl Campbell, whom the Oilers were able to draft after acquiring the number-one pick in a trade that sent tight end Jimmie Giles and four draft choices to Tampa Bay.

Campbell, the Heisman Trophy winner from Texas, was a one-man demolition team. At 5-11, 233 pounds, he usually was seen with multiple opponents draped from various limbs; yet, he had the speed to outrun many defensive backs. Campbell rushed for 1,450 yards in 1978, becoming the first rookie to lead the NFL since Jim Brown in 1957. He also helped the Oilers to a 10-6 record and playoff victories over Miami and New England.

His finest hour was a Monday night game against the Dolphins. Miami's Bob Griese was brilliant that evening, completing 23 of 33 passes for 349 yards and 2 touchdowns. But Campbell was better than brilliant. He ran for 199 yards, including a late 81-yard burst that sealed the 35-30 victory.

"We actually felt we were doing a good job on Campbell," Dolphins linebacker Rusty Chambers said. "But the thing we noticed was how he seemed to get stronger. Every time he got the ball, he seemed to run harder."

A month-and-a-half later, the Oilers had a date with Pittsburgh in the AFC Championship Game. "We expect a knock-down, drag-out fight," Phillips said before the game. "We're gonna sever diplomatic relations with 'em. That's what you do when you're declarin' war, isn't it?"

Houston was too one-dimensional to beat the powerful Steelers, though. When the two teams met in the freezing rain at Three Rivers Stadium, Pittsburgh walked away with a 34-5 win. That same day, Dallas waltzed to a 28-0 victory over the Rams, setting up the first rematch in Super Bowl history.

RECORDS SINCE THE 1970 AFL-NFL MERGER

AFC	W- L -T	PCT.	DIV. TITLES	PLAYOFF BERTHS
Miami	238-120-2	.664	10	14
Oakland/Los Angeles	227-127-6	.639	9	15
Pittsburgh	212-147-1	.590	10	14
Denver	202-152-6	.569	7	10
Cleveland	178-179-3	.499	6	9
Cincinnati	175-185-0	.486	5	7
Kansas City	168-185-7	.476	2	6
Buffalo	169-189-2	.472	6	9
Seattle★	127-149-0	.460	1	4
Houston	164-194-2	.458	2	10
San Diego	159-196-5	.449	4	5
Boston/New England	158-202-0	.439	2	5
New York Jets	152-206-2	.425	0	5
Baltimore/Indianapolis	148-210-2	.414	5	6

NFC	W- L -T	PCT.	DIV. TITLES	PLAYOFF BERTHS
Dallas	227-133-0	.631	11	17
Washington	225-134-1	.626	5	13
San Francisco	212-145-3	.593	13	14
Minnesota	210-148-2	.586	11	15
Los Angeles Rams	203-153-4	.569	8	14
Chicago	186-173-1	.518	6	9
Philadelphia	171-183-6	.483	2	8
New York Giants	169-189-2	.472	3	7
Detroit	160-196-4	.450	3	5
St. Louis/Phoenix	151-203-6	.428	2	3
Green Bay	150-202-8	.428	1	3
New Orleans	148-208-4	.417	1	4
Atlanta	144-212-4	.406	1	4
Tampa Bay★	81-194-1	.295	2	3

★entered NFL in 1976.
Note: The AFC holds a 562-530-8 edge over the NFC in interconference games during the regular season, 1970-1993.

Opposite: **Houston's Earl Campbell rumbled across the NFL landscape in 1978.**

And what a rematch it was. The Cowboys' offensive combination of Staubach (3,190 passing yards and 25 touchdowns) and Dorsett (1,325 rushing yards) looked even more imposing than the previous year.

The Steelers, with at least six future Hall of Fame enshrinees in their starting lineup, had become more than a football team in Pittsburgh. They were a symbol of civic pride in a steel city that was feeling the crunch of a grinding recession.

Emotions were running high on both sides. Dallas linebacker Thomas (Hollywood) Henderson, the most engaging interviewee of Super Bowl week, managed to insult Bradshaw, tight end Randy Grossman, and even Jack Lambert. "I don't care for the man," Henderson said of the Steelers' middle linebacker. "He makes more money than I do, and he don't have no teeth. He's Dracula."

The fans at Miami's Orange Bowl couldn't have asked for more. Bradshaw threw 4 touchdown passes, 2 to John Stallworth, to build a 35-17 lead. But Staubach led Dallas in a furious rally, throwing 2 touchdown passes in the final three minutes to shave the Steelers' lead to 35-31. The threat didn't end until Pittsburgh's Rocky Bleier recovered an onside kick with 22

Many people still consider Super Bowl XIII the best ever. Above: Pittsburgh's Terry Bradshaw fades back into the pocket.

THE NFL: READY FOR PRIME TIME

His vision was pro football as prime-time television entertainment—more cameras, new angles, graphics and information, commentary, and dramatic halftime highlights. The American sports audience never had seen anything quite like what Roone Arledge sprang on it September 21, 1970.

When Joe Namath and the New York Jets visited Cleveland to play the Browns that Monday evening, there was little evidence that pro football was venturing into a new frontier of television sports. "None of us had any idea what would happen," recalled Dennis Lewin, who was in charge of slow-motion replay that evening and, as senior vice president of productions, is the only person from that first broadcast still connected to ABC's "Monday Night Football."

The Monday-night venture was Arledge's project. "He wanted to combine football and entertainment," Lewin said. "We wanted to show people that pro football was more than a game of *Xs* and *Os*. If we wanted *Xs* and *Os*, we wouldn't have had Cosell."

But they did have Cosell—Howard Cosell, the outspoken and controversial commentator who complemented Keith Jackson's play-by-play and the analysis of Don Meredith. They formed an interesting team in the booth, but, as Lewin told it, the team almost didn't take the field.

"We did a practice game the week before, in Detroit, that never got on the air," he said. "Meredith thought it was so bad he wanted to quit. Roone talked him back into it."

It took just one game for Arledge and his colleagues to know they had a hit TV show, one that would be going strong nearly 25 years later. "The days after that first game, ABC was bombarded with phone calls and letters," Lewin recalled. "Half of them said Cosell was anti-Joe Namath; the other half said he was anti-Leroy Kelly [Cleveland's star running back].

"We had great ratings. And when that started to happen, the other networks took their best shots at us. Over the years we have gone up against Lucy, Rhoda, and Murphy Brown, and we've continued to have great success.

"'Monday Night Football' has been a happening," Lewin said, "on television and in the stadium. It's a show everyone wants to see. It started what some people call appointment television: People set the time aside and made a point to see it."

Nothing has changed recently. Offices still clear out and freeways empty every Monday evening. Thanks to "Monday Night Football," America's weekends are just a little longer each fall.

---

seconds left. Bradshaw, who finished with 318 passing yards, was the most valuable player.

"I think we're the only team that could've beat Pittsburgh," Staubach said, "and we almost did. Offensively, we had them confused. We moved the ball the whole game...we just came up short."

Fran Tarkenton had moved the ball for 18 NFL autumns. When the quarterback retired after the 1978 season, he owned league career passing records for pass attempts (6,467), completions (3,686), yards (47,003), and touchdowns (342).

Chargers Learn the Rules

There were more rules changes on the books in 1979, focused primarily on keeping players healthy. The changes outlawed blocking below the waist on special-teams plays and wearing torn or altered equipment or exposed pads. Also, any play would be whistled dead when a quarterback clearly was "in the grasp" of a tackler. It was a concept that would elicit heated debate in coaches' meetings and barrooms for years to come.

Less controversial was the decision to award the 1980 AFC-NFC Pro Bowl to Honolulu, Hawaii. What started as a one-year decision would become an annual tradition.

The NFL took a broadside when Ohio State linebacker Tom Cousineau, the first choice in the 1979 draft, rejected the Bills and signed with Montreal

"It's like standing blindfolded in the middle of Interstate Seventy-five, dodging the cars and trying to tackle the biggest truck out there."

—GARY BURLEY,
CINCINNATI BENGALS DEFENSIVE END,
ON TACKLING HOUSTON RUNNING BACK
EARL CAMPBELL

Taking advantage of recent offensive-minded rules changes, San Diego's Dan Fouts passed for an NFL record 4,082 yards in 1979.

"Everyone has some fear. A man who has no fear belongs in a mental institution. Or on special teams."

—WALT MICHAELS,
NEW YORK JETS HEAD COACH

of the Canadian Football League. Eleventh-hour overtures by Bills officials came too late. "We were even calling Cousineau's coaches at Ohio State," Bills personnel director Norm Pollom said in the book *Hard Knox*. "We were even calling his relatives. Longest night of my life."

At San Diego, the Chargers emerged with a frightening passing attack. Rookie tight end Kellen Winslow joined wide receivers John Jefferson and Charlie Joiner as targets for Dan Fouts, who set an NFL standard with 4,802 passing yards. "Air Coryell," the Chargers offense was called, though it received contributions from offensive coordinators Bill Walsh (pre-Coryell) and Joe Gibbs (under Coryell).

"We were going to have success throwing the ball regardless of the rules changes," Fouts said. "But they did affect us positively. Our offensive line was really big, and that was before it was common. We had a 300-pound tackle in Russ Washington and a 295-pound guard, Ed White, right next to him. And they did learn how to use those big bodies, to extend their arms and all that."

The only team to match the Chargers at 12-4 was Pittsburgh, which won its sixth consecutive AFC Central title. All offensive cylinders were firing in sync for the confident Steelers, though their aging defense had slipped a notch. Houston (11-5) again mounted a challenge behind Earl Campbell's 1,697 yards and 19 rushing touchdowns, but again lost to Pittsburgh in the conference title game, this time 27-13.

In the NFC, Dallas knocked Washington out of the playoffs with a 35-34 victory in the final week of the season. That win required not just one, but two comebacks. The Cowboys fell behind 17-0, took the lead at 21-17, fell behind 34-21, and finally won 35-34 on a touchdown pass from Staubach to Tony Hill with 39 seconds left. Only a game, right? As Tom Callahan wrote the next day in the *Washington Star*: "When a house collapses, does the contractor say it was only a house?"

The Final Curtain

Tampa Bay also made the playoffs, behind a suddenly fearsome defense. Just two years earlier, the Buccaneers were in the midst of a 26-game losing streak; now they faced the Rams in the NFC Championship Game.

In many ways, however, the Rams were even more of a curiosity. Their turbulent year had begun with the death of club owner Carroll Rosenbloom, who drowned off the coast of Florida and was succeeded by his wife, Georgia. On the field, injuries forced Los Angeles to play four different quarterbacks. The team finished with a 9-7 record and, with its lame-duck status in the Los Angeles Coliseum (the team moved to Anaheim in 1980), didn't exactly win the hearts of the home crowd.

Still, 9-7 was good enough to give the Rams their seventh consecutive division crown, a league record. Their subsequent 9-0 victory over Tampa Bay was the first championship game in NFL history that didn't include a touchdown. Three field goals by Frank Corral did the trick, thanks to a defensive effort that limited the Buccaneers to 177 total yards and 7 first downs.

In the Super Bowl, the Rams were heavy underdogs to the defending-champion Steelers. Quarterback Vince Ferragamo had started only seven NFL games; his counterpart, Bradshaw, had started 17 postseason games. Surprisingly, Los Angeles led 19-17 at the start of the fourth quarter. Then

the clock struck midnight as Pittsburgh scored twice in the final 15 minutes, including a 73-yard touchdown pass from Bradshaw to Stallworth. The final score: 31-19.

"That was a terrible game," said Bradshaw, who admitted it was his worst Super Bowl performance even though he passed for 309 yards and won his second consecutive MVP award. "We played against [defensive coordinator] Bud Carson, against the defense he designed with the Steelers. They knew our audibles; they knew our offense. It was the hardest game I've ever played in my life."

Walking off the field, Bradshaw could see the writing on the wall. More than 20 Steelers had made national television commercials, and Terry Bradshaw Peanut Butter was readily available in Pennsylvania supermarkets. The team was beginning to wilt under the spotlight.

"That entire offseason, I thought about retiring," Bradshaw said. "I should have retired. We won four Super Bowls in six years. And just the stress—not the pressure, but the stress—of winning had taken its toll. Emotionally, I was fatigued.

"You could see in that game that our football team would slowly start dismantling."

It was harder to discern which team would supplant the Steelers as the NFL's next dynasty. The answer soon became apparent, but you couldn't have guessed in 1979: The 49ers, under first-year head coach Bill Walsh, finished 2-14.

John Stallworth's 73-yard touchdown reception sank the upstart Los Angeles Rams in Super Bowl XIV. It was the Steelers' fourth NFL championship of the decade, but age soon would bring a close to their dynasty.

TEAM *of the* SEVENTIES

more and more were using running backs and tight ends in the downfield passing game. Defenses kept pace by switching to the 3-4, which featured two inside linebackers to handle the run and two outside men to join coverage—and apply pressure to the quarterback. And no one rushed the quarterback like Taylor.

The Giants used Taylor almost exclusively as a stand-up defensive end. At first teams tried to block him with a tight end or running back, but eventually they were forced to use an offensive tackle, at the very least. What made Taylor unique was his unprecedented combination of speed and power; at 6-3, 243 pounds, he was swift enough to run around a tackle and strong enough to run through him.

"To be honest with you, coming out of college I didn't think there was anything I couldn't do," Taylor said. "Looking back, I guess I was right."

In a 13-year career, Taylor produced 142 sacks (officially he had $132\frac{1}{2}$ because the NFL did not record sacks until Taylor's second year), many of them savage, blind-side hits that resulted in fumbles. Only Reggie White had more official sacks when Taylor retired after the 1993 season. Taylor was voted to the Pro Bowl in each of his first 10 seasons, an NFL record, and many believe he is the finest linebacker ever to play the game.

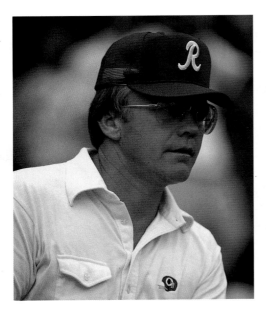

Unfortunately for Washington head coach Joe Gibbs, both he and Taylor arrived in the NFC East the same year. Gibbs later would say that Taylor caused the Redskins more trouble than any other defender. Which was saying something because the coach was an offensive wizard.

In With the New

Gibbs had been the offensive co-ordinator at San Diego when Fouts and Coryell made all the headlines. When Jack Pardee followed the

Washington's Joe Gibbs (above left) and Denver's Dan Reeves, both of whom were hired in 1981, would lead their teams to a combined six Super Bowl appearances in the decade.

legendary George Allen with a 24-24 record over three seasons, owner Jack Kent Cooke turned to Gibbs, who improved the Redskins to 8-8 from 6-10.

The Denver Broncos also improved two games, to 10-6 from 8-8, under a rookie head coach. And while Gibbs, a studious tight end, had played under Coryell in college, he never made it in the pros. Dan Reeves, on the other hand, played for eight seasons under Tom Landry in Dallas, the last two as a player-coach. At 37, Reeves was the league's youngest head coach when he joined Denver in 1981.

George Rogers, a Saints' rookie, led all rushers that year. He gained 1,674 yards, finishing a scant 28 yards ahead of Dallas's Tony Dorsett. They were two of an unprecedented group of 15 runners who produced 1,000-yard seasons. The Chargers again had three receivers with 1,000 yards, including tight end Winslow, whose undeniable will would become the symbol of one of history's greatest football games.

In a divisional playoff game on January 2, 1982, San Diego and Miami

Humid Beings

At Miami's Orange Bowl on January 2, 1982, late in the first quarter of an AFC Divisional Playoff Game, the San Diego Chargers extended their lead over the Miami Dolphins to 24-0 on a pass from Dan Fouts to James Brooks. The way tight end Kellen Winslow remembered it, he and his Chargers teammates were having the time of their lives. All of them, that is, except wide receiver Charlie Joiner.

"You don't come to Miami and do this to a Don Shula team," Joiner told Winslow. "He's gonna pull [quarterback] David Woodley, put in [Don] Strock, and we're gonna be here all day.'"

Sure enough, when Miami took possession with 12:05 to go in the second quarter, Shula inserted Strock, the eight-year veteran backup, at quarterback. With 8:31 left, it was 24-3. With 2:46 left in the half, it was 24-10. With 6 seconds left in the half, Miami had a first-and-10 at the San Diego 40. Strock passed to Duriel

Harris at the 25. Harris lateraled to Tony Nathan, and Nathan raced into the Chargers' end zone. "I haven't seen that since high school," said San Diego head coach Don Coryell.

The 1958 NFL Championship Game was the NFL's first sudden-death overtime game, but the 1981 playoff between San Diego and Miami was the NFL's first *continuous-death* overtime game. Condi-

tions were anything but conducive to stamina and presence of mind: 79 degrees and humbling humidity.

The Dolphins forged ahead in the second half. It wasn't until 58 seconds remained in regulation that Fouts found Brooks with a 9-yard touchdown pass to tie the game. Miami had a chance to win in regulation, but Winslow blocked Uwe von Schamann's 43-yard field-goal attempt on the final play to force overtime.

Leaden with fatigue, the teams traded possession six times in the extra period. Finally, Rolf Benirschke won it for the Chargers 41-38 with a field goal after 13:52 of overtime.

For much of the game Winslow suffered dehydration from the heat and humidity, and numbness in his arm related to a shoulder injury. He broke two sets of shoulder pads. When the game was over, he had to be carried to the locker room by teammates Eric Sievers and Billy Shields (inset), so intense were the cramps in his shoulders, back, and thighs.

played an epic game that resulted in NFL playoff records for points (79) and total yards (1,036). Kicker Rolf Benirschke's 29-yard field goal with 13:52 gone in overtime gave the Chargers a 41-38 victory. A dehydrated Winslow finished with a staggering (literally) 13 catches and 166 yards. He also blocked a Miami field-goal attempt on the final play of regulation time.

One week removed from the balmy Orange Bowl, the Chargers lost a chilling AFC Championship Game 27-7 in Cincinnati. Temperature at game time was a record-low 9 degrees below zero and the swirling winds at Riverfront Stadium made the chill factor minus-59.

"I talked to the players before the game and I told them they were going to be uncomfortable regardless of what they did," said Bengals head coach Forrest Gregg. "I said we were going to have to work in this discomfort."

The ability to deal with the elements helped the Bengals reach Super Bowl XVI, the first to be played in a northern city. The Pontiac (Michigan) Silverdome was the showcase for the league's two most accurate passers, Cincinnati's Ken Anderson and San Francisco's Joe Montana.

San Francisco led 20-0 at halftime, but the plays of the game belonged to its defense. Cincinnati scored on its first possession of the third quarter and later drove to a first down at the San Francisco 3. Following a 2-yard gain, the 49ers stopped the Bengals three straight times from the 1-yard line. And though Cincinnati cut the score to 20-14, kicker Ray Wersching's third and fourth field goals of the game gave the 49ers their final margin of 26-21.

"Playing middle linebacker is like walking through a lion's cage in a three-piece pork-chop suit."

—CECIL JOHNSON,
TAMPA BAY BUCCANEERS
OUTSIDE LINEBACKER,
ON WHY HE WOULDN'T CHANGE POSITIONS

Washington's John Riggins was like a runaway locomotive during the 1982 postseason. He had four consecutive 100-yard games, including 166 against Miami in Super Bowl XVII (above).

"Football is football. The best high school players usually make the best college players, and the best college players usually make the best pro players. It's just that the cream gets a little thinner as you go along because the weave of the strainer gets tighter and tighter."

—KENNETH SIMS,
NEW ENGLAND PATRIOTS DEFENSIVE END

Anderson set a Super Bowl record by completing 25 of 34 passes as the Bengals became the first team to outgain a Super Bowl opponent (356 yards to 275) and lose. Montana, who passed for 157 yards, was the MVP.

A Striking Departure

The NFL was riding high heading into the 1982 season. Regular-season attendance in 1981 (13.6 million) had broken the record for the fourth consecutive season and, moved by record-setting ratings, the three major television networks signed new five-year contracts.

The first two weeks of the regular season provided their usual thrills, but there were storm clouds on the horizon. At midnight on September 20, following a "Monday Night Football" game between the Packers and Giants, the NFL Players Association called for a strike. Quite simply, the players wanted a bigger piece of the pie.

So, for 57 days, there was no professional football. Seven games were lost as the owners and players negotiated, sometimes bitterly, over a new Collective Bargaining Agreement. In the end, the spirit of compromise prevailed.

The players won a minimum salary schedule, while training camp and postseason pay were increased, along with medical insurance and retirement benefits. The two sides also agreed on a severance-pay system to help with career transition, a first in professional sports. The owners were granted the right to continue the NFL draft through 1992.

The dispute was resolved in time to allow for seven additional games, which meant a nine-game regular season and a highly irregular playoff format. A week after Dallas running back Tony Dorsett exploded for an NFL-record 99-yard run at Minnesota in the final regular-season game, 16 teams, eight from each conference, entered the Super Bowl tournament. They were seeded according to their regular-season records.

Two losing teams, Detroit and Cleveland (each 4-5), made the tournament (but lost in the first round). In fact, the two eventual survivors were among the league's best during the regular season, bringing order to the proceedings.

Washington, which had the NFC's best mark (8-1) under Gibbs, dispatched the Lions and Minnesota with ease before defeating Dallas 31-17 in the conference final. Miami was 7-2, behind only the 8-1 Raiders in the AFC. The Dolphins eliminated New England and San Diego before advancing to Super Bowl XVII with a muscular 14-0 victory over the New York Jets. The Jets had reached the second AFL/AFC Championship Game in their history with a 17-14 victory over the Los Angeles Raiders, a win sealed by 2 Lance Mehl interceptions in the final three minutes.

The season's final game, played in the Rose Bowl, was an American Beauty. It was an ecstatic exclamation point to a turbulent year. Washington running back John Riggins delivered the game's most dramatic moment. Ever the iconoclast, he had mesmerized the press corps with a stream-of-consciousness monologue while dressed in army fatigues. But now, in the fourth quarter, with Washington trailing Miami 17-13, Riggins merely wore a grass-stained number 44.

On fourth-and-1 at Miami's 43-yard line, Riggins cut to the left, broke through Don McNeal's tackle, and bolted all the way to the end zone. On the Redskins' next possession, he carried 8 times in 12 plays to set up Joe Theismann's 6-yard touchdown pass to Charlie Brown, which gave the Redskins a 27-17 lead, the final margin.

Riggins finished with 38 carries and a Super Bowl-record 166 yards, and Washington won its first NFL title in 40 seasons. It was that kind of year.

Playing With Conviction

On December 12, 1982, the Patriots had used the sweep play to beat the Dolphins. Problem was, the pivotal player in the bizarre episode was Mark Henderson, an inmate at Norfolk (Massachusetts) State Prison.

In a blizzard at Schaefer Stadium, the Dolphins and Patriots had played to a bitter scoreless tie when, with 4:45 left in the game, New England kicker John Smith lined up for a 33-yard field-goal attempt. Patriots head coach Ron Meyer called a time out. He had an idea.

"I was saying, 'Let's get the sweeper out there,'" Meyer remembered. "Here was a guy who could really help us, but I had to find him. Finally, I spotted him on the ten-yard line. I ran down there and screamed, 'Get on that tractor! Get on the field and go do something!'"

Henderson, a convicted burglar who was on a one-day work release from Norfolk, jumped on a John Deere 314 tractor and drove into history. As Smith and holder Matt Cavanaugh chipped at the ice with their cleats, Henderson drove innocently down the 20-yard line. The Dolphins scarcely noticed him because he had been clearing the yard lines all day, but Henderson suddenly veered toward Smith and Cavanaugh.

The kick, from a clear patch of turf, was good. The Dolphins were furious but referee Bob Frederic ruled it legal. The Patriots won 3-0. It was that kind of year.

CENTURY MARKS

Baseball batters strive to hit .300, football rushers set their sights on 1,000 yards, basketball players shoot for a 20-point average. For NFL quarterbacks, the magical number is a 100 rating. The NFL rates passers on a complex system that focuses on completions, touchdowns, interceptions, and yards, all in relation to number of attempts. In 1989, 49ers quarterback Joe Montana completed 271 of 386 passes (70.2 percent) for 3,521 yards and 26 touchdowns, with only 8 interceptions.

Montana's rating that year was an NFL single-season record 112.4. Quarterbacks have achieved a rating of more than 100 only 19 times in league history:

QUARTERBACK, TEAM	YEAR	RATING
Joe Montana, San Francisco	1989	112.4
Milt Plum, Cleveland	1960	110.4
Sammy Baugh, Washington	1945	109.9
Dan Marino, Miami	1984	108.9
Sid Luckman, Chicago Bears	1943	107.5
Steve Young, San Francisco	1992	107.0
Bart Starr, Green Bay	1966	105.0
Roger Staubach, Dallas	1971	104.8
Y.A. Tittle, N.Y. Giants	1963	104.8
Bart Starr, Green Bay	1968	104.3
Ken Stabler, Oakland	1976	103.7
Joe Montana, San Francisco	1984	102.9
Charlie Conerly, N.Y. Giants	1959	102.7
Bert Jones, Baltimore	1976	102.5
Joe Montana, San Francisco	1987	102.1
Steve Young, San Francisco	1991	101.8
Len Dawson, Kansas City	1966	101.7
Steve Young, San Francisco	1993	101.5
Jim Kelly, Buffalo	1990	101.2

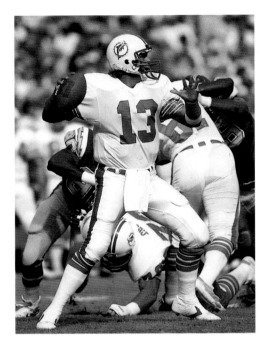

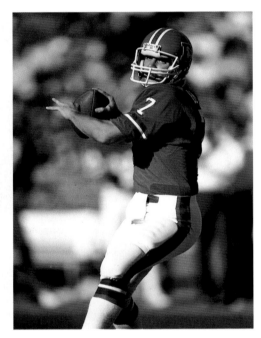

The talent-rich 1983 draft featured a half-dozen quarterbacks selected in the first round. Of the six, the most lasting marks were made by Dan Marino (top) and John Elway.

The Jets' Freeman McNeil was the rushing leader with a nine-game total of 786 yards. Raiders running back Marcus Allen led all scorers with 14 touchdowns. Pittsburgh's Terry Bradshaw, San Diego's Dan Fouts, and San Francisco's Joe Montana each threw 17 touchdown passes.

It also was in 1982 that Mike Ditka, a Dallas assistant under Tom Landry for nine years, was named head coach of the Chicago Bears. Not since the fourth coming of George (Papa Bear) Halas (who was 76-53-6 from 1958-1967), had Chicago experienced a winning coach.

Ditka, who had more than a little of Halas's gruff manner, would change all that, but not before suffering through a 3-6 rookie season.

A Class for the Ages

More than a decade after the Class of '83 descended on the NFL, it is difficult to fully measure the impact six of its first-round quarterbacks had on the game.

Taken that spring day in New York City, in order of appearance: Stanford's John Elway (first overall, to Baltimore), Penn State's Todd Blackledge (seventh, to Kansas City), Miami's Jim Kelly (fourteenth, to Buffalo), Illinois's Tony Eason (fifteenth, to New England), Cal-Davis's Ken O'Brien (twenty-fourth, to the New York Jets) and Pittsburgh's Dan Marino (twenty-seventh, to Miami).

They were the best and the brightest, based both on their college performance and the enormous potential they held as professionals. On virtually every level, they delivered.

"You can't compare anything to 1983, because nothing before it and nothing after it can compare to the class," said Miami coach Don Shula. "I don't think anything will ever top it."

Elway, who was traded to Denver a week after the draft, believed the attention given the Class of '83 actually drove the principals to greater heights.

"When we first came into the league, it was a real competitive situation for

CLASS REUNION

The 1983 NFL draft was a gold mine for quarterbacks, with six being taken in the first round. The selection was so deep that rifle-armed Dan Marino was the last of the six to go, with 26 players selected before him. A look at how the elite half-dozen have fared in their NFL careers (through 1993):

PLAYER	SELECTION, TEAM	ATT.	COMP.	PCT.	YDS.	TD	INT.	RATING
John Elway Denver 1983-present	(1, Baltimore)	4,890	2,723	55.7	34,246	183	167	75.9
Todd Blackledge Kansas City 1983-87; Pittsburgh 1988-89	(7, Kansas City)	881	424	48.1	5,286	29	38	60.2
Jim Kelly Buffalo 1986-present	(14, Buffalo)	3,494	2,112	60.4	26,413	179	126	86.0
Tony Eason New England 1983-89; N.Y. Jets 1989-1990	(15, New England)	1,564	911	58.2	11,142	61	51	79.7
Ken O'Brien N.Y. Jets 1983-1992; Philadelphia 1993-present	(24, N.Y. Jets)	3,602	2,110	58.6	25,094	128	98	80.4
Dan Marino Miami 1983-present	(27, Miami)	5,434	3,219	59.2	40,720	298	168	88.1

all of us," he said. "It was the fact that we all knew we were going to be compared to each other."

The results, of course, speak for themselves.

And while Elway and Kelly also are Hall-of-Fame-caliber players, it is Marino, the last quarterback taken in the first round, who is destined to be first in the record books. Marino is likely to set all-time marks for attempts, completions, yards, and touchdowns.

All the scouts agreed Marino had one of the quickest releases they ever had seen. But alleged knee problems and unsubstantiated rumors concerning his personal life left him on the drafting table for the surprised Shula, who made his decision in seconds.

After 11 seasons in a Miami Dolphins' uniform, Marino, who led Miami to Super Bowl XIX, holds numerous NFL records and has produced statistics that border on the surreal, including 40,720 passing yards (third in NFL history) and 298 touchdowns (second).

Elway hasn't been as prolific as Marino; of course, he hasn't been supported in the same style. One of the finest athletes ever to play the position, Elway, who has guided the Broncos to three Super Bowls, has produced an amazing 32 game-saving, fourth-quarter drives through 11 seasons, and has maintained the best won-lost percentage of the six draftees. In 1993, at the age of 33, Elway had the best season of his career, leading the AFC in passer rating (92.8), yards (4,030), and touchdowns (25).

Kelly signed with the rival United States Football League and threw 83 touchdown passes in just two seasons. After eight seasons in Buffalo, he was the fourth-rated quarterback in NFL history and had led the Bills to four Super Bowls.

Eason was a modest 29-24 over eight seasons, but he did guide the Patriots to Super Bowl XX. O'Brien made his mark as an efficient passer; his percentage of interceptions remains the NFL's third-lowest career figure. Blackledge, the only member of the quarterback class to win a college national championship, made only 29 career starts with two teams over seven seasons.

The only downside: All six passers were drafted by AFC teams; given the recent strength of the NFC, their combined record in the Super Bowl is a dreary 0-9.

"We're still young enough," Marino said. "I like to think I or Jim or John is going to win one of those things. That's the one thing missing from the picture."

Fleet Sixteen

While the Class of '83 was learning hard lessons in the pocket as rookies, NFL running backs ran as never before. Sixteen rushers—a total that has yet to be exceeded—gained 1,000 or more yards. The laundry list, ranked by yards, reads like a Who's Who of runners: Eric Dickerson, William Andrews, Curt Warner, Walter Payton, John Riggins, Tony Dorsett, Earl Campbell, Ottis Anderson, Mike Pruitt, George Rogers, Joe Cribbs, Curtis Dickey, Tony Collins, Billy Sims, Marcus Allen, and Franco Harris.

Five of those players (Campbell, Harris, Payton, Riggins, and Dorsett) already are enshrined in the Pro Football Hall of Fame, and Dickerson and Allen are likely to join them in the future.

THE FEW.
THE PROUD.
THE HOGS.

It was the spring of 1983. Bob Winckler, a 290-pound offensive lineman from the University of Wisconsin, freshly picked by the Washington Redskins in the sixth round of the NFL draft, had a goal. "To be able to say you're a Hog …let's just say it's something I would really want."

No. There was no "wanting" to become a Hog. Once the original Hogs had acquired their porcine nickname during training camp in 1982, the fraternity was locked. It started one day on the practice field, where offensive coordinator Joe Bugel said, "Okay, you hogs, let's go down to the bullpen and hit those blocking sleds."

Some players might have resented the name, but these guys loved it. From that moment, a camaraderie began to build: Hogs T-shirts were to be worn one day a week at practice, with violators forced to pay a $5 fine that went into a kitty for a postseason party; Hogs poker games every Friday night; satin Hogs jackets to wear on road trips.

Pay attention to the five interior Hogs' dimensions: center Jeff Bostic (6 feet 2 inches, 245 pounds), left guard Russ Grimm (6-3, 275), right guard Mark May (6-6, 285), left tackle Joe Jacoby (6-7, 295), right tackle George Starke (6-5, 260), plus tight ends Don Warren and Rick Walker. Reserves Donald Laster and Fred Dean were Hogs, too. Toward the end of the season, running back John Riggins became an honorary Hog.

During that 1982 season, which was shortened to nine games by a 57-day players' strike, the Hogs imprinted their collective image on the NFL consciousness by leading Washington to an 8-1 record.

PASSING ATTACKS GET FORTY-SIXED

The NFL's liberalized passing rules finally had a measurable effect in 1980, their third season. Footballs began flying like mad. More passes were thrown, per game, for more yards than at any time in history. In San Diego, Air Coryell was in full flower—Dan Fouts operating off a quick drop, throwing to superb receivers such as John Jefferson, Charlie Joiner, Chuck Muncie, and Kellen Winslow, who worked as a slot back or second tight end.

It was a one-back formation, the same one Don Coryell had used in St. Louis. Old Chargers fans recognized the strains of Sid Gillman football in the San Diego attack—except that Gillman never had a tight end like Winslow, a phenomenally gifted 250-pound player with agility and terrific hands. Joe Gibbs, a former Coryell assistant, took the one-back formation to Washington in 1981, and a year later the Redskins were in the Super Bowl.

In 1981, three teams topped the previous mark for most pass attempts. The Vikings, once a power-running team, headed the list with 709 attempts, more than 44 a game, a record that still stands.

"Guys today score a touchdown every 30 seconds and don't even get dirty," the *Boston Globe's* Leigh Montville wrote. "The quarterbacks just hand the ball a boarding pass and lead it to the gate. Everything is in the air."

In San Francisco a new dynasty was on the horizon, with head coach Bill Walsh as its architect. The horizontal passing game so firmly in place today belongs to Walsh, who won a Super Bowl with it in 1981, thanks largely to a third-year quarterback named Joe Montana. Walsh traced its development to his old San Jose State coach, Bob Bronzan—"a great innovative thinker, highly underrated," he said; to his year spent with the Raiders, where the Gillman system had filtered down; and to his eight seasons as an assistant at Cincinnati, where Paul Brown gave him leeway to develop the offense any way he saw fit.

Film study since has unearthed its mysteries: underneath crossing patterns, flooding an area and putting pressure on a linebacker, use of the fullback as a possession receiver underneath, scripted plays with no sequence repeated from previous games, option reads by the receivers, and breakout patterns at the end of routes.

And there were the great instincts of Montana, who could read just a little bit more, get through his progression more quickly, throw the ball with better timing, and pass better on the move than any other quarterback of his day.

The strike-shortened 1982 season was a quirky reversion to power. Gibbs's one-back set, featuring the thundering hoofbeats of 240-pound John Riggins and the feared Counter-Trey (in which the offside guard and tackle, two of the Redskins' five Hogs, pulled and led the other way), won a Super Bowl title.

Meanwhile, Bears defensive coach Buddy Ryan was building a scary operation in Chicago. It was an offensive coordinator's nightmare called the 46 defense, which covered each offensive lineman with a man head-up, loaded one side with two outside linebackers (either of whom might rush), and occasionally sent six or seven men at the passer.

"Son-of-a-gun made me change my draft philosophy," the Raiders' Al Davis said. "To play against the forty-six you've got to have a great center."

Ryan's 46, with its relentless pressure and great front fours ("Neanderthal Football," the Giants' Bill Parcells called it), earned the Bears the Super Bowl XX crown and later got his Philadelphia Eagles into the playoffs.

Pass rushing was becoming a fine art. A new position was created, the rush-linebacker, who would pursue the passer, often from a wide angle, with few pass-coverage responsibilities. The Giants' Lawrence Taylor was the best of all time at the position.

While the passers were having their decade, the running game seemed to be dying. A new type of offensive lineman had come into the league, 300 pounds, fortified by years of weight training—and, in some cases, anabolic steroids, which became a problem for the league in the 1980s.

These new linemen were able to bench press 450 pounds and pass-block effectively, but were less nimble on run-block techniques. "Belly-bumpers," former Colts coach Frank Kush called them. It had become that type of game.

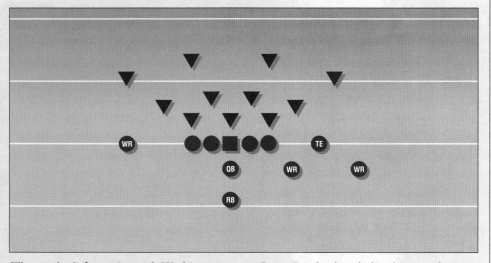

The one-back formation took Washington to two Super Bowls, then declined in popularity.

Superb coaches also were at work in 1983. Bill Parcells took over a New York Giants team in disarray, and though his rookie record was a disappointing 3-12-1, the Giants would reach the playoffs in each of the next three seasons. Chuck Knox of the Seattle Seahawks and the Los Angeles Rams' John Robinson had more immediate effects.

Robinson left the University of Southern California and coaxed the Rams to a 9-7 record and a wild-card berth after the team had gone 8-17 over two previous seasons. Knox, formerly the Buffalo Bills' head coach, produced a more dramatic breakthrough: The 9-7 Seahawks made the playoffs for the first time since the franchise was born in 1976. Warner, the rookie running back from Penn State, carried 335 times for 1,449 yards and scored 13 touchdowns.

It was a bittersweet season in Chicago. Mike Ditka guided Chicago to an improved 8-8 record, but team owner George Halas, the last surviving member of the second organizational meeting that led to the formation of the NFL, died at 88.

Scintillating statistics spiced the regular season. Dickerson, the Rams'

Marcus Allen's twisting, against-the-grain, 74-yard run sank the Redskins in Super Bowl XVIII. At the time, few suspected it would be the AFC's last Super Bowl victory for at least a decade.

rookie running back, carried 390 times for 1,808 yards and 18 touchdowns. Philadelphia wide receiver Mike Quick caught 69 passes for a league-high 1,409 yards and 13 touchdowns. Raiders tight end Todd Christensen caught 92 passes for 1,247 yards and 12 touchdowns.

The Washington Redskins defended their championship with vigor. They ripped through the regular season with a 14-2 record, marking the first 14-win season for an NFC team, and they set an NFL record with 541 points. The Redskins disposed of the Los Angeles Rams 51-7 in their first playoff game. It was the biggest postseason spread in 26 seasons and the largest in the Redskins' 51-year history.

Not surprisingly, the Redskins were clear-cut favorites to beat the Los Angeles Raiders in Super Bowl XVIII. Experts pointed to a high-powered offense that featured Riggins, who at 34 had just completed the best season (1,347 yards, an NFL-record 24 touchdowns) of his career. They also cited Washington's wild 37-35 victory over the same Raiders earlier that season.

In one of the ultimate game's most surprising scores, the Raiders razed the Redskins 38-9, producing the most lopsided Super Bowl to that date. The score was 14-3 before Raiders linebacker Jack Squirek intercepted an ill-advised Joe Theismann pass at the Washington 5-yard line and ran it in for a touchdown with seven seconds left in the first half.

And things got worse for Washington. The Raiders' Marcus Allen reversed his field in the third quarter and brush-stroked a 74-yard masterpiece of a touchdown run. He finished with a Super Bowl-record 191 yards on 20 carries and won the MVP award. It was a triumph for the underdogs and the AFC savored its ninth Super Bowl victory in 12 seasons. Who would have guessed it would be more than a decade before the AFC won another?

The Science of Sweetness

The Chicago Bears were not a good team in 1974—far from it. They won four games under Abe Gibron and, in retrospect, the only positive residue of that season was the fourth overall pick in the 1975 draft.

The Bears sweated as Atlanta chose California quarterback Steve Bartkowski, Dallas followed with Maryland linebacker Randy White, and the Colts took North Carolina guard Ken Huff. Then Chicago secured a piece of history, drafting Jackson State running back Walter Payton.

Jackson State was not exactly a football factory, but Payton had scored 464 points there, a National Collegiate Athletic Association record that included 66 touchdowns, plus assorted field goals and extra points. He was a punter, too, but it was his running skills the scouts coveted.

Payton, a powerful, 5-foot 11-inch, 202-pound package, led the NFC with 1,390 yards his second year in Chicago, the first of a record 10 seasons he would clear the 1,000-yard mark. Were it not for the strike of 1982, he might have done it 11 consecutive seasons.

Payton, whose bouyant personality earned him the nickname "Sweetness," was a pugnacious competitor; he seemed to relish contact that would have sent many backs running out of bounds. Payton's longevity could be traced to his diligence in the weight room. He could bench-press 390 pounds and

PAYTON'S PLACE

Bears running back Walter Payton retired after the 1987 season, having gained an NFL-record 16,726 yards in 13 seasons. The league's top career rushers:

PLAYER	YEARS	ATT.	YDS.	AVG.	LONG	TD
Walter Payton	13	3,838	16,726	4.4	76	110
Eric Dickerson	11	2,996	13,259	4.4	85	90
Tony Dorsett	12	2,936	12,739	4.3	99	77
Jim Brown	9	2,359	12,312	5.2	80	106
Franco Harris	13	2,949	12,120	4.1	75	91
John Riggins	14	2,916	11,352	3.9	66	104
O.J. Simpson	11	2,404	11,236	4.7	94	61
Ottis Anderson	14	2,562	10,273	4.0	76	81
Earl Campbell	8	2,187	9,407	4.3	81	74
Marcus Allen	12	2,296	9,309	4.1	61	91

"Walter Payton is the alllll-tiiiiime greatest. Remember the word alllll-tiiiiime! All-time means that he's the greatest since they started keeping records. Maybe there was some other guy, who is now unknown to man, who carried a stone for more yards. Or maybe those guys who carried messages from city to city covered more yardage. You know, the guys in Greece. But as far as we know, Payton's the greatest."

—DARRYL GRANT,
WASHINGTON REDSKINS
DEFENSIVE TACKLE

Opposite: Chicago's Walter Payton set NFL records with 10 1,000-yard rushing seasons and 77 100-yard games.

INDISPUTABLE VISUAL EVIDENCE

In 1986, the NFL decided to test the power of the rewind button. Meeting in the spring of 1986, club owners voted 23 to 4, with one abstaining, to utilize limited instant replay to review officiating calls for the 1986 season. The device, until then just a nifty enhancement of a game telecast, literally was taken to a higher level. There would be a new man upstairs—a replay official seated in front of two television monitors.

The system concentrated on plays of possession (e.g., fumbles, receptions, and muffs); those involving the sidelines, goal lines, end lines, and line of scrimmage; and cases of more than 11 players on the field for a given team.

Field officials still would have the final say on infractions such as clipping, offsides, and pass interference.

Through instant replay's six years as an officiating aid, its bywords were: "The system will be used to reverse an on-field decision only when the replay official has indisputable visual evidence available to him that warrants the change."

One predictable complaint was that the process made games longer and slowed tempo.

"It was a big second-guess on the game," said George Young, general manager of the New York Giants. Young was a leading opponent of the system and led the movement that eventually put together enough votes to eliminate it in 1992.

Young remembered leaving the meeting after instant replay had been defeated. "Somebody grabbed me and asked, 'Aren't you happy about the vote?' I said, 'I'm happy about victories, not votes.'"

But in a way, Young, along with the more than 100 men in the officiating fraternity and a considerable percentage of pro football fans, had been vindicated. Upon further review, America stood behind its NFL field officials.

---

squat more than 600 pounds.

By the time he reached 30, a certifiable offensive line had developed in front of Payton. He reached the 10,000-yard plateau faster than legendary runners such as Jim Brown, O.J. Simpson, and Franco Harris, and on October 7, 1984, at Soldier Field, he left them all behind.

On the second play of the third quarter against the Saints, the Bears ran a play called Toss-28-Weak. Fullback Matt Suhey and left guard Mark Bortz hit the New Orleans line, leaving a small crease for Payton. Typically, he turned it into a 6-yard gain. That pushed Payton past Brown's 12,312-yard NFL record.

In 1987, Payton would finish his 13-year career with 3,838 carries and 16,726 yards, both all-time records.

The Sound of Broken Records

Payton wasn't the only star who put up breathtaking numbers in 1984.

The Rams' Eric Dickerson, in only his second NFL season, carried 379 times and gained 2,105 yards. That total broke the single-season record of 2,003 yards, set by O.J. Simpson in 1973 (Simpson posted his total in a 14-game season, while Dickerson did it in 16 games). Dickerson had a dozen 100-yard games, a record that would go unequaled until Pittsburgh's Barry Foster matched the feat in 1992.

Miami quarterback Dan Marino, also in his second season, torched NFL defenses for a record 5,084 passing yards. Marino surpassed the standard of 4,802 yards set by San Diego's Dan Fouts in 1981. To put it in perspective, understand that Marino passed for more yards than 11 other teams gained in the air *and* on the ground.

Marino also threw 48 touchdown passes that season, obliterating the mark of 36 shared by George Blanda and Y.A. Tittle. Marino passed for 400 yards four times and 300 yards nine times, both NFL records.

Washington wide receiver Art Monk, a powerful possession receiver who artfully used his body to ward off defenders, took his place in the record book. Monk caught 106 passes, 5 more than Charley Hennigan posted 20 years earlier for the AFL's Houston Oilers.

In the third year that sacks were charted as an official NFL statistic, New York Jets defensive end Mark Gastineau set a record that still stands. Using his astonishing outside speed, Gastineau flattened opposing quarterbacks 22 times. Seattle safety Ken Easley led the league with 10 interceptions.

No one managed to intercept the Colts when they left Baltimore on March 28. They had put the NFL on the map in 1958 by winning the epic overtime NFL Championship Game and, in effect, had helped to legitimize the merger with the AFL by losing Super Bowl III to the Jets.

But by the late 1970s, Robert Irsay's team had declined, and attendance followed suit. The moving vans delivered the Colts to Indianapolis, where they slipped from 7-9 to 4-12.

It was, in fact, a season of movement, as the New York Jets left Shea Stadium to share Giants Stadium with their NFC rivals. Meanwhile, three NFL teams changed hands. An 11-man group headed by H.R. (Bum) Bright bought the Dallas Cowboys, Canadian businessman Patrick Bowlen purchased the Denver Broncos, and real estate developer Alex Spanos assumed control of the San Diego Chargers.

Super Bowl XIX was advertised as a clash between flame throwers: Miami's Dan Marino and Joe Montana of San Francisco. True, Marino had outthrown Montana by more than 1,400 yards and 20 touchdowns, but the 49ers had a terrific defense and an underrated running game—an irresistible postseason combination.

The Dolphins led 10-7 after the first quarter, but the 49ers, playing close to home at Stanford Stadium, scored 3 touchdowns in the second quarter and ran away. The final score of 38-16 only hinted at San Francisco's dominance.

Montana, who completed 24 of 35 passes for 331 yards, presided over an offense that produced a Super Bowl-record 537 yards and held the ball for more than 37 minutes. Montana won his second MVP award in as many tries, but he received plenty of help from running back Roger Craig, who scored a game-record 3 touchdowns, and a defense that sacked Marino 4 times—the most in the young passer's career.

A Bear Market

Webster's dictionary defines the word *team* this way: "a group of people working together in a coordinated effort."

But it is far more complex than that. Each year, a handful of teams in professional sports combine the elusive traits of talent, diligence, execution, and personality, and champions are born.

The 1985 season was more than OK for Bears rookie William (Refrigerator) Perry.

On rare occasions, however, a team can transcend its sport. The 1985 Chicago Bears were such a collection.

They were the big, bad Bears, created in the image of their snarling head coach, Mike Ditka. They had more characters than a Dickens novel: wild quarterback Jim McMahon, stylish running back Walter Payton, wide-eyed middle linebacker Mike Singletary, cantankerous defensive coordinator Buddy Ryan, and a rookie defensive tackle named William Perry.

They called Perry "The Refrigerator" because of his ample size, which fluctuated between 320 and 380 pounds. And when Ditka called his number—on offense—in a Monday-night game in October, a star was born. Perry, flashing an infectious, gap-toothed grin, scored on a 1-yard run against Green Bay and made the lead block on two other scoring runs by Payton as the Bears raised their record to 7-0.

If the Miami Dolphins hadn't beaten the Bears 38-24 in another Monday-night game in December—the highest-rated prime-time game ever—Chicago would have been history's only 19-0 team. As it was, the Bears settled for 18-1.

It was Chicago's "46" defense that allowed the team to dominate. The brainchild of Ryan, the 46 was named for the number worn by former Bears safety Doug Plank. Pressure was the cornerstone of Ryan's defense.

With eight men on the line of scrimmage, offenses never knew exactly where the pressure was going to originate. Would it be from defensive ends Richard Dent and Dan Hampton? From the tackles, Steve McMichael and Perry? Outside linebackers Otis Wilson and Wilber Marshall? The Bears sacked quarterbacks 72 times in 1984, an NFL record that still stands.

After Chicago had roared through the regular season, Super Bowl XX, played in New Orleans, was anticlimactic. The Bears blanked the Giants 21-0 in their first playoff game; as it happened, it was their closest postseason contest. The Rams were dispatched 24-0, and that left the New England Patriots.

The Patriots were a proud team, featuring future Hall of Fame guard John Hannah and linebacker Andre Tippett, who had an AFC-high 16½ sacks. It was a team that had made history by winning three straight road playoff games as a wild-card entry. But the Bears were better …much better. New England was beaten 46-10 in a game that wasn't as close as the score suggests.

The margin of victory was the largest ever, and the Bears set 11

Not even Randy White could keep the Rams' Eric Dickerson from a playoff record.

The USFL eventually failed, both as a viable sports entity and in its lawsuit against the more established league. But it did feature a number of future NFL stars during its three years of existence, including the Houston Gamblers' Jim Kelly (left), the Memphis Showboats' Reggie White (middle), and the New Jersey Generals' Herschel Walker.

Super Bowl records and tied 15 more. Dent, who was in on 2 sacks and forced 2 fumbles, was named MVP. "We've been working hard the last two years to be the best ever," he said after the game. "I believe we're in the running, and if we're not, I'd like to see who's better."

America loved every moment. Regular-season ratings were up significantly at the three major networks. Super Bowl XX replaced the final episode of "M*A*S*H" as the most-watched television program in history. A total of 127 million Americans watched the game, and two months later an estimated 300 million Chinese watched a taped version.

Lost in the spectacle of the return of the Monsters of the Midway was an individual achievement that will be difficult to match. San Francisco 49ers running back Roger Craig, in his third season out of Nebraska, became the first NFL player to produce 1,000 yards both rushing and receiving in the same season. Craig ran 214 times for 1,050 yards and caught 92 passes for 1,016 yards. He even outgained teammate Jerry Rice (49 catches, 927 yards, 3 touchdowns), an elegant rookie receiver from Mississippi Valley State.

The Raiders' Marcus Allen was the rushing leader with 1,759 yards, ahead of Atlanta's Gerald Riggs (1,719). Eric Dickerson set an NFL playoff record with 248 rushing yards in the Rams' 20-0 victory over Dallas. He carried 34 times and scored on touchdown runs of 55 and 40 yards. On September 29, Kansas City safety Deron Cherry intercepted 4 passes, equaling a league record held by 15 other players.

The NFL got its last glimpse of Washington quarterback Joe Theismann in action on November 18, when Giants linebacker Lawrence Taylor sacked him and broke his leg. On the other hand, the league got its first glimpse of Virginia Tech defensive end Bruce Smith, who was the first pick, by Buffalo, in the NFL's fiftieth draft.

The NFL welcomed two new owners, Norman Braman in Philadelphia and Tom Benson in New Orleans. The arrival of both men would signal an upturn in fortunes for their teams.

Giants Find Use for USFL

In 1983, the NFL had experienced another challenge to its preeminence when the United States Football League began operating in the fallow period from March to July. The league's creator, New Orleans entrepreneur Donald

"Most football players are temperamental. That's ninety percent temper and ten percent mental."

—DOUG PLANK,
CHICAGO BEARS SAFETY

Phil Simms was as close as it gets to flawless in Super Bowl XXI. He completed 22 of 25 passes and directed a 30-point second half for Bill Parcells's Giants.

Dixon, believed that the months from September through January just weren't enough for a pigskin-hungry public. In some ways, he was right.

The USFL started in 1983 with 12 teams. The Michigan Panthers were the league's first champions, prevailing over the Philadelphia Stars. The following two seasons, head coach Jim Mora's Stars were the class of the fledgling league.

There were plenty of stars on display. Jim Kelly played quarterback for the Houston Gamblers, Herschel Walker ran for the New Jersey Generals, Steve Young called signals for the Los Angeles Express, and Reggie White crunched quarterbacks for the Memphis Showboats. Steve Spurrier coached the Tampa Bay Bandits, while general manager Bill Polian and head coach Marv Levy guided the Chicago Blitz.

After three seasons, the USFL planned to move to a fall schedule, but when the league failed to get a television contract, it placed its future in the hands of the federal court system. The USFL, which claimed the NFL had, among other things, monopolized the television market for professional football, filed a $1.7 billion antitrust suit against the league.

On July 29, 1986, after an 11-week jury trial in U.S. District Court in New York, the USFL was awarded a single dollar (automatically trebled to $3 under antitrust law) for its time and effort. The verdict would be upheld two years later with a unanimous decision by the 2nd Circuit Court of Appeals in New York.

Many of the defunct league's stars already had signed with NFL teams; in all, 178 USFL players, such as new Washington Redskins Kelvin Bryant and Gary Clark, would wind up on NFL rosters.

The Giants were particularly wise in their USFL signings. Head coach Bill Parcells said he believes that winning a Super Bowl, let alone two, wouldn't have been possible without punter Sean Landeta, center Bart Oates, fullback Maurice Carthon, and guard Chris Godfrey.

The Giants reached Super Bowl XXI with a classic formula: a powerful running game and a suffocating defense. Running back Joe Morris gained 1,516 yards behind the blocking of a polished offensive line, with added muscle from Carthon and tight end Mark Bavaro. The defense, led by linebacker Lawrence Taylor and his league-high 20½ sacks, allowed barely 80 rushing yards per game.

The Giants finished 14-2, then routed the San Francisco 49ers 49-3 in frightening fashion. In the NFC Championship Game, New York beat the Redskins for the third time that season, 17-0.

The Denver Broncos, 11-5 in the regular season, lived dangerously in the playoffs. With quarterback John Elway making all the plays, they edged New England and escaped from Cleveland 23-20 in overtime in a memorable AFC Championship Game that featured "The Drive," a 98-yard march in hostile environs that ended with an overtime-forcing touchdown. But the Broncos did not have an answer for the Giants.

Denver led 10-9 at the half, but New York scored all of the third quarter's 17 points and eventually won 39-20 in the Pasadena, California, Rose Bowl. It was the Giants' first NFL title since 1956. And when it was over, Giants linebacker Harry Carson doused Parcells with a vat of Gatorade in his trademark style. "I know one thing," Parcells said. "We buried all the ghosts today. They are all gone."

Giants quarterback Phil Simms, quite simply, had the game of his life when it mattered most. The game's most valuable player completed 22 of 25 passes for 268 yards and 3 touchdowns. His completion percentage of .880 was a Super Bowl record.

Subject to Review

In some ways, the athlete under the most scrutiny in 1986 was one who never appeared on the field. Bo Jackson, the 6-foot-1, 225-pound Auburn running back, was the first pick in the NFL draft, going to the Tampa Bay Buccaneers. But the Heisman Trophy winner, the man Bill Walsh said "has a guaranteed Hall of Fame career," opted to play baseball instead.

Jackson, the quintessential natural, signed with the Kansas City Royals, learned how to hit the curveball, and began swatting prodigious home runs. The Buccaneers suffered in silence.

But the Los Angeles Raiders, figuring a part-time Bo was better than no Bo, drafted Jackson in 1987. He played in seven games and finished as the Raiders' second-leading rusher, with 554 yards on just 81 carries, an average of 6.8—the best among the league's leading runners. When Jackson retired from football after the 1990 season because of a debilitating hip injury, NFL fans were left to wonder what might have been.

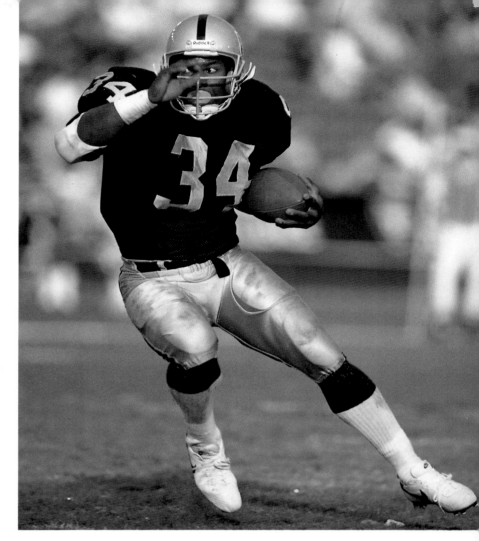

There were four new head coaches at work on the NFL sidelines in 1986, and though not one of them produced a winning record that season, all four soon would be consistent winners.

Jerry Glanville, who had taken over for Hugh Campbell with two games left in 1985, went 5-11 with the Oilers. Jim Mora, of the defunct USFL's Philadelphia-Baltimore Stars, was 7-9 in New Orleans, and former Chicago defensive coordinator Buddy Ryan was 5-10-1 in Philadelphia. Buffalo general manager Bill Polian hired his old friend Marv Levy when Hank Bullough was fired at midseason; the Bills were 2-5 under Levy, only marginally better than Bullough's 2-7 start.

Miami quarterback Dan Marino continued to dazzle. He passed for 4,746 yards, the third-highest total in NFL history and 338 yards short of his all-time mark set two years earlier. Marino also threw 44 touchdown passes, 4 short of his 1984 record. Miami's "Marks Brothers," Clayton and Duper, combined to catch 127 passes for 2,463 yards and 21 touchdowns.

For the first time in league history, officials' rulings were scrutinized by the NFL's new instant-replay system, which had been approved in March. By the end of the season, the league's officials had been vindicated; of 374 plays that were closely reviewed, only 38 were reversed.

The NFL cast another eye to the future that season, addressing the global future of professional football. On August 3, the Chicago Bears beat the

America of the late 1980s couldn't get enough of Bo Jackson, who paved the way for a new wave of two-sport stars. Jackson excelled as both a running back for the Los Angeles Raiders and an outfielder for the Kansas City Royals.

Dallas Cowboys 17-6 at London's Wembley Stadium, in the inaugural American Bowl. The game drew a sellout crowd of 82,699, most of whom cheered every play enthusiastically.

"We think football can succeed on a worldwide basis," explained Tex Schramm, Cowboys president and chairman of the league's competition committee, which originated the idea of football abroad. "Football has more elements than, say, soccer. In time, we could be everywhere."

In the coming years, there would be preseason games in foreign cities such as Tokyo, Berlin, and Montreal. Soon, sales of NFL merchandise outside the United States would surge past $100 million.

The NFL went cable in 1987 when it signed a contract allowing ESPN to televise 13 games. Above: the studio team of Pete Axthelm, Tom Jackson, and Chris Berman.

"Football is a tough game. Physically, if you don't want contact, you'd better grab a tennis racquet."

—DOUG WILLIAMS,
WASHINGTON REDSKINS QUARTERBACK

Replacement Parts

Once again, the NFL hummed on its axis and enjoyed unprecedented success and popularity. The league had set an all-time attendance record in 1986 with 17,304,463 fans. Television ratings were superb and the three major networks all signed on for three more years.

And there was a new wrinkle: ESPN, the cable sports network, signed a three-year contract to televise 13 prime-time games each season. The NFL's debut on ESPN produced the two highest-rated sports programs in basic cable history. The Chicago-Miami preseason game was seen in 3.81 million homes; two weeks later, the Raiders-Dallas game reached 4.36 million.

Before the season, the league announced a new program to benefit NFL veterans who played before the Bert Bell Pension Plan was created and made retroactive to 1959. Each vested player would receive $60 a month for each year of service in the league. On July 1, 400 former NFL players from the pre-1959 era received their long-overdue pension checks.

Then, once again, a dose of labor reality was visited upon Utopia. With the Collective Bargaining Agreement expired, the NFL Players Association called its second strike in five years on September 22, 1987, effective immediately after the New York Jets-New England Patriots game on Monday night.

Games scheduled for the third week were canceled. But while representatives of the owners and players negotiated the issues, the league—remembering the painful strike that cut the 1982 season short by seven games—made plans to play without its rank-and-file. The NFL's 28 teams, heavily taxing their personnel departments, scrambled to sign replacement squads.

For three weeks, this collection of hopefuls and walk-ons—plus a few stars who crossed the picket lines—performed in NFL uniforms. In their own way, the three replacement games colored the season.

The Giants, for instance, didn't take the concept seriously until it was too late—they lost all three games. Their bid to repeat failed to gain momentum when the regulars returned for the seventh week of the season on October 25. The Washington Redskins, on the other hand, moved quickly to secure the best available players and won all three replacement games under coach

WHO WERE THOSE MASKED MEN?

The 1980s was the decade in which pro football players began looking like Neil Armstrong—not the former coach of the Chicago Bears, but the first man on the moon.

Darth Vader-like visors made players look like moon walkers. And new, ultra-light equipment made them lighter on their feet.

Frank Pupello, Tampa Bay's equipment manager, introduced the dark shields to the pro game in 1984, when Buccaneers linebacker Hugh Green needed protection after a serious eye injury. At the request of other equipment men around the league, Pupello rigged up more visors, which had been modeled after motorcycle–helmet shields. Manufacturers soon took over and applied a coating so the visor would not fog up. The NFL eventually passed a rule limiting the new shields to those players who had eye problems.

They came along just at the right time for players such as defensive end Mark Mullaney, whose right eye was severely damaged in 1984 while he was playing for Minnesota.

"I have to wear it," Mullaney said. "If I got hit in the other eye, I'd be blind."

Adding to the astronaut chic, the NFL again dabbled in radio helmets—with about as much success as Paul Brown had in the 1950s. The noise in domed stadiums prompted the league to experiment with radio transmitters and receivers in the 1985 preseason.

"If every player on the offense could communicate through radio receivers, it would eliminate the crowd noise and even speed up the game," said then-Dallas Cowboys president Tex Schramm, a proponent of the devices. "You could all but eliminate the huddle."

By the end of the decade, the huddle still was in use…but radio helmets were not. They never appeared in a regular-season game because the bugs couldn't be eliminated.

The air impact system, however, took a foothold in the 1980s. Byron Donzis developed lighter, stronger equipment using air cushions to protect players. It caused a revolution in shoulder pads, which previously were made of hard foam. The new pads distributed blows to a wider area, thus diminishing them.

Adding a taste of old to the new, plastic facemasks reappeared for the first time in 30 years, only this time they were practically unbreakable. One player put his

Tinted shields: a child of the 1980s.

to the ultimate test. He drove his truck over the mask, which bounced back to form.

Players' hands and feet were covered like never before. When stickum was outlawed early in the decade, receivers turned to tackified golf gloves, which had the sticky stuff built in for better grip. It didn't take long for companies to produce specialized football gloves. Even quarterback Jim McMahon wore gloves when he directed the Chicago Bears to their Super Bowl XX victory inside the New Orleans Superdome.

"After McMahon put on the gloves," said Bears back-up quarterback Mike Tomczak, "I think everybody realized it was all right to wear them."

However, when McMahon wore a series of headbands in the 1985 postseason, it was *not* all right. Watching for the quarterback's next message or company logo became a national obsession in the build-up to Super Bowl XX, but the league reminded him of existing uniform codes…with a hefty fine.

The air impact system produced pads that were both lighter and stronger in the '80s.

Jerry Rice, drafted out of tiny Mississippi Valley State in 1985, quickly became a feared receiver for the 49ers. He set an NFL record with 22 touchdown catches in the strike-shortened 1987 season.

Joe Gibbs. The Redskins extended the winning streak to five games and eventually won the NFC East by a commanding four games.

It was a disjointed season all around.

Six days after the strike ended, the game's most prolific runner, Eric Dickerson, was the center of a monstrous trade that involved three teams and 10 players and/or draft choices.

Dickerson had led the league in rushing his first two seasons, and his first four years with the Los Angeles Rams had resulted in an incredible 6,968 yards. Now, in midseason, he was dealt to the Indianapolis Colts for six draft choices and two players.

The Buffalo Bills were the third team involved in the transaction. They received the rights to Alabama linebacker Cornelius Bennett, a fierce pass rusher taken second in the 1987 draft, from Indianapolis by sending running back Greg Bell and three draft choices to the Rams. The Colts sent running back Owen Gill and three more draft choices to the Rams.

In a delicious piece of irony, Dickerson's combined total of 1,288 rushing yards for the Colts (1,011 yards) and Rams (277) was the league's second-best figure…behind the Rams' Charles White, who posted 1,374 yards.

Second-Quarter Earnings

When it came to scoring points, San Francisco's Jerry Rice was in a class by himself. Catching the bulk of his passes from Joe Montana, Rice reeled in 22 touchdown passes in 1987—to shatter the record of 18 set by Miami wide receiver Mark Clayton in 1984. Rice also scored once by running, giving him 23 touchdowns and 138 points.

He was the first nonkicker to win the scoring title since the Raiders' Marcus Allen in 1982, and the first pure receiver to do it since the 1951 exploits of Elroy (Crazylegs) Hirsch. Rice set another record by scoring at least 1 touchdown in 13 consecutive games.

For perspective, consider that New Orleans kicker Morten Andersen kicked 28 of 36 field goals and converted all of his 37 point-after attempts and still placed second with 121 points. The nearest nonkickers? New York Jets running back Johnny Hector, Philadelphia wide receiver Mike Quick, and the Rams' Charles White, with 66 points.

Philadelphia's Reggie White registered 21 sacks, giving him 39 in two seasons since joining the Eagles from the USFL.

Certainly, the Washington Redskins were not the NFC favorites to reach Super Bowl XXII in San Diego. (The 49ers were 13-2 and the Saints were 12-3).

The Redskins trailed the Bears 14-0 at Chicago in a divisional playoff. Ultimately, however, cornerback Darrell Green won the game with a brilliant 52-yard punt return for a touchdown, and Washington was in its fourth NFC Championship Game in six seasons.

A week later, the Redskins beat the Minnesota Vikings 17-10 on a fourth-quarter touchdown pass from Doug Williams to Gary Clark and advanced to the Super Bowl for the third time in the 1980s.

The Denver Broncos, in their second consecutive Super Bowl, led 10-0 after the first quarter. But Washington spontaneously combusted in the second quarter. Exploiting Denver's smaller defense, the Redskins scored 35 points on five possessions in a total possession time of just 6 minutes 27 seconds. The Broncos didn't score. Williams threw touchdown passes of 80, 27, 50, and 8 yards.

It was the most stunning one-quarter outburst in the history of the National Football League.

"I kept looking up at the little thirty-five in the second-quarter box of the scoreboard," said Washington tight end Don Warren. "It was almost unreal. You just don't score thirty-five points in a quarter, especially against the Denver Broncos, especially in the Super Bowl."

When it was over, the Redskins were 42-10 victors, and Williams was the most valuable player. Washington rookie running back Timmy Smith carried 22 times for 204 yards, a Super Bowl record.

"I can't put my finger on it," Williams said. "The receivers just ran great routes and I just put the ball in their hands."

Winds of Change

The 1988 season was a point of transition on many levels.

Dallas coach Tom Landry opened his twenty-ninth season with Dallas, tying the longevity record set by Earl (Curly) Lambeau, who had guided the

QUARTERBACKS' ENEMIES LIST

The term "sack" was coined by former Rams Hall of Fame defensive end David (Deacon) Jones. But, officially, Jones never was credited with any sacks. That's because the statistic was not recognized until 1982, eight years after he retired. In 1984, Jets defensive end Mark Gastineau posted 22 sacks, a record that still stands. Here is how the NFL's career sack leaders stood prior to the 1994 season:

PLAYER	CAREER SACKS
1. Reggie White	137
2. Lawrence Taylor	132½
3. Richard Dent	124½
4. Rickey Jackson	115
5. Greg Townsend	107½
6. Bruce Smith	106
7. Andre Tippett	100
8. Jacob Green	97½
Dexter Manley	97½
10. Steve McMichael	92½

WHY DAWGS HATE HORSES

The Drive. The Fumble. In Denver, they are monuments. In Cleveland, they are nightmares. Anywhere around the NFL, say either one and most folks know what you mean.

The Drive was what enabled the Denver Broncos to tie and eventually defeat the Cleveland Browns in the 1986 AFC Championship Game. Its Driver, John Elway, took the Broncos 98 yards, to a part of Cleveland Stadium called the Dawg Pound. In this end-zone enclosure, named in honor of the Browns' scrapping defense, fans had taken to wearing dog masks, barking like hounds, and pelting the field with dog biscuits. With 5:32 to play and Cleveland leading 20-13, the real Dawgs were on the field, eager for a piece of Elway.

Pressure? Not for the men in orange. "Expectations would have been totally different if we'd started from, say, our

Mark Jackson celebrated his game-tying touchdown at the end of "The Drive."

thirty," Elway said. "With ninety-eight yards to go, if we do it, we're heroes; if we don't, well, hey, that's the way it goes."

Former Browns tight end Ozzie Newsome remembered that as he stood on the Cleveland sideline, it was "a very happy moment in my life."

Newsome's look at life soon did a flip as Elway passed and scrambled his club upfield. His 5-yard scoring pass to Mark Jackson with 37 seconds left and Rich Karlis's extra point made it 20-20. The Browns had first possession in overtime, but were forced to punt. Two passes by Elway put Karlis in position for the game-winning 33-yard field goal.

A year later, the same teams met in the AFC title game at Denver's Mile High Stadium. The Browns trailed 38-31 late in the game. They were driving for the tying touchdown and appeared to have it when, on second-and-5 from the Broncos' 8, Earnest Byner saw a clear path to the goal line.

But Denver cornerback Jeremiah Castille raced up, stripping the Cleveland running back of the ball at the Broncos' 5. Castille fell on it at the 3. The Broncos eventually took an intentional safety, and the Browns were Super Bowl spectators again.

Green Bay Packers from 1921-1949. It would be Landry's last season.

The taciturn coach, whose fedora-framed profile came to symbolize success in the NFL, left a powerful legacy. Starting from scratch in 1960, Landry produced 20 consecutive winning seasons from 1966-1985. Dallas reached five Super Bowls and won two of them.

The Cowboys' core of stars began to age in the middle 1980s, but it was a testament to Landry's skill that Dallas managed to win the NFC East in 1985 with a 10-6 record. Landry might have retired on that high note, but he insisted on rebuilding the Cowboys himself. Dallas fell to 7-9 the following year, then 7-8, and, finally, 3-13.

By 1989, Arkansas oilman Jerry Jones would purchase the team from H. R. (Bum) Bright and replace Landry with his old college roommate, University of Miami coach Jimmy Johnson.

There were other unsettling changes in the NFL. Art Rooney, the founder and owner of the Pittsburgh Steelers, died at 87 before the season began. The team that made history with four Super Bowl victories in the 1970s was left in the capable hands of his son, Dan. Meanwhile, real-estate developer Ken Behring purchased the Seattle Seahawks from the Nordstrom family.

Cardinals owner William Bidwill, citing a lack of community support, moved his team from St. Louis to Phoenix. The change in venue did little to affect the on-field product; the Cardinals were 7-9 at Sun Devil Stadium, after going 7-8 at Busch Stadium the year before.

Outside linebacker Wilber Marshall switched stadiums, too, in unprecedented fashion. Marshall, known for his expertise in avoiding the blocks of tight ends, left the Chicago Bears and signed with Washington as a free agent. As a result, the Bears received the standard compensation of two first-round draft choices, albeit low ones, given the Redskins' string of success. The transaction underlined the league's limited system of free agency and foreshadowed the monumental movement that would come four years later.

Marshall's old head coach, the volatile Mike Ditka, suffered a heart attack on November 2, but missed only a single game, a 28-10 victory over the Tampa Bay Buccaneers. "Iron Mike" returned for a resounding 34-14 win at Washington. "I thought he did very well," said a keen observer of his actions, his wife Diana. "He behaved like a perfect gentleman."

After prodding the Bears to a 12-4 regular-season record, Ditka was voted coach of the year by several organizations. The day Ditka returned to the sidelines, November 13, was Darryl Rogers's last game as Detroit's coach. The Lions, off to a 2-9 start, fired Rogers (18-40 overall) and made popular defensive coordinator Wayne Fontes interim coach. The Lions went 2-3 under Fontes, who formally was named head coach after the regular season.

The surprise team of 1988 was the Cincinnati Bengals. Only one year removed from a last-place 4-11 record, Sam Wyche's Bengals got mean. They won the AFC Central at 12-4, tying Chicago and Buffalo for the NFL's best record.

Quarterback Boomer Esiason, an engaging left-hander, was the league's highest-rated passer, throwing for 3,572 yards and 28 touchdowns. And, behind the blocking of state-of-the-art offensive tackle Anthony Muñoz, Cincinnati led the NFL in rushing and total offense.

Eric Dickerson of Indianapolis won his fourth rushing title in six seasons, carrying 388 times for 1,659 yards and 14 touchdowns. Philadelphia quarterback Randall Cunningham passed for 3,808 yards and led the Eagles in rushing, with 93 carries for 624 yards and 6 touchdowns.

Fog and San Francisco

Cunningham's extraordinary versatility was grounded by forces beyond his control in January. When heavy fog rolled in from Lake Michigan during the first quarter and enveloped Chicago's Soldier Field, the game looked like the set of a mystery movie.

Cunningham passed for 407 yards and guided the Eagles inside the Bears' 26-yard line 10 times, but Philadelphia could manage only 4 field goals by Luis Zendejas. "I could only see twenty yards downfield," Cunningham said afterward. "So, with a seven-step drop, that meant we were using all ten- to fifteen-yard routes. The Bears knew it, and jumped all over those routes."

Chicago's poet laureate, Carl Sandburg, must have seen it coming 72 years earlier when he wrote:

> "The fog comes
> on little cat feet.
> It sits looking
> Over the harbor and city
> on silent haunches
> and then moves on."

John Taylor's 10-yard touchdown catch was the exclamation point to Super Bowl XXIII. It took a brilliant performance by San Francisco's Joe Montana to get past the feisty Bengals.

EXPLOSION IN THE AIR

In 1978, rule changes liberalized pass blocking and restricted the contact a defensive player could make on a receiver. By the early 1980s, teams such as San Diego and San Francisco were taking full advantage of the new rules. Productivity increased dramatically, and the 4,000-yard season—an elusive achievement until first attained by Joe Namath in 1967—fell within reach of NFL quarterbacks:

4,000-YARD PASSERS			
1920s	0	1960s	1
1930s	0	1970s	1
1940s	0	1980s	14
1950s	0	1990-93	5

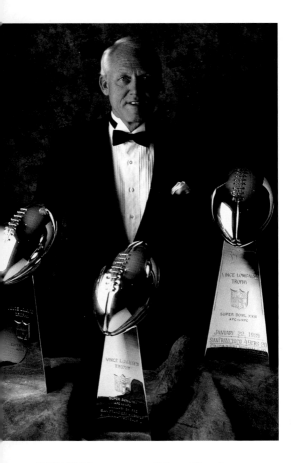

Bill Walsh, master of the offensive game plan, earned some impressive hardware at San Francisco: three Vince Lombardi Trophies.

"Joe Montana is not human. I don't want to call him a god, but he's definitely somewhere in between."

—CRIS COLLINSWORTH,
CINCINNATI BENGALS WIDE RECEIVER

The Eagles went home; the Bears moved on to the NFC Championship Game and a date with San Francisco. *Sans* fog, the 49ers throttled the Bears 28-3 to set up a Super Bowl XXIII matchup with Cincinnati.

The game pitted the NFL's two highest-rated offenses, as created by mentor (the 49ers' Bill Walsh) and pupil (Cincinnati's Wyche). But for nearly three quarters, Super Bowl XXIII lurched along in Miami like a kicker's training film; there were no touchdowns.

Then, finally, the game lived up to its name. The Bengals eventually led the 49ers 16-13, and San Francisco had the ball on its 8-yard line with 3:10 left to play. San Francisco also had quarterback Joe Montana, and he engineered a masterful drive. Eleven plays later, with 34 seconds left, Montana slipped a pass past diving cornerback Ray Horton and into the hands of John Taylor. It was a 10-yard touchdown pass and it was good for a 20-16 victory.

Montana completed 8 of 9 passes on that final drive and finished the game 23-for-36 for a record 357 yards. Still, teammate Jerry Rice, who caught 11 passes for a record-setting 215 yards, was named the game's most valuable player.

"I'd give the MVP to Joe any day," Rice said. "He really took control out there at the end."

It was the fifth consecutive victory for the NFC over the AFC and it elevated the 49ers to a rarified place in history; only the Pittsburgh Steelers had won more Super Bowls. Now, could San Francisco match Pittsburgh's record of four and, simultaneously, become the first NFL team to repeat since the Steelers' teams of 1978-79?

A Man for the Season

Under Commissioner Pete Rozelle, the NFL had risen to a preeminent place in American professional sports. Since 1960, he had guided the league through turbulent times while an evolving nation struggled with itself. He had successfully navigated a thicket of lawsuits, grappled with the vagaries of television technology, and managed to make more than two dozen rich and powerful men and women understand that the league always came first.

But, at the NFL's annual meeting, on March 22, 1989, in Palm Desert, California, Rozelle stunned the owners by announcing his retirement. Certainly, the demands of the job had taken a toll in recent years, but no one saw this coming.

The search for a successor began immediately. After 50 hours of committee debate, a total of four meetings at sites scattered around the country and 11 ballots, NFL counsel Paul Tagliabue prevailed over New Orleans Saints President Jim Finks.

Tagliabue, 48, gradually had won the ear of Rozelle in league matters, and was the choice of the NFL's younger, more progressive owners. A core of long-time owners had supported Finks. When Tagliabue's selection was announced on October 26, 1989, he sounded a conciliatory note.

"To me, the most important thing was the future of the league," Tagliabue said. "I think it will be a minor problem bringing people together. I feel I can have a very good relationship with all twenty-eight owners. I like to think that's why I was a serious candidate."

If Rozelle's beginnings in public relations had equipped him to market the

LIGHTS...CAMERA...

It started in the most humble of offices more than three decades ago—two rooms on the second floor above a Chinese laundry in Philadelphia, a lone Bell and Howell 16-millimeter camera their most prized possession.

Today, home is an 87,000-square-foot archive of pro football history in Mt. Laurel, New Jersey. There seems to be an award for each square inch of space. Perhaps the most cherished tribute is a framed letter from former NFL Commissioner Pete Rozelle to Ed Sabol and his son Steve. Rozelle praised them for their love of the game and their efforts to romanticize it and mythologize it.

"What we have here is a labor of love," Steve Sabol said. "Pete loved the fact that we brought a flair to the game with what we did. On film, we changed [pro football] from black-and-white to color, from marching music to music of today.

When we did something, we thought about the drama. There was a story line."

Ed Sabol filmed Steve playing for Haverford School in Pennsylvania, but he saw more than a game through the camera; he saw his future. So Ed got out of the business of making overcoats and into the business of filming football. He bid $3,000 for the rights to film the 1962 NFL Championship Game between the New York Giants and the Green Bay Packers.

NFL Films was born three years later, and it really took flight in the 1980s. The Sabols' studio has become a vehicle that takes the NFL fan into the heart and soul of the sport.

"When cable boomed in the eighties," Steve said, "everything was set up for us. We had been a significant part of 'Monday Night Football' when we packaged those highlights together for the popular halftime show with Howard Cosell. Then came HBO, which had its NFL show each week, using our stuff.

"Now we were going on prime time, thanks to cable. 'This is the NFL' is the longest-running syndicated sports show in history—twenty-seven years."

NFL Films captures the players as they are swept by human emotions. There are classic battles and comical situations, legendary plays and overlooked greatness. The films go beyond the score.

"What we put together took the NFL all over the globe," Steve said. "Some NFL people tell the story of how, during the first game played in Japan, fans started to protest. All they had seen of the NFL were our films, with all the dramatic plays one right after another. The Japanese fans at the game didn't understand the time outs, commercials, or halftime."

Alas, life can't quite imitate the art of NFL Films.

league with a flair, Tagliabue was a lawyer in an age of litigation. He had represented the NFL in several lawsuits, including the Raiders' suit and the antitrust action brought by the USFL. With a labor agreement seen as the key to the future, Tagliabue clearly was the man for the job.

Less than a year later, Tagliabue had negotiated a four-year television package worth $3.643 billion, overhauled the league's uneven drug program, shortened games significantly, enlivened the playoff format, and opened a dialogue with the players concerning a long-overdue labor agreement.

One thing Tagliabue couldn't influence was Bill Walsh's sudden departure from the 49ers. Four days after San Francisco's Super Bowl XXIII victory, Walsh stepped down as head coach. He had won three Super Bowls in three tries, compiling a 10-year record of 102-63-1. Walsh, who would go on to broadcasting and then return to coach at Stanford University, was succeeded in San Francisco by defensive coordinator George Seifert.

The 49ers did anything but wilt without Walsh; in fact, they might have been shaken out of a potentially complacent season. With Joe Montana setting a record for passing efficiency (his quarterback rating was a stratospheric 112.4, erasing Milt Plum's standard of 110.4 set in 1960), the 49ers won 14 of 16 games.

San Francisco never really was challenged in the playoffs, either. The Minnesota Vikings went quietly, 41-13 in a divisional playoff, and the Los Angeles Rams fell 30-3 in the NFC Championship Game.

THE NEW 'BOYS

In 1989, Jerry Jones, an Arkansas businessman who had forged a financial empire in oil and gas exploration, purchased the Dallas Cowboys and their stadium leases from H.R. (Bum) Bright for a reported $140 million, a record price for an American sports enterprise at the time. The new owner promptly fired Tom Landry, the only head coach the team had known in its 29-year history.

There went the neighborhood. It was only a matter of time until club president and general manager Tex Schramm followed Landry out the door. Over the years, the two had elevated the Cowboys from a ragtag bunch that debuted with a record of 0-11-1 in 1960 to the stature of "America's Team," a widely popular piece of football machinery that appeared in five Super Bowls and won two.

To replace Landry, Jones brought in his old University of Arkansas teammate and roommate, Jimmy Johnson, who had put together a 52-9 record at the Univer-

sity of Miami from 1984-88, including a national championship in 1987. At a press conference, Jones mock-admitted to the media, "Jimmy Johnson would be the first to tell you that he couldn't carry Tom Landry's water bucket." But Jones came right back with, "I wouldn't have bought the Dallas Cowboys if Jimmy Johnson couldn't be my coach."

Jones, stressing his bottom-line image, then chiseled his name into the walls of Texas Stadium with what has become known as "the socks and jocks quote":

"I will sell my house in Little Rock and move to Dallas. My entire office and my entire business will be at [the Cowboys'] complex. I want to know everything there is to know, from player contracts to socks and jocks and television contracts. This is my company, and I will be making all the decisions. The Cowboys will be my life."

Over the next five seasons, Johnson and his perfect haircut proved equally flamboyant, with straightforward opinions and occasional predictions. Jones cut costs, Johnson nurtured a youth movement and built a team in his own image, and the Cowboys won Super Bowls XXVII and XXVIII before Johnson abruptly resigned in March, 1994.

A month earlier, veteran Dallas columnist Skip Bayless had written in the *Insider* newsletter: "For more than 30 years, most Cowboy fans held Landry up to heavenly standards unfair for even the finest mortal."

The standards were even higher for the brash new Cowboys leaders...and they lived up to them.

And, for the third time in four seasons, the Denver Broncos awaited the NFC champion. The two previous games had been disastrous for the Broncos as they were outscored by 19 and 32 points by the Giants and Redskins. Incredibly, the 49ers did even better in Super Bowl XXIV.

The final score was 55-10, the widest margin in the game's history. The 49ers scored touchdowns on four of their six first-half possessions on the way to a 27-3 lead. Montana, who won his third MVP award, completed 22-of-29 passes for 297 yards and a Super Bowl-record 5 touchdowns, 3 to Jerry Rice.

So, the 49ers managed to repeat as NFL champions and, with four Super Bowl titles, draw even with the celebrated Steelers—all with Seifert, a rookie head coach, holding the reins.

Shakeups

There were two other highly visible coaching changes in 1989. In the off-season, Cleveland head coach Marty Schottenheimer had resigned, despite his rather glowing credentials. (He had landed the Browns in the 1986 and 1987 AFC Championship Games and produced a playoff berth four years running.) Schottenheimer's new team, the Chiefs, improved from 4-11-1 to 8-7-1.

In Los Angeles, Hall of Fame offensive tackle Art Shell replaced Mike Shanahan as head coach on October 3, four games into the season. Raiders owner Al Davis made his former star the first black head coach in modern NFL history, and the first since Fritz Pollard coached the Akron Pros in 1921.

Two weeks later, the earth moved again in California, this time in a literal sense. The Bay Area Earthquake overwhelmed San Francisco's resources, forcing the 49ers to relocate for one game. San Francisco gathered itself and, on October 22, beat the New England Patriots 37-20 at Stanford Stadium.

Facing litigation from the players over the issue of free agency, the NFL created a new system of player movement in the offseason. It was called Plan B, and it permitted teams to protect front-line players, leaving the rest free to negotiate with other teams.

When the first signing period ended on April 1, 229 free agents had changed teams. When the regular season kicked off, 111 Plan B free agents had landed roster spots, and many made significant contributions.

The new player with the most impact was in Detroit, where rookie running back Barry Sanders carried 280 times for 1,470 yards and 14 touchdowns.

From a team standpoint, the statistical gem belonged to the Washington Redskins. So egalitarian were Redskins quarterbacks that each member of "The Posse"—Art Monk (86 catches, 1,186 yards), Ricky Sanders (80, 1,138), and Gary Clark (79, 1,229)—cleared 1,000 yards.

Earlier in the season, Dallas made a blockbuster deal with the Minnesota Vikings that would serve as a catalyst for the Cowboys' success in the 1990s. Owner Jerry Jones and head coach Jimmy Johnson shipped their only Pro Bowl player, running back Herschel Walker, to Minnesota in the largest trade in NFL history, involving 18 players or draft picks and the San Diego Chargers.

When the Cowboys traded quarterback Steve Walsh to New Orleans for an additional handful of draft choices, the handwriting was on the wall. Players drafted or acquired as a result of the two deals—including running back Emmitt Smith, defensive tackle Russell Maryland, offensive tackle Erik Williams, and cornerback Kevin Smith—would go on to play pivotal roles in the Cowboys' championships in 1992 and 1993.

Barry Sanders made his mark quickly, rushing for 1,470 yards as a rookie in 1989.

TEAM *of the* EIGHTIES

THE TEAM THAT WINS TOGETHER

There had been many proud moments in a very proud decade for the San Francisco 49ers. Funny that Eddie DeBartolo, the excitable owner of the 49ers, couldn't remember feeling prouder than he did right there, right then, on the end-zone floor of Veterans Stadium. Funny because this was the third game of the 1989 season, and nothing of great substance was on the line, other than the 49ers getting off to a 3-0 start.

But DeBartolo, as the clock wound down, had wet eyes and a hoarse voice. "God," he said, "I love this team. They're spunky. I'm prouder of them right now than I was at our Super Bowls."

And then, as his players came off the field, DeBartolo grabbed as many as he could, hugging safety Ronnie Lott ("I'm so proud of you, Ronnie!"), jumping into the arms of running back Roger Craig ("I love you guys, Roger!"), and thanking quarterback Joe Montana and wide receiver Jerry Rice ("What a game, guys!").

These 49ers were on their way to their fourth Super Bowl triumph of the eighties, and what a perfect frame this game was for their greatness. Not all the most significant players of the eighties played in San Francisco. Lawrence Taylor invented a new position—terroristic pass-rusher—and brought the Giants to great heights. Anthony Muñoz of the Bengals was the prototypical left tackle for a sport that, in one decade, got faster and stronger. Kellen Winslow of the Chargers played the type of athletic, physical, and speedy tight end that we'd never seen before, and haven't since. Chicago running back Walter Payton put the all-time rushing record 4,000 yards beyond what anyone ever had fathomed. Great players all.

But the 49ers defined the decade. Their truly great players—Lott in the defensive secondary, Rice at receiver, Craig as the most versatile back of his day, Montana at quarterback—endured and flourished under the decade's resident genius, Bill Walsh. Not to overstate this 38-28 regular-season win at Philadelphia in 1989, but it showed in so many ways why these players, and this team, are one of the special groups ever to play.

Four reasons why:

1. It was on the road.

Fathom this: From 1981 to 1989, the 49ers had a better regular-season road record than any other NFL team had at home. Honest. San Francisco treated its players wonderfully on the road, traveling two-seats-to-a-person on the charter flights, giving most of the players private rooms at road hotels, going to the road site on Friday instead of Saturday so the team could have two restful nights in the hotel and a day and a half to focus on the task at hand.

"What Bill always drummed into us," said offensive lineman Randy Cross, "was winning on the road. He talked about how it was us against the entire city, about how tough we had to be, about what a thrill it would be to take that win away from that team in its home stadium."

Bill Walsh was a fine judge of talent and a superb offensive mind, but he deserves more credit than he has gotten for mastering the details of building a winner.

2. Montana.

This might have been the best game of his life. Blasphemy? Yes or no, it was a perfect example of why, when the NFL turns 100 in 2020, a lot of the old-timers will say he's the best they ever saw.

After getting sacked 7 times in the first three quarters, and after his running game had produced the grand total of 8 yards, Montana had the ball four times—not including a late kneel-down—in the fourth quarter. In those four possessions he completed 11 of 12 passes for 227 yards, including touchdown passes of 70, 8, 25, and 33 yards to four different receivers...and all against a pass rush that had three Pro Bowl players chasing him on every throw. The 49ers trailed by 11 twice in the fourth quarter, but as a typically blasé Montana said later: "You relish being in those situations."

Joe did. Most others preferred nice, 14-point, fourth-quarter cushions.

3. Explosiveness.

Early in the game, Rice burned the Eagles for a 68-yard lightning score. John Taylor streaked for a 70-yard touchdown in the fourth quarter. And when the Eagles, down 31-28, tried to salvage the game with three minutes to go, *boom!*— Lott intercepted a pass by Randall Cunningham, setting up an insurance touchdown scored, of course, by Rice. "Jerry Rice," Dallas receiver Michael Irvin once said, "is Michael Jordan in cleats."

4. Pride.

The 49ers almost unwittingly followed in the footsteps Walsh choreographed. It seemed a damnable offense to lose football games. In the locker room afterward, there was nothing to distinguish this game from the horde of other nice 49ers victories over the decade. "We're warriors," Craig once said. "We're not coming out of games when we're hurt. And in the offseason, we'll train harder than anyone. That's what we do."

One thing Walsh drilled into his guys was that having high expectations was the only way to succeed. Why else would Rice and Lott be doing five-hour offseason track workouts? Because they, like so many of their teammates, were determined never to accept second place. "Every game we go into, I can't imagine us losing," safety Jeff Fuller said in 1989.

The only other club to place four people on the team of the eighties, Chicago,

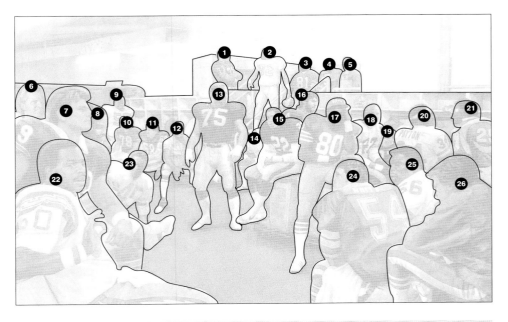

1) John Hannah, guard; 2) Reggie White, defensive end; 3) Billy Johnson, punt returner; 4) Sean Landeta, punter; 5) Steve Largent, wide receiver; 6) Morten Andersen, kicker; 7) Dan Hampton, defensive tackle; 8) Mike Singletary, inside linebacker; 9) Dwight Stephenson, center; 10) Anthony Muñoz, tackle; 11) Russ Grimm, guard; 12) Ronnie Lott, safety; 13) Howie Long, defensive end; 14) Mike Nelms, kickoff returner; 15) Mike Haynes, cornerback; 16) Jim Covert, tackle; 17) Jerry Rice, wide receiver; 18) Mel Blount, cornerback; 19) Ted Hendricks, linebacker; 20) Walter Payton, running back; 21) Eric Dickerson, running back; 22) Kellen Winslow, tight end; 23) Kenny Easley, safety; 24) Randy White, defensive tackle; 25) Lawrence Taylor, outside linebacker; 26) Joe Montana, quarterback .

looked at mid-decade as though it might give San Francisco a run for team of the decade. The 49ers had the offensive genius of Rice at wide receiver; the Bears had the wondrous Payton at running back. The 49ers had the ferocious and bright Lott quarterbacking the secondary; the Bears had middle linebacker Mike Singletary, just as ferocious and just as bright, quarterbacking the front seven. The 49ers didn't have an interior defensive lineman as imposing as Dan Hampton of the Bears, nor a pass protector as good for as long as Jim Covert.

The difference in the staying power of the Bears versus that of the 49ers? Walsh has to be one reason. He built a stronger front office and coaching staff than the Bears. But look behind the center. Jim McMahon started about half the Bears' games in his Chicago career. Montana

missed only a few. And he was as consistent a player as the eighties featured, not the yo-yo of a performer and a physical being McMahon was.

Maybe that's why we've grown to admire these 49ers over the years. In a game that so regularly beats down its heroes, and so consistently clobbers pretenders to long-term greatness, the 49ers refused to give in to mediocrity.

Back to that weekend in Philadelphia, one last time. On Saturday afternoon, in his airport hotel room, new coach George Seifert pondered a question about why the 49ers kept winning. Put talent aside for a minute, he was told. Why else?

Seifert looked straight ahead. "It's expected of us," he said, without a second's pause. Talent, plus such great expectations, can do wonders for a football team. It did for this one.

A LONG, LONG WAY FROM CANTON, 1920

After a good day at the race track in 1933, 32-year-old Art Rooney bought an NFL franchise for $2,500, and the Pirates (renamed the Steelers in 1941) joined the 10-team NFL. In 1993, the NFL's twenty-ninth and thirtieth franchises were awarded to Carolina and Jacksonville. The price tag was $140 million each.

Clearly, a lot had happened in 60 years, and it can't all be explained by the inflation rate. The National Football League, which spent decades struggling for financial stability and popular approval, had become a powerful, global corporation by the dawn of the 1990s.

It did not come without a cost. Gone were the innocence and small-time charm of earlier eras. Billion-dollar television contracts and licensing agreements spelled better times for a lot of people involved with the sport, but they also contributed to big-business headaches such as strikes, holdouts, autograph fees, and scalpers asking $1,000 for Super Bowl tickets.

On the field, however, the sport had become more competitive and more lively than ever. Offseason weight and fitness regimens, improved diet, and the use of videotape and computer analysis created NFL players who would have seemed like supermen to the brawlers of the 1930s.

Fortunately, one thing has not changed throughout the 75-year history of the league: On game day, two teams still fight each other like hell—and the best team wins.

Hurry Up and Win

The Buffalo Bills didn't go anywhere in 1987, but on September 20 of that season quarterback Jim Kelly had used the two-minute offense to lead his team to touchdowns in its final two possessions. As a result, Buffalo beat the Houston Oilers 34-30. In 1989, the Bills had won three different games by

While Troy Aikman (8) and the Dallas Cowboys were soaring to the top in the 1990s, Raiders defensive end Howie Long (75) was wrapping up his brilliant career.

Buffalo's No-Huddle offense got most of the headlines, but Raiders quarterback Jay Schroeder learned that the Bills' defense also could be formidable.

"When you get old, everything is hurting. When I get up in the morning, it sounds like I'm making popcorn."

—LAWRENCE TAYLOR,
NEW YORK GIANTS LINEBACKER,
AFTER 12 YEARS IN THE NFL

scoring on their final two possessions with the hurry-up offense.

Why, asked offensive coordinator Ted Marchibroda, don't we use it all the time? On the surface, it was a radical thought. But upon further inspection, the No-Huddle offense began to make a great deal of sense.

After all, in Kelly the Bills had a quarterback who had a knack for successfully reading defenses on the fly. And then there was the vast offensive talent at Kelly's disposal: primarily, versatile running back Thurman Thomas, wide receiver Andre Reed, and a muscular offensive line.

With such gifted personnel, the Bills rarely made substitutions. Why, reasoned Marchibroda, give the defense a chance to make its own changes? By calling out plays and formations to his teammates at the line of scrimmage, Kelly prevented opponents from bringing in specialists from the sidelines. That created favorable mismatches for the Bills. It also had a tendency to leave defenses exhausted.

The Bills committed to the philosophy in the final four games of the 1990 regular season, a year in which they led the NFL and set a club record with 428 points. Kelly was the league's top-rated passer (101.2) and Thomas led all runners for the second consecutive year with 1,829 yards from scrimmage. Reed caught 71 passes for 945 yards and 8 touchdowns.

In the playoffs, the No-Huddle offense had no peer. In two games, the Bills scored a breathtaking 95 points and gained 995 yards. The game that landed Buffalo in its first Super Bowl was a not-to-be-believed 51-3 victory over the Raiders in the AFC Championship Game. The Bills set an NFL playoff record by scoring 41 points in the first half. When the Raiders switched to six defensive backs in the second quarter, the Bills ran the ball 11 straight times on the way to a touchdown. Buffalo finished with 202 rushing yards, underlining the No-Huddle's versatility.

Buffalo head coach Marv Levy downplayed the scheme. "We haven't invented the Salk vaccine," he said. "It's just players playing together and getting better at it."

Tim Rooney, the Giants' director of pro personnel, knew better as his team prepared for Super Bowl XXV. "The No-Huddle, it's awesome," Rooney said. "The Raiders couldn't blitz, they couldn't do anything. Having good players has a lot to do with it, but Buffalo's game is so well-conceived that you can't entirely credit it to the talent."

The Bills' offense wasn't the only new wrinkle of the 1990 season. As part of a new television contract, a bye week was added to the schedule for 1990-92, and two bye weeks in 1993.

The playoff structure was altered, too, with a third wild-card team added in each conference. That meant six teams from each conference would make the playoffs, and the division winner with the poorest record in each conference would play a wild-card team in the first round.

In the summer, Art McNally retired after an 18-year run as the league's director of officiating. Jerry Seeman, an NFL official for 16 seasons, was named as his successor.

After going 35-35 in five seasons in Houston, Jerry Glanville took the head coaching position in Atlanta. Jack Pardee, who played linebacker for legendary Paul (Bear) Bryant at Texas A&M, left the University of Houston for the vacated Oilers' post. Meanwhile, Bobby Beathard, architect of five Super Bowl teams in Miami and Washington, arrived in San Diego as the Chargers' new general manager.

A Field Goal Here, a Field Goal There

As the season progressed, the San Francisco 49ers seemed headed for their third straight NFL title. After finishing the 1989 season in a blur by winning eight consecutive games, the 49ers opened 1990 with 10 victories to run their streak to 18 (including postseason). The Los Angeles Rams finally caught up with the 49ers, beating them 28-17 at Candlestick Park on November 25. Nevertheless, the 49ers would not lose a road game for the remainder of the season, giving them another NFL mark: 18 consecutive victories away from home (19 including postseason).

Houston quarterback Warren Moon turned in the season's best individual performance, completing 27 of 45 passes for 527 yards against a strong Kansas City team at Arrowhead Stadium. Moon's yardage total was the second highest in NFL history, after the 554 posted by the Rams' Norm Van Brocklin in 1951. Wide receiver Haywood Jeffires caught 9 of Moon's passes for 245 yards.

Kansas City kicker Nick Lowery had only a single field goal in that 27-10 Houston victory, but he kicked 34 of 37 field goals for the season and led

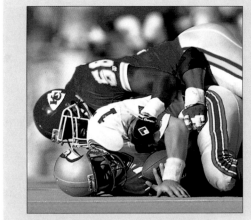

SEVEN'S NOT ENOUGH

"**I** was on a mission today," said Kansas City's Derrick Thomas.

The Chiefs' outside linebacker had just finished putting Seattle quarterback Dave Krieg on the ground 7 times, an NFL record. This was Veterans Day, November 11, 1990, and Thomas's use of "mission" was no casual choice. Before the kickoff, four U.S. Air Force A-10 jets flew over Arrowhead Stadium in memory of his father, Robert, a captain who died in Vietnam in 1972 while flying on a mission called, ironically, "Operation: Linebacker Two."

Mission was accomplished by Derrick Thomas, but it didn't leave him satisfied. With four seconds remaining and his team leading 16-10, he had his arms wrapped around Krieg, but couldn't pull him down for number 8.

Instead, Krieg eluded Thomas's grasp and threw a 25-yard touchdown pass to Paul Skansi that tied the game. Norm Johnson kicked the extra point, and Seattle won 17-16.

In the locker room afterward, Thomas said, "I'd trade every one of those sacks for a *W*."

The Chiefs sacked Krieg 9 times during the game, a statistic he tended to shrug off in retrospect. "I took every offensive snap that year," he said. "[The nine sacks] did have an effect, though. That was a long day."

Krieg finished 16 of 23 for 306 yards and 2 touchdowns.

After rushing for 1,486 yards in the regular season, the Cowboys' Emmitt Smith added 132 in Super Bowl XXVIII.

DON'T TOUCH THAT DIAL

On January 30, 1994, nearly 135 million fans—the largest American audience ever—gathered around television sets throughout the U.S. to watch Dallas beat Buffalo in Super Bowl XXVIII. Super Bowls dominate the list of the most-watched domestic TV programs of all time:

PROGRAM	DATE	NETWORK	*VIEWERS
Super Bowl XXVIII	Jan. 30, 1994	NBC	134,840,000
Super Bowl XXVII	Jan. 31, 1993	NBC	133,400,000
Super Bowl XX	Jan. 26, 1986	NBC	127,000,000
Super Bowl XXI	Jan. 25, 1987	CBS	122,640,000
M★A★S★H (Special)	Feb. 28, 1983	CBS	121,624,000
Super Bowl XXVI	Jan. 26, 1992	CBS	119,700,000
Super Bowl XIX	Jan. 20, 1985	ABC	115,936,000
Super Bowl XXII	Jan. 31, 1988	ABC	115,000,000
Super Bowl XXV	Jan. 27, 1991	ABC	112,140,000
Olympic Fig. Skating	Feb. 23, 1994	CBS	110,530,000

*watched some portion of the broadcast
Based on A.C. Nielsen figures

"The Southeast is a terrific area for sports and the NFL," explained Commissioner Paul Tagliabue. "As we looked at the population and the growth of that area, having six teams [Atlanta, Carolina, Jacksonville, Miami, New Orleans, and Tampa Bay] is the preferred option."

The Carolina Panthers, headed by former NFL player Jerry Richardson, and the Jacksonville Jaguars, led by shoe executive Wayne Weaver, began preparations for a 1995 kickoff.

They weren't any more anxious to start playing than Joe Montana. The celebrated quarterback had thrown just 21 passes in 1991-92, thanks to an elbow injury that threatened to end his career. But Montana wasn't ready to quit, even with a dazzling résumé that included 2,929 completions, on 4,600 attempts (63.7 percent), 35,124 yards, 244 touchdowns, a 93.5 passer rating, and four Super Bowl rings.

With Steve Young established in San Francisco as one of the league's best quarterbacks, Montana persuaded the 49ers to trade him to the Kansas City Chiefs. There, at 37, Montana prepared to start over. He wasn't alone in that respect.

In Super Bowl XXI, Bill Parcells's Giants had defeated Dan Reeves's Broncos. In 1993, they traded conferences. Reeves, who was 117-79-1 at Denver, left to become Giants head coach after Ray Handley was fired. Parcells, after two years in the broadcast booth, returned to head coaching, this time at New England. Each man had an enormous impact; the Giants went from 6-10 to 11-5 and the playoffs, while the young Patriots started slowly, but finished the season with four straight wins.

Quarterback Challenges

In college, Drew Bledsoe and Rick Mirer had proved themselves to be the best quarterbacks in the nation. In the NFL, the first and second overall picks in the 1993 draft suffered their share of disappointment as starters for the New England Patriots and Seattle Seahawks, respectively. The last time quarterbacks had gone one-two in the draft was 22 years earlier, when Jim Plunkett was the Patriots' choice and Archie Manning went to the New Orleans Saints.

Bledsoe and Mirer met in the season's third week, and the Seahawks came away with a 17-14 victory at Foxboro Stadium. By season's end, Mirer held a similarly slight statistical edge over Bledsoe. Mirer passed for 2,833 yards (an NFL rookie record), 12 touchdowns, and 17 interceptions, while Bledsoe's numbers were 2,494 yards, 15 touchdowns, and 15 interceptions. Mirer's final rating was 67.0, compared to Bledsoe's 65.0. Still, both quarterbacks established themselves as heirs apparent to stars such as John Elway and Dan Marino, who had entered the NFL a decade earlier.

Miami coach Don Shula finished the season with a 9-7 record, giving him 327 victories over a 31-year career. That was three more than Chicago's legendary George Halas, the previous record-holder.

There were record numbers in other phases of the game. Green Bay wide receiver Sterling Sharpe produced an incandescent 112 catches, breaking the record of 108 he had set a year earlier. Sharpe became the first NFL player to catch 100 passes in two different seasons, let alone consecutively.

San Francisco's Steve Young led all quarterbacks with a rating of 101.5, based on 4,023 yards, a completion percentage of 68.0, and 29 touchdown passes. Young became the first player to lead the NFL in passing three consecutive years. Dallas's Emmitt Smith won his third consecutive league rushing title with 1,486 yards, despite missing the first two games because of a contract dispute. Rams rookie Jerome Bettis was second, with 1,429 yards.

Montana finished as the AFC's second-rated passer, but he missed several games with an injured hamstring. Kansas City teammate Marcus Allen, another former Super Bowl MVP, led the AFC with 15 touchdowns. Allen's former teammate, Howie Long, the Raiders' magnificent defensive end, retired after his thirteenth season.

The Houston Oilers won their last 11 games to capture the AFC Central title, but the Buffalo Bills made history by advancing to their fourth consecutive Super Bowl—and by losing their fourth consecutive Super Bowl, again to Dallas.

The Cowboys won Super Bowl XXVIII 30-13 at the Georgia Dome, becoming only the fifth team to repeat as Super Bowl champion. Dallas quickly erased a 13-6 halftime deficit when safety James Washington returned a Thurman Thomas fumble 46 yards for a touchdown. Smith, laboring with a separated shoulder, was the MVP, carrying 30 times for 132 yards and 2 scores.

"I'm not much of a historian," said Dallas head coach Jimmy Johnson. "I just know we won the Super Bowl the last two years in a row."

True historians were surprised two months later when Johnson stepped down as head coach. The Cowboys aimed to play a significant role in the future of the NFL, as they had in its past…but, starting in 1994, they would have to do it without Jimmy Johnson.

FIRST 325 ARE THE HARDEST

Don Shula never has been one to dwell on specific plays or moments from the 325 victories that made him the winningest coach in NFL history.

"There are games that will never be blotted from your mind," Shula said. "But it's pretty hard to go back and recount what happened in each and every one of those wins."

We can help. On September 22, 1963, in the second game of his head coaching career, Shula's Baltimore Colts rallied for 10 fourth-quarter points at San Francisco, and the Colts won 20-14. It was his first NFL victory.

And how did Shula fare against George Halas, the man whose prodigious record he eclipsed? Shula beat him five of nine, after losing the first two.

Flash-forward to Veterans Stadium, Philadelphia, November 14, 1993—six Super Bowl appearances later. Were Shula's 1993 Dolphins feeling extra pressure as number 325 approached?

"I tried to keep that from happening," he said. "I tried to talk about team objectives versus personal accomplishments and personal goals.

"I wanted [number 325] to happen in a year when the team was successful."

The Dolphins' 19-14 victory over the Eagles improved their record to 7-2, but Shula's wish for a year of team success fell one victory short. The Dolphins missed the playoffs at 9-7.

STARS *of the* NINETIES

Competition for the hearts and minds of sports fans could lead to holographic replays and in-seat interactive games based upon the action on the field.

slippery I-beam, that sort of thing."

Competition for sports fans will be stiff, but the even more daunting competition could be the stadiums against the television industry. "Probably all stadiums will have to be redone," Schramm said of the next 30 to 50 years. "You'll get more of a racetrack thing of seats at tables for comfort and enjoyment."

The spectators will want large screens and more of them. They'll need keypads at their seats for playing the interactive games available to home fans. In most cases, they'll be indoors. Many domes will be retractable, but if most shopping centers already are indoors, people aren't going to want to tolerate the weather at football games a generation from now. "We'll find a way to grow grass inside economically," McCaskey said.

Either that, or hydraulic technology will make it possible to grow a field outdoors and move it into the dome for games. That would give domes a greater variety of uses when the grass is outside.

The League

In the early days of the NFL, players switched jobs so frequently that they often signed contracts for only a game or two. The stars won't be doing that again anytime soon, but pro basketball has 10-day contracts for marginal players. However player movement eventually shakes down, one thing is clear right now.

"Free agency has become the new rudder to the ship," Wyche said.

Before the decade ends, Plumb guessed, only the stars will have contracts for longer than one year. "If you produce, you'll make more next year. If you don't, you'll take a big pay cut."

Careers will be shorter because younger players will be cheaper. Former Cardinals punter Rich Camarillo went to his third consecutive Pro Bowl after the 1993 season, his option year. He looked forward to a big raise from $550,000. New coach Buddy Ryan offered him a $300,000 cut. Nothing personal—Ryan just decided the salary cap left him with no more than $250,000 for a punter. Even veteran coaches could price themselves out of the market.

Stars will price themselves out of town. If Troy Aikman, for example, commands more than one-quarter of the salary-cap budget, the Cowboys very easily could say they'd rather spend the money on more players, and Cowboys fans very easily could let out a howl that would be heard all the way to Aloha Stadium in Honolulu. The non-stars will switch teams more than before, but maybe not as often as people expect.

The others, composing the majority of the players' union, will revolt. It could change the union leadership in the next few years, but it won't lead to a strike, not during the Collective Bargaining Agreement that lasts through the century. Even after that, union leaders will be reluctant to strike against owners who have committed a percentage of revenues for player salaries.

In the long run, players will have other places to play.

Any NFL expansion in North America will continue to move at its recent pace, only slightly faster than an old-growth redwood expands. Mexico City and Montreal might be the next NFL expansion cities, while St. Louis, Baltimore, Oakland, and Memphis become cornerstones in other leagues.

Eventually, there will be football leagues in other countries, perhaps comparable to the European basketball leagues of today. Jerry Vainisi, the World League's director of operations, said former NFL commissioner Pete Rozelle told him in 1986 that he expected the NFL to generate more revenue internationally than domestically in the early 2000s. The NFL will have its own stake overseas, but it probably won't be able to control the market entirely.

The league already has a strategy for developing football in a foreign country, and the strategy is working well in England. The first step is sponsoring clinics and working with amateur teams to teach them the game. At the same time, it contracts with licensees to sell hats, T-shirts, and other NFL paraphernalia, and to put NFL highlight shows on television, whetting the sports fans' appetite. Then comes an American Bowl game to give fans a taste of live action, followed by a World League franchise to give them an entire meal.

"Now there's enough interest that the World League and NFL television rights are worth more, plus there's more licensing," Vainisi said.

The World League will resume play with six European teams in 1995. "Three to five years after that," Vainisi said, "we'll have a Pacific Rim division with teams in Tokyo, Sydney, Honolulu, and Seoul."

It will remain a minor league for 30 years or so, gradually incorporating local talent that is good enough to jump from the club level to the World League.

As American football programs improve overseas, so will the World League and any other overseas leagues. Eventually the English and Spanish teams, for example, using primarily Englishmen and Spaniards, will reach the level of Lithuanian basketball teams and beyond. "That will be your Super Bowl in a generation or two," McCaskey said. The winner of the World League championship game between the European and Pacific conferences will play the winner of the NFL championship game between the National and American conferences.

"I think that's the whole future of all sports," Schramm said. "People are going to think in terms of national competition more than individual. That's why the Ryder Cup has become a big event. Football will definitely become the world sport because football is the best television sport. I don't care where you are, the sport that's best on television is going to be the biggest sport."

The players will be bigger people wearing smaller pads, but there still will be 11 on a team. The coaches still will stay up nights looking for an edge. The players still will win games by making plays that human beings should not be able to make. It will be football.

FOOTBALL FOR THE MASSES

League executives often have repeated that the Super Bowl will be on free TV for the rest of the century. Does this mean Super Bowl XXXIV in January, 2000, already is scheduled for pay-per-view? Not necessarily, said Art Modell, owner of the Cleveland Browns and chairman of the NFL Television Committee. In the foreseeable future, and not before the next century, pay-per-view will offer only expanded options. Retirees in Florida, for example, can watch their previous home teams from New York or Detroit instead of the Dolphins or Buccaneers games that the local network affiliates are carrying.

"It will be a long time before we make the hazardous jump to pay-per-view at the exclusion of free television," Modell said. "There would be Congressional problems and public-relations problems. People are so accustomed to getting their games free. God only knows what you could get for a Super Bowl on pay-per-view, but it's unthinkable."